TITLES BY T. D. JAKES

He-Motions

Follow the Star

God's Leading Lady

The Great Investment

Maximize the Moment

The Lady, Her Lover, and Her Lord

His Lady: Sacred Promises for God's Woman

Woman, Thou Art Loosed! The Novel

PRAISE FOR OTHER BOOKS BY T. D. JAKES

The Great Investment

"Jakes's most important book to date."

—*The Ethnic Newswatch Philadelphia Tribune*

The Lady, Her Lover, and Her Lord

"A groundbreaking book . . . Jakes argues that high aspirations and achievements are not incompatible with love, marriage, and sacred duty."

—*People*

"If you want to know the secret to a fulfilling life as a lady, if you want to know how to strengthen your relationship with your love, and most of all, if you want to establish a stronger fellowship with your Lord, then this book is for you. Bishop T. D. Jakes is a breath of fresh air. . . . Take it from me, the material within this book does make a difference."

—Natalie Cole

"[Jakes] demonstrates an unusual ability to inspire, uplift, teach, and comfort. An eloquent wordsmith . . . [he] writes with an abundance of memorable metaphors and yet speaks to women's hearts in practical, often humorous terms. . . . This masterful preacher offers all women sound advice and gentle, respectful encouragement."

—*Publishers Weekly*

Maximize the Moment

"To me, there is no man of God who is more gifted, more compassionate, more articulate, more anointed to reach and touch lives, small and great, than T. D. Jakes."

—Oral Roberts

"A handbook for reaching one's full potential. . . . You'll want to read this one."

—*Fort Worth Star*

"Jakes reminds us that 'Sometimes . . . His will collides with our loves.' Out of those collisions comes 'a clearer view of God's grace'—a gift more valuable than a dozen SUVs. In other words, a life lived in tune with God's will is always more abundant than a life guided by our own headstrong wishes."

—*Beliefnet.com*

God's Leading Lady

Out of the Shadows and into the Light

T. D. JAKES

BERKLEY BOOKS, NEW YORK

A Berkley Book
Published by The Berkley Publishing Group
A division of Penguin Group (USA) Inc.
375 Hudson Street
New York, New York 10014

Unless otherwise noted, Scripture quotations are from the New King James Version of the Bible. Copyright 1979, 1980, 1982 by Thomas Nelson, Inc., Publishers. Scripture quotations noted NIV are from The Holy Bible, New International Version. Copyright 1973, 1978, 1984 by International Bible Society. Used by permission of Zondervan Publishing House.
All rights reserved.

Copyright © 2002 by T. D. Jakes.
Cover design © 2002 by Walter Harper.
Cover photograph © Robert Daly/Getty Images/Stone.
Book design by Stephanie Huntwork.

All rights reserved.
This book, or parts thereof, may not be reproduced in any form without permission. The scanning, uploading, and distribution of this book via the Internet or via any other means without the permission of the publisher is illegal and punishable by law. Please purchase only authorized electronic editions, and do not participate in or encourage electronic piracy of copyrighted materials.
Your support of the author's rights is appreciated.
BERKLEY and the "B" design are trademarks belonging to Penguin Group (USA) Inc.

PRINTING HISTORY
G. P. Putnam's Sons hardcover edition / June 2002
Berkley trade paperback edition / July 2003

Berkley trade paperback ISBN: 0-425-19016-1

The Library of Congress has catalogued the
G. P. Putnam's Sons hardover edition as follows:

Jakes, T. D.
God's leading lady : out of the shadows and
into the light / T. D. Jakes.
p. cm.
ISBN 0-399-14883-3
1. Christian women—Religious life. I. Title.
BV4527.J325 2002 2002023152
248.8'43—dc21

PRINTED IN THE UNITED STATES OF AMERICA

10 9 8 7 6 5 4 3 2

Most Berkley Books are available at special quantity discounts for bulk purchases for sales promotions, premiums, fund-raising, or educational use. Special books, or book excerpts, can also be created to fit specific needs.

For details, write: Special Markets, The Berkley Publishing Group, 375 Hudson Street, New York, New York 10014.

To the women all across the country and around the world who have shared their testimonies, their secret burdens, their dreams, and aspirations with me. Their open expressions have enrolled me into the school of life in an inspirational way. Because of their encouragement and support, I am reminded, in the midst of all that I do, that what I do is an expression of God's heart for them. Every word I have ever written was penned to inspire them to be all that they can be. Wonderfully, the dividend they received from my investments has been reciprocal and has greatly enriched me as a person, a counselor, a husband, a father, and a friend. I, too, have been challenged and inspired to be all that I can be. For that I am eternally grateful.

To the women who have made significant investments and immeasurable contributions to my life: my wife, Serita; my late mother, Mrs. Odith P. Jakes; my sister, Jacqueline Jakes; my spiritual mother, Pastor Christine McCaskill; and Ms. Geraldine Bullard, the lady whose constant witness eventually led me to go beyond superficial religion into a salvation experience and a deeper walk in the Spirit. Each of these women has profoundly affected my life in significant ways. While some may not have the notoriety of the biblically referenced heroines, or the social brilliance or business acumen of the entrepreneurs exemplified in this book, they are no less distinguished.

Therefore, I dedicate this book to those who might traditionally be behind the scenes, but who have helped to create a light far brighter than this world could ever comprehend. To each woman who wrote to me, stopped to encourage me, or in any way enhanced my stay here on this earth, please accept this dedication as my thanks. And to the many more who are the unsung heroes of other men and women around the world, you will always epitomize my idea of "God's Leading Ladies." May your lights shine brighter and brighter unto a glorious and perfect day.

Acknowledgments

THERE ARE MANY people who invested in the development of this project who must be and should be acknowledged. Without them I would not have been able to meet the stringent demands of my life and still provide the quality information that was essential to this kind of project. Their investment in me makes it possible for me to invest my message and thoughts in you.

My gratitude to my wife, Serita, and my entire family, who generously shared me with this manuscript. I will always appreciate your love and support. I also want to acknowledge the compassion and encouragement that I consistently receive from my church family.

Thank you to Denise Silvestro, who tirelessly labored to enhance this project with her insights and creativity. Her grace to race as we edited and developed this book was a significant component in reaching the deadline and getting this timely message out to the people who needed it most.

Thank you, Joel Fotinos, for your enthusiasm, encouragement, wisdom, and for believing in my message and my method.

Thank you to everyone at Putnam. You all treated me and my work with great dignity and integrity. My gratitude to Susan Petersen Kennedy, Marilyn Ducksworth, Dan Harvey, Dick Heffernan, Martha Bushko, and everyone at JMS Marketing & Sales, Inc.

Special thanks to Mr. Dudley Delffs, whose prolific literary experience and ability enhanced my ideas and inspired me personally.

Contents

PART TWO
Dress Rehearsals: Trials of a Leading Lady

PART THREE
Encore: Legacy of a Leading Lady

God's Leading Lady

INTRODUCTION

Waiting in the Wings

AN ASTRONAUT SOARS into the glittering expanse of God's handiwork in the heavens. An entrepreneur risks her life savings and leads her fledgling company to the heights of the Fortune 500 list. An abused rag doll of a little girl overcomes the heinous stains of shame, guilt, and fear from her abuser's violation and pens a novel that stirs the hearts of readers and wins every literary prize in sight. A stunned mother holds the miracle child that doctors once told her she could never birth.

Twenty-first-century women arguably have more opportunities for greatness than ever before. They can bring to life their girlhood dreams. They can overcome barriers of sexism, racism, economic and social oppression, and the demons of childhood abuse and family dysfunction. They can soar with a beauty and majesty that their Creator intended when He first fashioned them in His own likeness: ". . . in the image of God He created him; male and female He created them" (Genesis 1:27).

So why aren't more women fulfilling their dreams and soaring as their Creator intended?

While opportunities and inspirations have multiplied, so have the weights of responsibility, the pressures of others' expectations, and the temptations of mediocrity. Like wildflowers straining to press through the cracks in a crumbling sidewalk, women strive to bloom within the confinements of this jumbled and segmented stretch of concrete called Life. Yes, numerous freedoms have brought numerous opportunities for many women. Still many barriers threaten a woman's ability to answer God's call of greatness upon her life. It is a struggle for a woman just to keep the tender bud of her dreams alive.

Smells Like a Storm

WHEN I WAS a boy growing up in West Virginia, folks would gather on the porch in the morning or along the sidewalks in the afternoon to exchange a friendly word or a piece of juicy news. Weather always provided a popular topic of conversation and inevitable speculation. What impressed me most were the older gentlemen and ladies who claimed they could smell a storm coming, even on a sun-gleaming, sultry afternoon with nary a cloud to be seen. Gentle breezes ruffling the emerald-green leaves carried a scent for those who'd been around long enough to recognize it. What smelled moist and clean in the air to me, signaled something harsher and harmful on its way. Most times they were right, and banks of clouds rolled in like marching soldiers in gray columns.

Have you smelled the storm building in your own life? Like the scent of impending rain clouds telegraphed on a balmy breeze, there may be indications that the storms of life are coming, if they're not already pouring down on you.

As one set of pressures collides with another, a massive life-storm mounts across a woman's inner landscape. External pressures—maybe in the form of a looming deadline at work, an under-appreciative boss, or a final notice, overdue bill that demands remittance—billow like a hot air mass from the Gulf Coast on one front. These winds sweep and pound against a woman's purposeful stride, but she pushes on. Then more personal pressures converge into a cold front, sweeping in with added demands and obligations. Her kids need a nurturing strength from her that she's not sure she has; her husband claims to love her but seems distanced by their hectic lives; her parents are deteriorating before her eyes and beg her care; some friends want to know her but there's never enough time.

And at the center of this storm is its power source—a woman's battle with her self. This may take the form of an inner critic whispering a scathing judgment in her ear that she's not good enough, smart enough, pretty enough, loving enough to be who she should be. It may drape her soul with the unending needs of others, suffocating any and all attempts for her to allow her soul to breathe. It may take the shape of career confusion and relational uncertainty that is paralyzing her, keeping her in a state of indecision. It may be the weariness of the mundane rumbling through the darkness of her heart's depression.

The storm churns and ravages her being until a bolt of lightning sears her to her core. With its flickering light, this bolt illuminates that something must change. The electrical energy streaking inside her can short-circuit her life and cause a total blackout.

Or it can be harnessed and used as a source of energy.

Weather Beater

WHEN I WAS a young man just starting out, I worked as an assistant manager of a local paint store. There I was often approached by customers who had trouble with their paint adhering properly. Generally, excess moisture was the recurring problem. I often recommended a paint called Weather Beater. Its advertisements used to show freshly painted shutters buffering the pounding rain of a midnight storm, or the pristine exterior siding of a house, also newly painted, resisting the bitter teeth of a New England snowstorm. For our West Virginia cold winter winds and torrential spring rains, Weather Beater paint proved itself a critical protector of a homeowner's greatest investment. You see, many customers wanted not only the beauty of a freshly painted dwelling but the security of knowing their investment could withstand the elements and ravages of time, and endure—perhaps even becoming an heirloom to pass down through the following generations.

But a woman's life is more than an item to be passed on to the people who love her. She is a priceless resource of strength and vitality, and if she is not only to survive, but to thrive in the life God calls her toward, a woman must be a "weather beater" as well. She must know how to prepare for life's storms, how to smell the wind and know when a storm is brewing, how to look for shelter and rise above the tumult.

If a woman is fortunate enough to have weathered some of life's storms in the past, then she knows that this latest one will pass as well. Perhaps she's experienced enough of these storms to see what causes them, the way the external and internal pressures crash into one another to create a larger force against her. This storm-tossed woman may know herself and her past well enough to know which windows to barricade, which doors to lock. She may have learned enough to take shelter in the security of her true identity or in the warm embrace of a supportive partner. Most of all she may know to take refuge on the rock of faith in her loving Lord.

But even if she knows how to be a "weather beater" on life's journey, she may not be sure of her path. Storms leave her disoriented and disappointed. Like Dorothy swept up by the tornado in *The Wizard of Oz,* a woman finds herself dazed and uncertain of her surroundings. She realizes that she's "not in Kansas anymore," and there's no yellow-brick road to guide her to her heart's true desires. Her world may be turned upside down by life changes. Perhaps she lost a loved one in the world-shattering events of September 11, 2001, in this country. Maybe she's losing a parent to cancer or Alzheimer's, or losing the security of her marriage to the devastation of divorce.

Or perhaps it's a quieter storm, one driven from the inside out, as a woman wonders what has happened to the hopes and dreams that used to burn in her breast. Maybe what used to seem important no longer commands the same energy and commitment. Her life has become a series of treadmill motions, quiet disappointments, and angry resignations. She may feel like she's living inside a child's snow globe—one of those toys that peppers the tiny people inside with silvery flakes when you shake it. Her life may feel suspended, contained, and claustrophobic. She finds herself shaken and stirred by a yearning that taunts her, that's just out of reach. She finds that outside circumstances rock the priorities that once nestled her safely in place.

"I'm Every Woman"

AS A MAN, I certainly can't pretend to know what it's like to be a woman. I respect you too much to pretend that I know how you feel. Only *you* know how you feel. But perhaps I can help point to the reasons why you feel the way you do. After twenty-five years of ministry, I have watched life's play acted out by the many people I have counseled and personally loved. Yes, I am a man who has had a chance to love and to know and to pray for just about every kind of woman imaginable. I know what I don't know. But I also know what I do know. And I do know what I see in the eyes and hearts of the women I counsel, the women I love—my wife, my daughters, my mother—and the women I've been privileged to work and minister alongside.

A while back Whitney Houston had a hit single entitled "I'm Every Woman" in which she proclaimed the many roles and kinds of women that must exist inside every female. Starting out slow and leading to a pulse-pounding dance rhythm, the song captures a bit of truth here in the diversity of a contemporary woman's reality.

But women also know the flip side to this single: In learning to be "every woman" and conform like a chameleon to the ever-changing environment around them, they lose sight of the *one* woman they were created to be. When they do catch a glimpse of this unique creature, her gaze may seem as distant and unfamiliar as a stranger's on the subway. Who is she? Who are *you* when you're not busy trying to be everything to everybody?

Imagine a woman sitting alone in a darkened room. Her face conveys a weariness beyond her years, and her makeup is smeared from the tears coursing down her cheeks. Her beauty has frayed at the edges. She feels torn apart by all the roles she plays: wife, lover, mother, daughter, sister, friend, entrepreneur, hostess—the list goes on and on. In these rare moments when the house is quiet and she is left with only herself, a voice rises within her like a mighty tide from the ocean floor: "Where am I going with my life? Do I even know who I really am? What have I settled for? Do I even know what I really want?" While she has faced her past, it continues to haunt her at odd moments. While she loves her family, they don't always care to understand and appreciate her. While her work provides a paycheck, it leaves her soul as cold and obscured as a winter's fog. Her marriage, though filled with all of the images of intimacy, seems so hollow as she struggles to be heard in a relationship that often leaves her feeling like those who love her are hearing-impaired. Her dreams are starting to fade, and she feels locked into mediocrity by barriers beyond her control. Behind her smile and vivacious personality, there is an inner ache and a piercing cry for help. But those around her cannot hear her screaming plea and the relentless storm raging within her. Her family goes about their lives, not noticing that lightning has streaked her sky and thunder rumbles in her soul.

As lonely as she may feel, she is not alone. The irony is that every woman must face these moments within her self if she is to rise above the corporate, domestic, and personal storm clouds hovering overhead. She may be a single mother raising her children in the inner-city chaos of crack and calamity. She may be a prominent businesswoman and leader in her affluent community. She may be a respected role model in her church. She may be struggling to make ends meet and keep her heart in her marriage. She may be thriving in her high-powered career and relishing her singleness. This woman questioning herself and her dissatisfaction with life may wear Armani suits and diamond rings or she may slip on the same Payless shoes and Kmart special day after day. She could be white or black, Hispanic or Asian, young or old. She yearns for more out of life. She can't quiet the questions of who she is and what she was created for any longer; she is more than ready to drop all the bit parts she's playing and find a way to live the one role for which she has been created: a Leading Lady.

Your Time Has Come

IT'S LIKE A modern-day fairy tale, a Cinderella story of disaster and despair turned into a showstopper of discovery and destiny. A beautiful blond ingenue spotted on a stool at a drugstore counter. A backup singer forced to perform in the star's place at the microphone. A secretary recognized for her ingenuity and promoted above her boss. Many women want to be recognized for who they really are and the talent they possess. Unfortunately, too many women wait passively for some fairy godmother to flit through their overburdened lives and make success happen for them.

But most women truly at home with themselves and the excellence that is their pursuit know that you have to be your own fairy godmother. There is no magic wand turning pumpkins into coaches. There is no record producer eavesdropping on your impromptu karaoke as you wail out an Aretha Franklin classic along with the radio. There is no pixie dust turning your blue-light special into a Broadway spotlight. But, praise God, there is the magic of faith coupled with the actions of a relentless woman whose commitment to her dream wields the wand of her destiny. Turning your faith into action is critical. Forcing your dream to move beyond the pillow of last night's sleep and into the possibility of today's conquest transforms fanciful ideas into glorious achievements. Moses held his power in the rod that he walked with, and my question to you is the same as God's question to him: "What is that in your hand?" (Exodus 4:2). Then wave it, sister, and let the magic begin!

How do you unleash the magic of your faith put into action? Oprah Winfrey is famous for her "aha!" moments, those small moments of epiphany in one's life that have monumental consequences from then on. If you are reading the words on this page, then let this be an "aha!" moment for you. Your time has come.

If you are no longer content with the misguided attempts to be every woman but yourself, then your time has come. If you are no longer satisfied to compare yourself to the shortsighted expectations of others around you, then your time has come. If you are no longer fulfilled by the remnants of your dreams being shoved to the back closets of your heart, then your time has come. If you are tired of ducking and hiding from the storms of life in whatever helter-skelter shelter you happen to find, then your time has come.

The time has come for you to step out of the shadows of your life and into the spotlight. Jesus made it clear that He came not just to free us from our failures but that we might be free to succeed. "I have come that they may have life, and that they may have it more abundantly" (John 10:10). Every woman has the potential to be one of God's Leading Ladies, to move beyond the edges of the stage where they have watched life's drama unfold before them, and to stride onto center stage and fulfill the role of their lifetime. Make no mistake, becoming God's Leading Lady does not require play-acting or pretending to be something you're not. On the contrary, becoming a true leading lady requires stripping away all the other roles and bit parts you may have settled for and acted out before. It means discovering who you are and what you are truly about and exercising faith in your Divine Director to guide you through the only authentic performance of which you are capable.

Little did Rosa Parks know that when she refused to surrender her seat and move to the back of the bus, more was at stake than a ride home. She was moving center stage by being herself. No games, no lines, no makeup—this was the real Rosa, and God shined a light on her soul that made history. God's light has come to shine on your efforts as well. That is what makes greatness shimmer in the midst of mediocrity. One brief shining moment is all it takes.

Arise, shine;
For your light has come!
And the glory of the LORD is risen upon you.

ISAIAH 60:1

All the World's a Stage

ONE OF THE best known lines from William Shakespeare's comedy *As You Like It* reminds us, "All the world's a stage,/And all the men and women merely players." Although it's not necessarily what the Bard was getting at, I find that the word "merely" conveys both understatement and great truth. We are merely players because God's great drama of redemption and grace is being carried on with or without us. Yet He chooses us—all of us, you and me—to play a unique part unlike that of any other of His sons and daughters in the production. Yielded to His direction, fueled by the vision of our fulfilled selves in service to purposes far greater than any we have ever dreamed, we take our place on the world's stage.

This book is designed to empower you in your pursuit of that place. I hope to challenge you to true excellence, to fan the dying embers of your desire for more out of life, to help you discover what the Creator had in mind when He formed you as female, and to enable you to recognize the incredible impact you can have on the world around you. Whether that world is the safe haven of a cherished homefront for your family or the boardroom where you lead a national conglomerate to greatness, whether it's the Sunday school classroom before dozens of hungry hearts or the bedroom alone with the passionate heart of your husband, you are a leading lady in your life's theater.

It's what God created you for. These desires for greatness, this yearning to step into the best role of your life, are nothing new. Women, as well as their leading men, have been wrestling with the harshness of life and the hope of a higher purpose since the Lord breathed life into Adam and Eve. Throughout time God has been calling out His Leading Ladies to take the stage and fulfill the challenge of their lifetime. And it's clear from Scripture that He doesn't choose the women that the Hollywood directors would choose for their next romantic thriller. So who does He choose and how do you become His Leading Lady?

He chooses *you.* If you're reading this book, you've likely experienced something of this gentle tugging on your heart. To help you answer His call, we will explore the great performances of many of His Leading Ladies of the past, and like a faithful understudy, we will glean all we can from women such as Rebekah and Sarah, Rahab and Mary Magdalene, Delilah and Bathsheba, Ruth and Joanna. Like purveyors of beauty in a grand museum, we will study each woman's dreams and failures, each one's unique contribution to the Holy Ladies' Hall of Fame. We will examine their legacies, see how other women have been inspired by them throughout history, and how their faith fuels their performances.

Leading Lady, your time has come to quit waiting in the wings and take your place onstage. This is your cue. The time is now!

PART ONE

Open Auditions:

Cast As a Leading Lady

CHAPTER ONE

The Director's Call

YOU NEVER KNOW when your time will come to take your place on a larger stage. Several years ago, I was invited to a conference commemorating the powerful events that happened at the turn of the century in Los Angeles, California, known as Azusa. This ministry phenomenon first started in 1906 when a number of Methodist bishops, led by a one-eyed black man named William J. Seymour, experienced a powerful revival at the small Apostolic Faith Mission located at 312 Azusa Street. They prayed together every single day for three years. Out of this fervency for God was born the Pentecostal movement as we know it. Since its dramatic yet humble beginning, the Azusa conference has become an annual time of celebrating and renewing the passionate fervor of God's Holy Spirit.

So I had been invited to Tulsa, Oklahoma, to celebrate the history-making power of God's Spirit working through Bishop Seymour and the others. It was my first Azusa conference, and I was so excited to see the diversity of people of all faiths and backgrounds gathered together in one concert of praise and worship. What an exhilarating experience it was for me! I was not a speaker, a singer, or on the program at all. I was just another face in the place. But what an excitement enveloped me as I sat in the crowd. That first night, amid the ten to twelve thousand people gathered in the auditorium, I took my seat high in the balcony, one man worshiping with the many, through the music, the preaching, the energy of the Body of Christ, gathered to celebrate. Nobody knew who I was or why I was there, other than to share in the service as we were all doing.

The next night my friend Sarah Jordan Powell, the talented Gospel singer, invited me to sit with her and her family in the front row. The view was different, of course, being up close and up front near the stage. I could see the powerful muscles in a soloist's face and neck as she strained to hit the perfect high note of her song. I could see the beads of perspiration forming along the forehead of one of the gifted preachers as he read Scripture beneath the white-hot stage lights. I could sense the nervous energy of those about to speak, their anticipation at being used by God's Spirit to deliver His message to the waiting throngs of people.

One preacher's message, in particular, caught my attention that night. Richard Hinton, pastor of the Monument of Faith Church in Chicago, used an analogy that became a precursor for how the Lord was about to use and bless me and my ministry. Bishop Hinton introduced the metaphor of being onstage in a play or show and explained how performers had to take their places in the shadows backstage and in the wings long before the lights went up and their scenes began. These actors had to be fully prepared in a matter of seconds to recognize their cue, hit their mark, and give all they had to the hungry audience. These actors had to be in makeup and their appropriate costume already; they had to know where and when to cross the stage; they had to have memorized their lines long before this moment in the darkness, waiting. These performers know that they are next in line to walk onstage and share their talent with the eager crowd. They are willing to do all it takes to prepare for their time onstage.

Bishop Hinton used this analogy to convey how we must be ready when God turns up the lights on the stage of our lives and we are thrust into positions of leadership, ministry, and responsibility that challenge us to the very core of our being. Positions that we may not have even dreamed about on our own, stages that seem distant and lofty from our starting places. He insisted that we must focus on our present purpose, our place in serving the King's company, if we expect to be stretched and extended to our full potential as men and women of God when He raises the lights on our next stage. If we do our part of preparation in the day-to-day tasks requiring our attention, then God will increase our responsibilities and use us to our fullest, and then some. "Whoever can be trusted with very little can also be trusted with much, and whoever is dishonest with very little will also be dishonest with much" (Luke 16:10, NIV).

I discovered this truth for myself; so much can happen in the space of 365 days! The following year I returned to Azusa not as a spectator or worshiper from the pews but as the speaker on the closing night. Suddenly I was catapulted onstage, beneath the blinding lights, before thousands and thousands of faces. Yes, the butterflies in my stomach felt more like hummingbirds beating against my rib cage, but there was also something to steady my resolve. I had taken

Hinton's message to heart. I had heard the Lord speak to me that night a year before. I had prepared to the best of my ability not just in the prior months but most of my life. You see, I believe that your successes and your failures help to shape your destiny. Both had worked as a team to develop the man who was to speak that night. Like partners under contract, all that I had won and all that I had lost labored together to define this one moment in my life. Was I ready to be seen onstage, to be heard echoing through the rafters where I had sat the year before, to be known in the naked vulnerability of one who puts himself before the Lord and His people? I wasn't sure. I didn't know. But often life will take you beyond ready answers and into the land of faith. And before my faith could reassure me, I was being introduced. But not just to the sizable audience there. I was being introduced to the next twenty years of my living. I was being introduced to the part of me that was waiting in the wings. Ready or not, here I come walking across the stage, taking on the challenge, and being thrust into the brightest blinding light my soul has ever known.

Shortly after I preached the closing night at Azusa, one opportunity after another began to fall into my path. Owners of the Trinity Broadcast Network contacted me about broadcasting my sermons. I had no cameras, no fancy church, and only a very small staff. All I had was a mandate from God, a burning sense of destiny, and a touch of real indigestion. Stage fright? Oh, yeah! But fright need not stop you when you have faith for that which you are afraid.

A little later I was able to acquire a spot on Black Entertainment Television. They, too, offered me a contract to broadcast my services. Speaking engagements emerged before larger and larger crowds of people. Days turned into years like pages blowing in an open book, and I found myself speaking before almost eighty thousand people at the Georgia Dome, breaking all records for attendance at the stadium. On September 17, 2001, I found myself on the cover of *Time* magazine. I tell you this not to boast or brag about anything I have done but to be willing to be who God made me. I was willing to take my place onstage, day in and day out, until the curtain went up and I found myself in the light of God's purpose. Ultimately, all that I went through was to prepare me to coach *you.*

The Potter's Shelf

FOR YOU SEE, this analogy of preparing to take your place onstage applies to you right now even as you're reading this. The message is not just to me and those in more public forms of ministry and leadership. It's not a message to those who already have it all together and want to be recognized for what they have done. No, it is a call to action wherever we are, especially for those God has brought through the wilderness to the Promised Land. I believe firmly that God prepares us for greater and greater opportunities if we are willing to trust Him and His timing in our lives. We must do our part and prepare with all our might, but then we must recognize the voice of His call as our cue to move onto the next stage of our lives.

So often we try to make it to a larger stage by ourselves. Our society tells us to "fake it till you make it." Well, I'm here to tell you that often we only stand in the way of something far greater than we could have ever staged ourselves. We must be willing to accept the leading role God has scripted just for us. We must be willing to transform our "acting" into an authentic performance that unleashes who we really are. May I tell you how much courage it takes to share who you really are? The fear of rejection is unbelievable. But remember, your strength is in your struggle, and your power is in your pain. So take a risk and come out of the shadows into the light.

How do you take those first steps? Another way of considering our preparation as we wait from cue to cue is to imagine the potter's shelf. If you've ever handled clay or even the Play-Doh that kids mold into every shape imaginable, you know how soft and pliant this material can be. It takes the shape of whoever handles it, and it conforms around the center of its gravity. That's why potters use revolving wheels with large hubs in the center around which to mold the clay. The moving hub provides the momentum to capitalize on the clay's submission to gravity. The potter's hands provide constant friction, the warm palms and fingers transforming the lifeless clay into a thing of beauty. After the clay has been shaped into a bowl, a vase, a cup, the potter sets it on his shelf until the piece can be fired in the kiln. The hot oven literally bakes the potter's work into the shape he has ordained for it, keeping the new form in place permanently instead of letting it shift back into a lump of clay.

Can you see how this compares to us taking our place onstage? God the Master Potter has been shaping and forming you through countless events and experiences. He has ordained your very being and set you in place for greatness. The Psalmist says that He has made us "a little lower than the angels" and crowned us with glory and honor (Psalm 8:5). Perhaps you can already feel the heat from the Refiner's fire casting you permanently into His shape, His likeness, into being His Leading Lady.

Or perhaps you are resisting the Potter's purpose for your life.

You are trying to shape yourself and mold your own form into what you think will make you a beautiful and perfect vessel. Maybe you're wrapped around the wheel of a man, trying to conform and mold your life and personality around his. You know it's not working because he can't provide you with that inner security and cherished love that comes only from yourself and your Creator. Or maybe you're rolling the clay of your life around your family, giving all you've got to hold them together, to keep your kids out of a gang, your husband out of the bars. But the vessel you've formed is cracking under the pressure. Your heart and energy are leaking onto the floor and you can't catch yourself.

No, you must allow the Potter to mold you into the beautiful, intricate design that He has imagined for you before time began. You must be willing to move from the events of your past and even your present into the permanent shape that He wants to cast you in. You must move beyond the Potter's shelf into the fire of greatness.

Sabotaging Self-talk

PERHAPS YOU HAVE caught the vision for yourself and what you need to do to become one of God's Leading Ladies. But I know from experience that many of you reading this are shaking your heads and rolling your eyes in frustration. "Yes, I hear you, Bishop Jakes," you're saying, "but you don't understand all I'm dealing with right now. There's my job—somebody's got to pay the bills and keep food on the table. There's my man—who knows how much longer we're going to hold it together? There's my kids—I'm scared to death for what they're facing in the back alleyways and school hallways of their teenaged lives. No, it's well and fine for all those other women to get ready to take their place onstage. Not this girl."

Others of you may be brushing away silent tears of shame and guilt, and trying to push away painful images from your past that stir up old fears and future doubts. You're thinking to yourself, "No one with my past can take her place onstage. Not with the kind of abuse I've had to endure. Not with the kind of guilt I feel over what I've allowed myself to do and whom I've allowed myself to do it with. There's nothing here the Lord can use. I might as well stop reading now."

Or maybe you're the kind of woman reading this book who knows her time has come. You're successful, you're vibrant, you seem to have it all. On the surface you may read about taking your place onstage and say, "Great. I'm ready. Let's get on with the show." But below the surface, deep within your heart, you're thinking, "Oh no, not another pep talk about being the perfect woman. I'm so tired of trying to be perfect. All I need is one more expectation to live up to, another demand to drain what little strength I have left. That sounds so exhausting. And I can't dare let anyone see how weary and insecure I really feel."

I hear all of you. The woman who feels like her life is going under amid the harrowing circumstances of her family. Perhaps you have children in jail and you wonder what happened and ask yourself how you failed them. Maybe your husband is cheating on you and you feel torn as to whether or not you have somehow brought this on yourself. Maybe your parents are losing their bodies and their minds to the ravages of some terrible disease even as they grow to depend on you more each day. I hear you.

To you, I want to recall the words of Paul as he wrote to the Corinthians:

For our light affliction, which is but for a moment, is working for us a far more exceeding and eternal weight of glory,

while we do not look at the things which are seen, but at the things which are not seen.

For the things which are seen are temporary, but the things which are not seen are eternal.

2 CORINTHIANS 4:17–18

You must realize that your present trouble is not going to last, but your role in the spiritual realm of God's kingdom is forever. You must see beyond the pain trying to blindside you. You are so much bigger than your present trials allow you to be.

Maybe the physical, sexual, and emotional abuse from the hands of someone you should have been able to trust has left you feeling powerless over your life. Or it could be your own addiction to alcohol, prescription drugs, or sexual promiscuity that has challenged your dreams and left you with nightmares. All of us face something—from overeating to overspending, from an unhealthy relationship with someone who is merely using you to an unhappy relationship with someone you are using. You may be ripped apart by the desire to love and obey your Lord even as you find yourself seducing a man at the bar or charging above your limit at the jewelry counter. It is a terrible feeling when you find yourself doing what you like but not liking what you do. "For what I am doing, I do not understand. For what I will to do, that I do not practice; but what I hate, that I do" (Romans 7:15).

I hear you. And to you, dear sister, I want to recall the truth that Paul sent to the Corinthians just a few lines down from his words above: "Therefore, if anyone is in Christ, *she* is a new creation; old things have passed away; behold, all things have become new"

(2 Corinthians 5:17). I have personalized the pronoun reference in this verse—the original, which is usually rendered "he," is generic and inclusive to all of us—in order to make sure you know that you are a new woman in Christ, a new being created in God's image. We will come back to this truth in many of the examples of the women God uses as His Leading Ladies, but for now let this taste be a drop of honey on your soul, whetting your appetite for more of what is true about you.

I hope many of you reading this have overcome whatever painful baggage of the past once weighed you down. I hope many of you have taken the initiative to stop playing victim to life's blows and have taken a stand for yourself. It's so good and so necessary to stand up for ourselves, to hold our heads high with the dignity God intended for His beloved creations. And yet, too often, I see women who have stood up and overcome their pasts, as well as their present painful circumstances, become brittle perfectionists. They project themselves with perfect makeup and impeccable accessories, with careful words and direct authority. They seek to control every detail of their lives and the lives of those they love, and they're simply not up to the task.

A woman I once counseled comes to mind. She was a beautiful, intelligent, gifted wife and mother with her own successful real estate business. She came to me because she felt like she could trust me. She initially said something about not knowing how to worship as demonstratively as she had seen others do at my services. She felt out of place and uncomfortable. As we continued she mentioned, "I go through the motions of worship and prayer, I go to church and volunteer as much as I can, but I don't sense any growth or connection with the Lord." As we talked and I got to know her, I observed that beneath the manicured nails, diamond tennis bracelets, and silk dress was a scared and weary little girl. Several conversations later, this woman shared some of the invisible scars tattooed on her heart. In her detached, tearless but weary-full voice, I detected the intractable commitment she had made to become invulnerable.

Like a twenty-first-century Scarlett O'Hara, this woman had vowed to protect herself and her image at any and all cost. "With God as my witness, I'll never go hungry again," she had proclaimed. But her soul was starving. In her resolve to overcome the pain of her alcoholic father and her abuse at the hands of an older brother, this woman had left no room for her own neediness. She had left little room for God to work in her life because she no longer trusted Him fully with her life. She clutched her little images of success like doll babies in the hands of the child she was inside. Her response is understandable, but there comes a time to move beyond where we are and step onto the next stage the Lord has for us. We must act in faith to take our place onstage and trust Him to see us through the performance.

Ex-cues and Excuses

THAT TIME IS now. In order to see God's cue for us, we must overcome what I call the "ex-cues," the ghosts of past opportunities and failures that attempt to blindside us in the present. An ex-cue can be any former stimulus that used to affect our behavior and how we think of ourselves. Like the way a certain song on the radio can bring a former flame to mind even though the embers have long since smoldered and died, an ex-cue prompts us to feel and believe something about ourselves that is no longer there, if it ever was.

Whether it's an old test score recording our underachievement or the shameful memory of receiving welfare, whether it's the baby we gave up or the marriage we let melt into mediocrity, our ex-cues must be abandoned. Just like an overripe melon pushed to the back of the fridge, an ex-cue is overdue for a toss into the waste bin. Its time has passed, and we must not hold onto its untimely message any longer, for fear of missing the very real cue that the Lord has for us now.

An ex-cue says, "It's too late; you'll never find your place onstage now. You're too old, too tired, too uneducated, too poor, too scared. You need to accept reality and resign yourself to where you are. You can't make it any better by pretending there's some pie in the sky around the next corner. And you sure don't have the power to make it happen for yourself." I'm sure you've realized by now how much "ex-cue says" sounds like "excuses." Because that's exactly what they are, excuses, standing in the way of exercising faith in action. Excuses are the lies of the enemy binding you to the past, straitjacketing you into accepting a pale imitation of who God created you to be. It's time to shed ex-cues and excuses and magnify what the Lord has planted in you: the seed to be His Leading Lady.

Mirror, Mirror

WHEN YOU LOOK in the mirror, what do you see? Every little girl loves to play out the roles of fairy tales, looking into her momma's hand mirror or the glass above the bathroom sink, saying, "Mirror, mirror, on the wall, who's the fairest one of all?" In the innocence and humility of the question, she knows that she contains that fairness, that beauty that bears her Creator's image and imagination.

It is only as we grow up and become conditioned by the harsh realities of life that our shame tarnishes our reflection and causes us to sneer at ourselves or to divert our tearful eyes.

The problem is, we're looking at ourselves but are focused only on the exterior. We scrutinize the contours of our face in the looking glass, desperately searching for something in our features to tell us who we are and what we're about. And if we don't like what we see, we make changing what we see our new goal, instead of trying to discover our true selves, our divine purpose.

Have you ever witnessed a makeover? It seems to be a feature of nearly every talk show or celebrity hour you see on television these days. A plain, frumpy woman is plucked from the audience, or perhaps her hip teenaged daughter or dissatisfied husband has written in to the show and volunteered her. In either case, this disoriented woman is trotted offstage and into a labyrinth of makeup artists, hairstylists, fashion consultants, and personal shoppers. Within the hour she's back onstage, this time with a sleek haircut, subtle, age-defying cosmetics, and the latest designer's chic outfit. Her own family members don't even recognize her, let alone the studio audience and the viewers at home. Amazing what a difference the right clothes, the right cut, and the right know-how can make in a woman! Yet I always wonder, is this woman any happier, any more satisfied than she was before her new look? Is being content just a matter of getting the right look or fulfilling the expectations of magazine editors at *Cosmopolitan* or *Essence*?

Don't get me wrong—I love to see a woman who feels comfortable in the beauty of herself and her accoutrements. It's nice to wear beautiful clothes and to take enough pride in our Lord's creation of us to fulfill His design. But if you've ever had a makeover yourself, or even simply tried a new look, then you know that it's not just what we see in the mirror that defines who we are.

How do we see beyond ourselves when we look in the mirror? How do we transcend the illusion of appearance and focus on the realities of God's calling? Well, we have to look beyond the reflection in the looking glass and embrace the vision God has created for us. We have to look into the mirror of our souls and be real about what we see. We must see beyond the past hurts, beyond the present afflictions, beyond the future uncertainties, and yield ourselves to the Lord's goodness, to the blessedness of becoming His Leading Lady.

Mary in the Mirror

LET'S LOOK AT the story of a woman who gazed into the looking glass and saw God's purpose for her. It wasn't what she expected to see. It wasn't a role she thought she could fulfill. She was a young woman, just little more than a girl, a teenager, informed with the news that she had been chosen to perform a leading role unlike any other in the annals of time and history. Her only audition was the simple faith and pure heart that defined her character. Imagine this strange scene between the woman and her surprising heavenly visitor.

Now in the sixth month the angel Gabriel was sent by God to a city of Galilee named Nazareth, to a virgin betrothed to a man whose name was Joseph, of the house of David. The virgin's name was Mary.

And having come in, the angel said to her, "Rejoice, highly favored one, the Lord is with you; blessed are you among women!"

But when she saw him, she was troubled at his saying, and considered what manner of greeting this was.

Then the angel said to her, "Do not be afraid, Mary, for you have found favor with God.

"And behold, you will conceive in your womb and bring forth a Son, and shall call His name Jesus.

"He will be great, and will be called the Son of the Highest; and the Lord God will give Him the throne of His father David.

"And He will reign over the house of Jacob forever, and of His kingdom there will be no end."

LUKE 1:26–33

Several startling truths emerge from this dramatic scene. First, Mary is already spoken for. Talk about the ultimate love triangle! The Lord sends His angel to an engaged woman, someone who clearly sees her life spread out before her in a particular direction. She will marry Joseph, a good man, a carpenter who has asked her to marry him and share his simple life. Nothing fancy, nothing glamorous, but life-changing nonetheless. She is a plain girl from an honorable family, but not from a dynasty of great wealth or power. We can presume that Joseph was a good catch for her, and not only that, but that she loved him and he loved her.

We're told that she is a virgin when the angel appears to her, reinforcing a wholesomeness to their relationship. Then as now, it wasn't uncommon for an engaged couple to partake prematurely of the physical delights of the marriage bed. But Mary and Joseph were honoring God and respecting each other. They were waiting to consummate the intimacy of their commitment to each other.

Gabriel greets this special woman: "Rejoice, highly favored one, the Lord is with you; blessed are you among women!" And Mary doesn't know what to make of it. "But when she saw him, she was troubled at his saying, and considered what manner of greeting this was." She knows that something's up, that the fabric of her life has been irrevocably altered by this strange messenger. It shakes her to the foundation of the life she had planned for herself. Her simple household—with her big strong carpenter and the certainty of their Jewish heritage—melted into an uncertain future. It melts into God's future, for the angel "reassures" her by telling her something even more stunning and fear-provoking. *She* will conceive God's Child! *She* will birth the Messiah, the great Son of the Most High, whose coming had been prophesied for centuries. It's not just that her future domestic bliss has been changed—it's been obliterated! It's not just that God is asking her to cook a meal or take a sacrifice to the Temple. No, He is asking for her inmost part, her sexuality, her vulnerability, her innocence, her nurturing, her mothering for His Son. He is asking her to forgo the natural course of her engagement and marriage to Joseph. He is asking for more than it would have been imaginable to give.

He asks the same of you today. You may not have Gabriel appearing in your living room, and you won't be called to birth, physically, the Christ Child. But we are all called to give up the future and the life that we have imagined for ourselves and yield to birthing God's greatness in our lives, just like Mary. He wants all of you, all you have to give, all of your ability to give yourself to His purposes, all of your ability to conceive and nurture His fruit in your life. We will talk more about the unique capacity of women as life-givers in chapter four, but for now realize how much God wants to ignite your potential in ways you can't even imagine. He has planted His seeds of greatness in your very being. Even your reading of this page may be one of his seeds planted to inspire your acceptance of His calling on your life. Look in the mirror and see the woman God wants you to be.

After hearing that she's soon to become a mother, Mary next asks Gabriel, "How can this be, since I do not know a man?" (Luke 1:34). While still a virgin, she knows the impossibility of her conceiving when no man has touched her, not even her fiancé. The angel explains that the Holy Spirit will overshadow her to conceive the Messiah in her womb. He then announces that her cousin, Elizabeth, a woman barren in her old age, has even conceived a son, as if to punctuate his exit line: "For with God nothing will be impossible" (Luke 1:37).

This is where Mary looks beyond the mirror image and sees the woman she was created to be. She no longer finds herself limited to the drape of her shawl or the color of her eyes in identifying her true self. Instead, she sees beyond the physical details and finds the impossible. God has chosen to magnify His purposes through her. He has chosen her to accomplish the impossible as we know it—to conceive a child without an earthly father. Instead of accepting the limits of her self as she has known before, she dares to believe in the God of the impossible, the God who shines His light through us until the world is aflame with His glory.

She doesn't see her past when she looks in the mirror. Sure, it's there—who she used to be and what she used to want out of life. She doesn't see her present when she looks in the mirror. And it certainly glares back at her. Here she is pregnant with a baby that was not fathered by her fiancé. What in the world will he think of her? Will he still trust her? What about her family, and the neighbors, and everyone in their village? What kind of woman gets herself pregnant before the wedding ceremony just weeks away? Mary had to look past all these questions and pressures of the present. And she had to look beyond the future she had already imagined for herself as well. No quiet, simple life as the wife of a carpenter for her. She would be known for generations as the mother of God!

Finally, Mary doesn't get hung up on her own desires when she looks into the mirror of her soul. She sees only God working through her. She has become a leading lady caught up in a role so much larger than herself and her life.

Larger Than Life

I BELIEVE GOD wants to use each of us in a way larger than our own lives. Like Mary, we must have faith in God and believe that through the Lord we can achieve so much more than we could ever accomplish on our own. Many women get so wrapped up in who they think they should be, not who they truly are. They feel pressure from their parents to pursue a certain career or a certain kind of boyfriend or husband. They feel pressure from the special man in their life to look a certain way, dress a certain way, and act a certain way. There's the pressure from their bosses and co-workers, even from their ministers and prayer partners, to be someone they may not be. These women wonder why they feel empty and detached from life. They have become mannequins dressed up in the showcase windows of other people's department stores, not the leading lady on a stage of God's greatness. Not only are they missing out on the authenticity of the woman inside them, they are likely missing out on what God has in store as well. For I believe that being true to ourselves grounds us in a way that allows us to hear the Lord's calling to His greatness. Mary thought she knew what was best for her, but God had other things in mind, and she had enough faith to simply say yes. Mary trusts that she doesn't necessarily know what is truly best for her. Marrying Joseph and living a quiet life may have once offered her the vision of security for her future, but she is wise enough to know that Life is larger than her intentions. And only God is larger than Life.

Too many people have their hands full of their own agendas and their minds full of their own greatness, so they don't have room for God to plant His seeds in them. Women so wrapped up in their own looks and appearances, all taken in by the latest seaweed facial wrap and herbal perfume, or women so consumed with their PalmPilots and cell phones in their attempt to organize the world—they don't have room in their lives for what is truly larger than life. We must drop our designer sunglasses and our consumption of the latest crisis brewing on the horizon and be real about what a role of true greatness looks like in our lives. We need not qualify our response to the Director's call on us. We should just open ourselves to His possibility, even if that looks like an impossibility to us. That's all He asks for right now, a simple yes.

What is the Lord calling you for today? How does He want you to magnify Him? What must you let go of in order to have room for Him to bless you and plant His seeds in you?

Like the mother of our Lord Jesus, women are still being called out to serve as leading ladies. It may require you to move beyond past shame and old wounds. Your response may require you to believe in the impossible, to respond like Elizabeth, "Blessed is she who believed, for there will be fulfillment of those things which were told her from the Lord" (Luke 1:45). Are you listening to what He wants to tell you? And your response may necessitate relinquishing your future hopes and dreams into His care for purposes exponentially greater than your fame or fortune. But this much I know: He calls us all onstage and wants to bless us with the fulfillment of His fruit in our lives. Put down this book for a moment and consider what magnificent role He is calling you to. What's holding you back from accepting His opportunities with humility, gratitude, and a larger-than-life perspective? It's time to take action, Leading Lady.

CHAPTER TWO

Center Stage

LITTLE GIRLS LOVE to play dress-up. They put on their momma's skirt and hat, earrings and makeup, and prance in front of the mirror pretending to be all grown up. They stare at their reflections, trying to look older, prettier, just like their favorite pop star. Their make-believe games are fun and fantasy-filled. One day they may be a recording diva on a sound stage; the next, they may be president of the United States.

This playacting is not limited to little girls. As anyone who has been around teenagers knows, adolescents spend countless hours in front of the mirror, making sure they have the right clothes, the right makeup, the right look of the day. *People* magazine and MTV provide guidelines and role models and fashion do's and don'ts. But this is okay. As we're growing up and developing into adults, all of us, women and men alike, try on different "clothes" and model ourselves after those we admire. There's nothing wrong with this modeling during our adolescence. Girls and boys must experiment and discover what works for them and who they really are.

However, many women become mired in the quicksand of other women's images, sinking slowly, gradually, year after year, further and further away from their true selves. The women they model themselves after may be wonderful, successful, godly ladies—their mothers, their older sisters, a teacher or a coach, a boss. They may try to emulate the charismatic charm and style of a movie star, gospel singer, talk-show host, or world-class athlete. And although it's wise to use others' admirable qualities as inspiration, problems occur when they try to force themselves into an image that doesn't fit who they really are. They mold themselves into the good girl, the wonder woman, the Christian martyr-mother-saint, and while they may appear to be successful and to have it all together, inside of them is a growing sense of dissatisfaction and dishonesty. It's like trying to squeeze into the wrong size shoes. You can cram your feet into them, and you might look good for a while, but sooner or later your toes start to cramp, your bunions ache, and blisters form on the back of your heels.

What's terribly unfortunate is that then these women suffer in silence, walking around in shoes that don't fit, afraid to remove them. They fear being branded an impostor or worry that their true selves won't live up to the image they've been portraying. Some women stay behind a mask of what their families and pop culture dictate as successful and beautiful, because the mask acts as a shield, protecting them from anyone getting too close. They have experienced so much hardship and anguish in life, and the mask is a defense, a facade that doesn't reveal their vulnerability, their weakness, or the pain churning within their souls. Saddest of all are the women who remain behind their masks because they've long forgotten their true selves. They have spent so much time and energy creating and maintaining the illusion of who they are supposed to be, that they've lost sight of who they really are. They've suffocated their extraordinary personality and buried their unique beauty. They worry that if they step out from behind their mask, they won't know who else to be.

Well, I say to all these women—I say to all of you reading this book—the time has come to drop the mask! Stop doing the impersonations and take your mark at center stage, fulfilling the role you were born to play. Do not forfeit who you are in pursuit of playing a role that was not designed for you. Be true to your character and boldly claim your place in the world!

I know it takes courage to drop the mask. Suppose you are rejected? Suppose people laugh at you? False friends may be appalled by your transformation, because when you change your role, they might be forced to change their own. Well-meaning family members may be concerned—after all, why should you change? You were everything they thought you should be. But you can't maintain the status quo at the expense of your destiny. You'll be shortchanging yourself and everyone in your life if you don't fulfill the promise of who you are meant to be. Think of all the potential you are squashing by not allowing yourself or the Creator to display the masterpiece of who you are.

My goal here is not just to inspire you but to admonish you that it is essential that you succeed in being you! You were created with a Divine purpose, and it is our Lord's desire to see you live up to the image *He* created for you. So, today we drop the mask by developing our own opinion, style, and personality. We drop the mask by developing the courage—and it can be developed—to risk being different from those who have influenced us. *Complementing*—not duplicating—the women who influenced them catapults great women into leading ladies. For you see, leading ladies do not imitate, they create. Have you discovered the creative powers, forces, and instincts that exist inside you? These are the energies that will build, equip, and empower you for your destined end. Today, let's begin the challenging task of dropping our masks and discovering the power within.

Sister, our Lord has sacrificed too much and blessed you too far to allow you to hide behind a mask. He delights in shattering those false masks and structuring the delicate shards into an intricate, rainbow-hued mosaic of the daughter He has formed in His own image. "For we are His workmanship, created in Christ Jesus for good works, which God prepared beforehand that we should walk in them" (Ephesians 2:10). Drop the mask and reveal the workmanship of the Master.

Blocking Your Stage

FROM MY EXPERIENCES as a playwright, I know that when I commit words to the page, I imagine scenes coming to life full-blown: my Jacob character stands next to the door when he says these words to Leah, and Rebekah hides in the fabric of the lush drapes and eavesdrops. The scene springs to life like a movie in my mind, and I merely try to capture the words and movements of the characters as they interact.

However, as a playwright I also know that when a director begins transferring my script to the concrete reality of an actual stage in a theater limited by physical dimensions, scenes can change. Bound by the square footage onstage, limited by the visibility from certain rows in the balcony, perhaps confined by certain props or special effects, a good director works with his cast to find the best way to frame each scene. This process is called *blocking.* As actors walk through their lines, the director experiments and choreographs the movement of each actor. Careful blocking and creative use of props can match the essence of a scene with the space of the stage like a brilliant diamond set into the most exquisite mounting of a golden ring.

How do you achieve this marriage of form and function in your own life's stage? You must be practical about what you have to work with and the resources available. You must appreciate the present apparent limitations on your performance while not losing sight of your ideal position on the ultimate stage. As we addressed before and will again, some of those limitations are self-imposed as the result of negative masks and sabotaging self-talk, an unwillingness to act in faith, and fears of changing the status quo we're mired in. Other limitations arise from outside our control, and these are the ones that require creativity, sensitivity, and an ability to see beyond the barriers everyone else takes for granted. It reminds me of the dramatic effects in many of the extravagant Broadway musicals of the last few years. As staged at the Majestic Theatre in New York City, *The Phantom of the Opera,* one of the all-time great romantic musicals, incorporates a scene in which the imposing chandelier of the Paris Opera House comes crashing down—nearly touching the heads of the audience seated close to the stage! It's obviously a sensational special effect that leaves us gasping in the audience as we become part of the drama. However, it took the imaginative vision of someone to move beyond the usual possibilities—you can't venture huge props out into the audience like that!—to see how exciting and dramatic the effect would be if you could transcend the limits of the stage.

For women, the stage limitations have often, sadly enough, been imposed by men, out of either fear or insecurity in their own manhood or their misguided aggression and desire for control. Cultural traditions, both within and beyond the Church, have also bound women into socially accepted roles that often suppressed or ignored their multitude of talents, gifts, and offerings. While we have seen great strides made in the way our twenty-first-century world greets and considers its women, some cul-de-sacs of sexism, racism, and self-righteousness still threaten to dead-end the dreams of women.

So does this mean you should remain in the shadows because that's where society has directed you? Should you wait in the wings hoping someday your cue to step forward will come? If you want to be a leading lady, you must take your place in the spotlight before life slips away. Sometimes one cannot afford to wait for society's permission to move forward. Take the limits off the stage of your life and know that true leading ladies are limited only by their own creative thought and their willingness to go beyond the familiar into the extraordinary. Realize that the only barriers that shackle you are the limits that you allow to diminish your own creativity. Recognize the barriers being imposed on you and determine how to step beyond them. Face your obstacles and devise ways to work around them. Block your scenes so that you make the best use of your stage and transcend the limits that hold you back. All the world is your stage—step up and allow yourself to shine.

Asking for What's Yours

TO BECOME A leading lady, you must raise the curtain and step forward. You must extend yourself beyond the self-imposed limits, external pressures, and patriarchal authoritarian control. You must strip away all traces of self-doubt and fear. Don't let yourself get weighted down by crushing despair over the way things are and defenseless resignation to glass ceilings and kitchen confinement. It is your time to soar! You must begin by separating fact from fiction and realize that our Lord created you in His image as a female for a distinct and sacred purpose. God is no respecter of gender distinctions when regarding His call to greatness—He calls and uses women and men with equal pleasure and glorification to Himself. I don't think God stopped to consider whether or not Mother Teresa would be limited in caring for thousands of infected and dying outcasts (and inspiring countless others) because she was a woman. I don't believe He paused to second-guess whether Harriet Tubman had the strength as a woman to lead hundreds of runaway slaves to freedom through the dark, treacherous outposts of the Underground Railroad.

God consistently shows Himself as a Father who gives generously and equally, even when gifting in different ways, to both His sons and His daughters. This truth emerges clearly from the request of the daughters of Zelophehad and God's response to them. Mahlah, Noah, Hoglah, Milcah, and Tirzah question the accepted patriarchal standard of Jewish law in which only sons were eligible to inherit their father's property. When their father, Zelophehad, dies in the wilderness without male heirs, his five girls muster their courage and dare to ask for what belonged to their father. "Why should the name of our father be removed from among his family because he had no son? Give us a possession among our father's brothers" (Numbers 27:4). Instead of allowing their uncles to absorb their inheritance, these sisters are willing to ask for their share.

Moses doesn't know what to do with this strange situation, but as a man of integrity, he brings their case before the Lord. God wastes no time laying down his verdict: "The daughters of Zelophehad speak what is right; you shall surely give them a possession of inheritance among their father's brothers, and cause the inheritance of their father to pass to them. And you shall speak to the children of Israel, saying: 'If a man dies and has no son, then you shall cause his inheritance to pass to his daughter' " (Numbers 27:7–8). Women have a right to power, to all that the Lord wants to bless them with in their lives.

Too often women have been conditioned not to ask for what is rightfully theirs. Like greedy bullies on the playground, men have divvied up the goods among themselves, afraid of sharing their authority and riches with the female coheirs in their lives. It's only been in the last hundred years that women in our country have been given the right to vote, to own property, and to make their voices heard in government and in the Church. I say "given," but in reality it was taken by courageous women who refused to remain in the assigned "appropriate" roles. These renegade women who attracted controversy only a few decades ago are now upheld as heroes. Are you willing to lead the charge for generations of women to come?

Our world still needs women who are willing to stand up as lightning rods for energizing those around them. Even today, with the dawn of a new century gleaming along the horizon of time before us, the Church continues to sidestep and suppress half the members of its body. It reminds me of the tragic consequences of a stroke victim, someone who has experienced deprivation of oxygen to the brain caused by the rupture or blockage of a blood vessel. Often one side of their body is left impaired with the brain unable to direct the fine-motor control of fluid movement and graceful agility. Instead, the damaged side of the face is drawn and sunken, the arm and hand of that weakened side drape clumsily to the body, the leg and foot drag and sweep behind. But like Jesus healing the paralytic, He has healed and continues to heal the way the Church relates to its women.

From my many years of ministry, I'm all too aware of the many controversies swirling around women's roles in the Church. Should we let her teach Sunday school? Do we let her read Scripture from the pulpit? Do we dare let her teach a mixed group or just a nice, quiet ladies' Bible study? Why isn't she happy to work with the children's ministry and organize the fellowship suppers? Surely we can never let her preach!

But my guess is that you know what men are just now starting to admit: Women have often been the driving force of the Church. Like a weary bus driver dutifully guiding her passengers to their many destinations, women have been hidden behind the gaudy advertisement of a man's name on the side of the bus. The old saying that behind every successful man is a supportive woman has often been a license for sexism. Many men have abdicated the hard work of ministry and its many details to women. They have created a double standard in which women can virtually do anything that needs doing as long as they let men have the voice and take the credit for it. Women have not been allowed to use their voice, because whoever speaks has influence. Whoever feeds the flock leads the sheep. I wish this were an overstatement that would make you laugh at the foolish fears and insecurities of a small handful of weak men. While I know that many men are not intimidated by women and welcome their contribution, there are still those who cling fearfully to the controls of life like the wizard behind the drapes. These men attempt to control Oz while masked behind the curtains of a few poorly interpreted Scriptures, leaving the women waiting for fate to claim what only faith can conquer. As an African-American, I realize that discrimination is a tragic reality, whether by gender or by race, that leaves many wounds deep in the flesh of the soul.

Cultural Evolution

SUCH LICENSE FOR sexism has expired and must never be renewed. You must realize that limiting a woman's role in ministry is a cultural defect and not a biblical effect. Yes, Paul has several things to say about women's behavior both in and out of the Church, as he does about men's actions as well. In his letter to his young protégé, Timothy, Paul writes:

> *I desire therefore that the men pray everywhere, lifting up holy hands, without wrath and doubting;*
> *in like manner also, that the women adorn themselves in modest apparel, with propriety and moderation, not with braided hair or gold or pearls or costly clothing,*

but, which is proper for women professing godliness, with good works.
Let a woman learn in silence with all submission.
And I do not permit a woman to teach or to have authority over a man, but to be in silence.
For Adam was formed first, then Eve.
And Adam was not deceived, but the woman being deceived, fell into transgression.
Nevertheless she will be saved in the childbearing if they continue in faith, love, and holiness, with self-control.

1 TIMOTHY 2:8–15

This passage has often been appropriated to silence women and deflect their contributions in the Church. But we must realize a couple of things to make sense out of what Paul is saying, let alone to apply it to women today. First, he's writing about cultural characteristics and how they interface with Christian character-building. Paul makes it clear that the principles he's expounding—modesty, propriety, godliness—are timeless in their appeal and application to women. But his examples of these are cultural—avoiding the accoutrements of temple prostitutes, and crass women hiding behind their wealth and class status. It's not that women today can't braid their hair or wear gold jewelry or pearl necklaces or designer clothing. For better or worse, our cultural roles have blended and shifted and blurred to the point where there is no clear-cut code of dress or hair fashion for women. Most of us know that character is not established by these mementos of femininity. I have seen promiscuous women dress like nuns. Humans look on the outer appearance and thereby assess who we are. But God's eyes are far keener, and He looks upon the soul.

Nevertheless, modesty, while not easily transferred into a specific dress code, is apparent to both the beholder and the transgressor. While we must realize that clothes do not make the woman, they may, when taken to extremes, leave clues that expose inner areas of insecurity and vulnerability. It's not in dressing to the standard of those she works with or even worships with, but as she pursues personal holiness that a woman will discover that God helps her determine where her wardrobe should have boundaries. Quite frankly, I find that the boundaries of personal holiness are determined by the condition of your heart toward God and how you feel you should represent Him.

The issue surrounding women in the Church and what some have deemed as their silent support has largely been hypocritical. How can the woman keep silent if she sings in the choir? What kind of church will not allow a woman to speak the words that she just sang in a hymn? Is that true silence? How can a woman be able to influence the finances of ministry, leave an impact on the teaching curriculum, write lyrics and sing them, direct plays and implement their production, and then be told that her gender exempts her from speaking? In truth, her checkbook speaks, her choir robe speaks, her teaching and writing and typing are all methods of communication relative to speaking in today's world. If Paul's words are to be taken literally by our society, then a woman in the Church should be silenced everywhere or nowhere at all.

Consider that a woman carried the first message that Christ has risen from the dead. She announced it to all the men. A woman ran from the well and witnessed to the men of Samaria, inviting them to come see the man who had told her about all the things she had ever done. A woman carried the Christ Child who was, in fact, the Word made flesh according to John's Gospel. Yes, women have greatly laid the foundation of our faith, but it doesn't stop there. What would the world of science be without women like Marie Curie? What would the Civil Rights movement be without pioneers like Sojourner Truth? What would medicine be like today without the contributions of women like Elizabeth Blackwell, the first woman to earn a medical degree in this country (1849), open a practice, and establish the first American hospital (1857) staffed entirely by women for women?

Women's contributions are many and manifold. They have danced on our stages, entertained us at war, educated us in universities, and inspired us with their songs. If the women were silent, we would have lost the voice of Mahalia Jackson out of our churches. We would've lost the voice of Maya Angelou from our poetry books. Oh, my sister, if women go silent, our cultural orchestras would cease and our world's creativity would diminish and wither. And our Risen Savior might still remain unannounced from the empty tomb.

For despite its suppression of women, the Church has been healed by its Katherine Kuhlmans, touched by its Aimee Semple McPhersons, fed by its Mother Teresas, and revived by its Jackie McCulloughs. It has been taught by its Marilyn Hickeys and instructed by its Joyce Meyers. Oh, look at what we would have missed had we silenced our sisters and our mothers—we would have missed so many miracles!

So sing, barren women, as Isaiah declared. Prophesy, you daughters, as Joel said you would. There is a new breed of men coming who welcome the resurrection of our women in leadership. Like Deborah, the woman who sat on the Board of Judges for Israel and was able to lead her nation to battle, now you need to lead us where your gifts enable you to do so. Preach the Word, sing the Word, type the Word, and e-mail the Word. But whatever you do, do not keep silent! We need to hear from you. And one day, when we put away childish things for good, we will apologize for the inconsistencies we have put you through. Maybe our punishment was, in fact, the loss of words and voices that would have comforted us through the tragedies of life. Perhaps our punishment is in the songs that were not recorded, the sermons that remain unspoken, and the many lost cities that could have been reached had a woman from our wells been allowed to speak.

Cultures evolve and change as circumstances require new responsibilities and time affords clearer perspectives about our past decisions. In recent years we've seen Pope John Paul II make a public apology for the Vatican's sometimes passive response to the heinous crimes of the Jewish Holocaust during World War II. Leaders of the Southern Baptist Convention have issued public apologies for their denomination's support of slavery during our country's Civil War. Looking back, it's easier and clearer to see the mistakes we've made, either by passively allowing injustice to occur or by actively participating in an injustice. Our culture has evolved in tremendous ways for women in the twentieth and now into the twenty-first century. The Church is slowly waking up to these seismic shifts that recognize the vitality and unique power of its women. Sing out, sister, and refuse to be silent ever again!

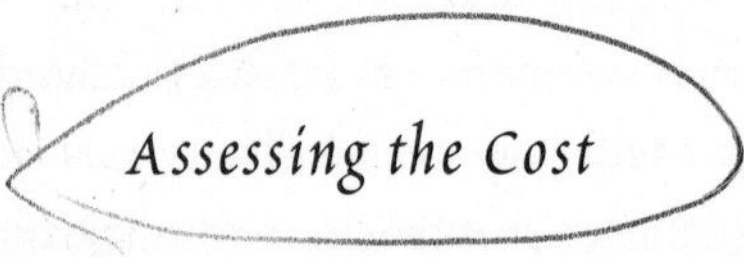

Assessing the Cost

YES, YOU MUST be realistic about the way our culture and society regard women, but no, ma'am, you must not be inhibited from giving all you've got. Sometimes you might even have to give more than you've got. You might have to stretch yourself beyond your limits. This is when you have to assess the cost of taking your place onstage. You need to know what sacrifices are necessary and when to make them. You must determine which risks are worth taking, despite how foolhardy they may seem, and which ledges of security are really precipices of dangerous mediocrity.

If the example of the Good Samaritan is any indication, we are all called to serve beyond our means at some point. While the priest and the Levite are too busy and pious to touch the wounded mugging victim on the side of the road, a certain Samaritan had compassion on him. The Samaritan not only comforts and bandages the poor man but places him on his donkey and checks him into an inn. He leaves two denarii, which is approximately two days' wages, with the innkeeper for the expenses of the injured man and promises to repay him the cost of any other items (see Luke 10:29–37). The Samaritan knows it will cost him not just in the present but in the future as well, and he anticipates the means required to complete the gift he has been called to give.

If you have been called to give and serve from your rich inventory of talents and gifts—and the Lord calls all his daughters to greatness—what is it going to cost you? Many women ask, How does a woman maintain her feminine grace and beauty as she climbs up the ladder of success? How does she maintain and balance the priorities of her husband and family while establishing herself as a conscientious entrepreneur? Can she really have it all? What is the cost of leadership for women in the twenty-first century?

Well, let me tell you, it might cost you some of your negligees and PTAs if you are going to take your rightful place onstage. You might have to invest the money set aside for a new dishwasher into your ministry or your fledgling cottage company. Or perhaps you have to put aside your Day Planner and PalmPilot and attend to matters more meaningful than mind-numbing meetings and dress-to-impress power lunches. You may be required to give up things that make you feel good in order to give in-service for the good of others. The cost of greatness sometimes means going beyond the anticipated resources and their prescribed purposes.

Going Over Budget

AS WE ASSESS our costs, it is wise to develop a budget. Budgets take into account the cost of our needs and how much we have to spend. They are intended to provide a clear and comfortable plan for how to reach our goals, financial or otherwise. Without a budget, we might overspend and fall short of our desired end.

> *For which of you, intending to build a tower, does not sit down first and count the cost, whether he has enough to finish it—*
> *lest, after he has laid the foundation, and is not able to finish, all who see it begin to mock him, saying,*
> *"This man began to build and was not able to finish."*
>
> LUKE 14:28–30

Have you counted your costs and made your budget so that you may fulfill your dreams and potential for greatness? Or do you find yourself without walls or a roof as the rains of misfortune fall upon you?

Have you ever gone over budget? I know some of us tend to make this a harmful habit because we don't realistically count the cost of our needs. Some folks live in denial about the price of what is required and, consequently, dig themselves into debt to merciless masters. These people must reconsider what their priorities are and how to plan for the future. They must realistically assess their costs, determine a budget, and make an unwavering commitment to adhere to it.

Budgets are wonderful things, but we must also consider the moments when apparent limitations challenge us to risk going over our resource budget as a matter of faith. Now, I'm not talking about reckless overspending—buying a BMW when you are on a Volkswagen budget. Nor am I talking about impulsive buying to give yourself a momentary rush of pleasure; those sexy red shoes or that new lipstick might make you feel good for the moment, but you won't be smiling when the bills come in.

No, I'm talking about going over budget as a way of putting your faith into motion. When you've discovered your role as a leading lady, heard your calling and stepped out from the wings, you may look around and see where the stage appears to drop off into the orchestra pit. At that moment you have to drop to your knees in prayer so that you can have the courage to step beyond the darkened edge of the stage.

Cathy Hughes knows what it means to "go over budget" in order to fulfill her calling at center stage. Ms. Hughes attended Creighton University and the University of Nebraska at Omaha but did not graduate. In 1969 she began working at KOWH, a black radio station in Omaha. In 1973 she became sales director at WHUR-FM, based in Washington, D.C., and two years later she became the station's first female general manager. She saved her pennies and worked inside the industry until she found a station she wanted to buy five years later. From a small Washington, D.C., AM station that she rechristened WOL, Cathy Hughes challenged the status quo on many levels. For one thing, she was an African-

American woman in an industry, like so many, run by Caucasian men. She managed to secure the necessary loans for WOL's acquisition despite the insistence of bankers who maintained that she must appeal to traditional white audiences to keep advertising dollars flowing. Ms. Hughes had a vision, however, for an African-American station that not only played appealing music—mostly classic R & B—but addressed vital issues of social justice and racism.

Those early years were bitterroot tough. Ms. Hughes was forced to sell her car and eventually her home in order to make the loan payments on the station. During the early 1980s, inflation and interest rates soared and challenged WOL's ability to turn a profit. When her marriage collapsed, she and her teenaged son were forced to move into the station. (Interestingly enough, despite all her own personal sacrifices, she would not compromise saving for her son's college fund. Today her son, Alfred Liggins III, is a graduate of the Harvard Business School and president of his mother's company.) She went without a paycheck herself to pay her tiny staff and keep the station afloat. She even worked as a radio talk show host in order to save money and discovered her natural gift as a thoughtful, articulate analyst of complex social issues.

Cathy Hughes used word of mouth and a clever advertising campaign to overcome the obstacles standing in the way of her business success. She addressed her listeners as a community and asked earnestly for their help in creating a larger listening family for WOL. She came up with the idea to ask "family members" to write "I listen to WOL" on their personal checks paid to Washington-area merchants. It worked so well that soon she was purchasing her next station and then her next one, all the while maintaining her formula for success. She knew what she was willing to sacrifice and she stuck to it, even in the hard times. Today, Hughes chairs the board of a media empire known as Radio One, valued at well over a billion dollars! In the summer of 2000, Radio One made history with its billion-dollar acquisition of a dozen radio stations from the conglomerate Clear Channel. It was the largest acquisition ever by an African American–run company.

Thelma and Louise Meet Deborah and Jael

OF COURSE, CATHY Hughes is not the first extraordinary woman to overcome apparently insurmountable odds to take her place onstage. While Hughes's shattering of the glass ceiling serves as a powerful contemporary example of a woman's sacrificial leadership, an even earlier example lends us a timeless paradigm for balancing strength with grace. In the Book of Judges, we find an incredible story of a woman who knew how to count the cost and take her place onstage.

Deborah is the only woman in Israel to serve as Judge. We aren't told much about her before her courageous reign at the helm of the oppressed Israelite nation. We do know that she was the wife of Lapidoth (Judges 4:4) and that she was a mother (Judges 5:7). But we're first introduced to her as a prophetess, the leader of her people during a twenty-year stretch of oppression at the hands of Jabin, a Canaanite king, and his army commander, Sisera. She holds court under the Palm of Deborah, and like her namesake, "a bee," this extraordinary woman buzzes with a certainty, strength, and deliberation that sharply contrasts with many of the weak and corrupt men surrounding her. God speaks through her to Barak with instructions about how to overcome Sisera and Jabin's army. It's clear that God will deliver the Israelites victorious and lead Sisera directly into Barak's path.

But here we have an interesting turn of events in the story: Barak turns to his commander in chief and says, "If you go with me, I will go; but if you don't go with me, I won't go" (Judges 4:8, NIV). Now certainly it's not unusual for a warrior to want the security and protection of his leader nearby as he goes into battle. However, it's simply amazing for Barak to make the ultimatum he makes. It's not just an invitation to his leader to boost morale by accompanying him to battle; it's a qualification predicated on this woman's willingness to crawl through the desert and face an enemy army of more than nine hundred iron chariots, quite a sizable unit for that time. It's unclear exactly why Barak feels so strongly that Deborah must accompany him to the front lines. Perhaps he wants to test her to see if she really has had this word from the Lord; surely she wouldn't risk her life if she hasn't indeed heard God's voice. Or maybe Barak trusts her leadership to the extent that he doesn't want to venture off without it. For whatever reason, it seems clear that the cost to Deborah was enormous.

Consequently, in her willingness to go with Barak, she makes it clear that girl power will rule the day. "Very well . . . I will go with you. But because of the way you are going about this, the honor will not be yours, for the LORD will hand Sisera over to a woman" (Judges 4:9, NIV). Because of the caveat Barak placed on his obedience to God, Deborah makes it clear to him that he will not share the honor to come from Sisera's fall. It's striking, too, that she doesn't hesitate with her reply. She doesn't say, "Let me call my husband and see what he thinks. Let me check with my girlfriends and get back to you. Let me pray about it and I'll let you know tomorrow." She doesn't make excuses by saying,

"I'm the leader of the country—I can't be off traipsing through the desert like a sheepherder. I'm not as physically strong as you men—I might get hurt. Besides, my husband and children need me here." No, Deborah doesn't use any of those lines, some of which might have been justified. Once more she is like her namesake, making a beeline for what needs to be done to fulfill her calling as God's Leading Lady.

The other point Deborah makes to Barak is her prophecy concerning Sisera's demise. It's almost as if she's saying, "If you can't trust God enough to do your part without me, big boy, then God's going to show you how well a strong woman can do the job." And sure enough, what follows is one of the most stunning murder scenes in all of literature. Deborah has kept her word and joined Barak near the Kishon River with an Israeli army of ten thousand men. When Sisera comes after them with his fancy chariot brigade, Deborah gives the word from the Lord and sends Barak after Sisera.

Once more, the story takes a turn as Deborah's prophecy is fulfilled. As the entire Canaanite army falls—"All the troops of Sisera fell by the sword; not a man was left" (Judges 4:16, NIV)—Sisera takes off on foot in an attempt to escape with his life. He runs into what he thinks is a friendly tent—King Jabin and the tent's owner, Heber, were on good terms. There Heber's wife, Jael, graciously invites him in and says, "Don't be afraid." After his flight through the desert wasteland evading Barak and his pursuers, Sisera is parched and asks Jael for a drink of water. Instead she gives him milk, a precious commodity and a sure sign of her gracious hospitality. He asks her to stand guard at the tent flap and lie that she hasn't seen him if the Israelites come knocking. Then Sisera collapses into the sleep of the exhausted for the last time, for his hostess, sweet and kindly Jael, picks up a tent peg and hammer and drives it into his skull! Talk about a stunning scene of bravado and immense courage.

Deborah's prophecy has indeed come to pass. Sisera and his armies are defeated, as is their king, Jabin, and the Israelites enjoy a rare peaceful interval of forty years. The story of Deborah concludes with the song of praise that she and Barak compose to glorify God with their victory. In many ways it's not just a song of worship and heroism, it's a song of women. Both Deborah and Jael are celebrated in the verses of this historic ballad, a true testimony to the fierce power of women committed to serving their God, their country, and their calling with an unquenchable fervor. Thelma and Louise don't have anything on this fearless female duo.

Worth Fighting For

WHAT IN YOUR life is worth fighting for? Certainly, most of us are willing to lay down our lives for our children, our country, our faith in God. But fortunately most of us aren't called to face a firing squad as martyrs in a blaze of violence.

No, most of us lay down our lives each day by how we expend our energy, give of our time, and fulfill our responsibilities. Do you force yourself to get up an hour early, while the place is still quiet, to work on that novel that's been brewing in your heart for years? Or do you roll over when the alarm goes off, convinced that it's a foolish pursuit with nothing in return? Can you see yourself fulfilling a dream and rising to a promotion by going the extra mile on this project, or can you see yourself complaining to the same empty cubicle this time next year? Are you saving your nickels and dimes so that you can go back to school next fall or so that you can have a shopping fling downtown next weekend? Whose faces come to mind when you consider for whom you are willing to give a little more and take a little less?

Of the many valuable lessons we've taken to heart after the wrenching tragedy enacted on our nation on September 11, 2001, one is to make sure you pursue your true priorities before it's too late. Many office workers and stockbrokers who were in the Twin Towers on that fateful day and survived the devastation of those terrorist acts changed careers. While some expressed the natural fear and shock of post-traumatic stress, many of these survivors saw this intense brush with their mortality as a wake-up call to their hearts. They knew they weren't pursuing their true potentials, their dreams and callings to greatness. They had simply taken a job because they needed a paycheck, and the months flipped over into years and the job became a career. Or else, the passion they once felt had long since melted and drained away, but still they went through the motions on empty, hoping something would come along and fill them up again.

It's sad that often it takes a crisis or tragedy to jolt us into an awareness of our lives and the way we live them. But perhaps what is sadder is when people come to the surface after such an event and aren't willing to risk pursuing their dreams when given this second or third chance. Don't wait until catastrophe strikes to count the cost of what you're living for! Take inventory today and compare the price tag on your vision of the future with what you're earning and spending today. Don't wait for someone to come through and place your future on clearance! Attaining your place onstage never comes cheap. It requires an honest assessment of the barriers that you may face, both personally and as a woman in your specific environment. It requires a willingness to count the cost of your dreams and set your budget so you may have a blueprint to your goals. Finding center stage means exercising courage and a sense of timing finely attuned to God and His directives for your life. Finally, it involves your sacrifices in the right places to pay those costs and reap a reward unlike any you've ever experienced before: the ability to look at yourself in the mirror with a love and respect for who you've become and where you've come from; the ability to know you're pouring out your gifts for worthwhile purposes that bless others even as you are blessed in the giving; and a peace within yourself that steadies you even as you attempt even more daring feats toward greatness.

CHAPTER THREE

The Art of Improvisation

I LOVE GOOD comedy. There is nothing like that laughter that comes from deep down within you and bursts forth with unrestrained mirth. It refreshes your spirit and brightens the mood, and succeeds like nothing else in bringing people together. After all, laughter is the same in any language and country, joining together cultures and creeds and all who share it. Good comedy takes you out of the moment and sweeps you up in fun and frivolity, allowing you for a short while to think of nothing else but the hilarity of humor.

I will always remember the first time I read Maya Angelou's *I Know Why the Caged Bird Sings.* It was embarrassing for me when I burst out laughing in the otherwise still and stately library. My loud laughter pierced the hallowed silence like a hot knife slicing cheesecake. Only the librarian failed to have an appetite for my boisterous emission of approval. She did not see the value of my reaction as others were studying for their exams. I just couldn't help myself. When I read the scene about the children who were sequestered into a church service that they would rather have missed, it struck me as funny. They had sat through the service in a bored daze, as I recall, until the religious, sanctimonious atmosphere was shattered by one of the sisters, who unconsciously lost her grip—not on her seat but on her teeth! I guess in the absence of Polident or denture adhesives, her loosely gripping gums gave way to gravity, and the unsuspecting pair of dentures leaped out into the aisle like a prostitute running for the altar. By the time I finished reading about the children who had slid out of the old wooden pews onto the floor, laughing all the while, I, too, had joined in their hysteria. Yes, I was laughing out loud. I saw the scene as the writer had intended for me, the reader, to experience it. I was nine years old again and everything funny happens in church when you are nine and your mother's lap is the only children's church in the building. Maya had done it for me. She had managed to bond with me and draw me into the wooden-floored church of some old beaten-down building in Arkansas. I was there listening to the upright piano squeak its way into a failed attempt at melodious music. I was there with the young children as they squirmed in their seats. And when amusement of the moment was so vividly brought to life in my mind's eye, Sister Maya delivered the punch line that knocked me out of my seat. She flawlessly described how the teeth flew out of the robust, weathered, and weary old woman, and I, along with the children in her story, were caught in a crescendo of humor so powerful we could not contain ourselves.

This is comedy, as intoxicating as scotch and as smooth as brandy. I was drunk with laughter and everyone knew it, even Mrs. Johnson, the librarian. Though she failed to appreciate the power of Maya's craft as she ushered me into detention hall, she knew why my shoulders were still shaking and my tears still gushing down my face like wind in a mine shaft. The power of laughter is a mighty force.

We can witness comedic talent when we watch contemporary performers like Chris Rock, Martin Lawrence, and the Wayans Brothers, or great masters of comedy like Bill Cosby or Lucille Ball. With his on-target, in-touch observations and razor-edged voice, a performer like Chris Rock paints a word portrait in the minds of his audience, hesitates for just a moment to create the mental thirst of expectation in those around him, and then, like a Michael Jordan rushing downcourt, he zings his punch line on them for a slam dunk. When the audience explodes with uproarious laughter, he knows he has succeeded in reaching them. Does he stop there and move on? No, he seizes the moment and goes into a little riff of wordplay about the clever joke he's just landed. He milks every moment for every ounce of its potential. Audience members' eyes stream with tears as bellies shake and heads bob with unending laughter.

We have also all experienced comedy that doesn't work. Maybe it's the office clown innocently telling an off-color joke at the water cooler that only succeeds in offending those gathered around. It might be an older family member—an uncle or grandfather—who tells the same stale jokes and outdated punch lines at every family reunion or holiday get-together. Or maybe it's a nervous newcomer attempting her stand-up comedy routine for the first time at an open-mike night at a club. Her jokes come off stiff, and she makes no eye contact with her audience.

So what makes one person funny and the other seem dense? Is it just a matter of having good material? Certainly that's part of it, but the real key to successful humor is talent and timing. A comedian must instinctively know how and when to land a joke on the runway and taxi to the gate of a waiting audience's uproarious approval. He or she must interact with the listeners and play off their reactions and responses. Comedians must venture into the spontaneity and energy of the live audience before them, and trust their instincts and the synergy of the moment as they relate to the people receiving their words. They can't be afraid to put aside their prearranged scripts and carefully laid plans and go with what works in the moment. They must master the art of improvisation.

Improv Training

MOST OF US can relate to the mistakes of amateurs in failing to connect with the pulse of their audience and in not waiting for the right timing for their lines. We have all had our moments when we didn't realize where our audience was coming from, which resulted in misunderstanding and hurt feelings. You may have interpreted a co-worker's silence as complicity as you shared an opinion, only to learn later that she disagrees with you. Or you made light of an awkward moment of vulnerable sharing, realizing later the immense gravity it held for your spouse. Perhaps you enthusiastically chimed in when your girlfriend started tearing down her husband after an argument. It was only after they made up that you understood that she just wanted to vent and didn't appreciate you slamming her man. Now she's not talking to you!

Similarly, our timing can be off, as confused and off-balance as a cuckoo clock wound too tight. You ask for a raise just as the boss is about to chew you out for coming in ten minutes late that morning. You scold the kids for being home late from school only to learn that they were helping another child who'd been injured in a fight. You prepare a romantic candle-lit dinner for your husband, and then discover his message on the answering machine relaying that he has to work late.

As human beings, we're all fallible and therefore susceptible to such mistakes. However, it is vital to your performance as a leading lady to learn to engage with the reality of the moment instead of relying on tired old scripts or half-baked plans that don't account for the unpredictability and ever-changing circumstances of life. This means reacting to the present and not obsessing over the scar-kissed wounds of the past or the unborn possibilities of the future. This means getting rid of your canned speeches and predictable plot lines and responding to the drama that is unfolding before you. This means releasing regret and the aborted opportunities from your past and maximizing the moments at hand. You must trust in the Lord enough to risk deviating from the script when necessary and leave yourself open to the joyful surprise of the unexpected.

Our Lord delights in sweeping us up in His lap and surprising us with unexpected treasures. Imagine a loving father surprising his beloved little girl with a favorite chocolate bar or a new paper doll, for no other reason than he loves her and wants to bring her joy. He hides the small treasure in his coat pocket and then picks her up and swings her in the air. She squeals and giggles as she rummages through the overcoat to find her treat. Your Father wants to bestow gifts on you as well. Let yourself be open to the possibilities. Don't tie yourself to some cliché-ridden script and lock yourself into a predictable outcome. Learn to improvise and be in the moment—for your moment is now!

Your Cue Is Now

I KNOW MANY people, ladies as well as some men, who love to watch the afternoon soaps. Their "stories," as they call these programs, usually portray flawlessly attractive people in melodramatic conflicts soaking like dirty laundry in a schizophrenic spin cycle of turmoil. Much of what viewers love about these shows is that even though the plots are drastic and life-changing for the characters, little actually changes from episode to episode. The pretty heroine contemplates dating the new bad boy in town. The trusted matriarch wonders if her beloved husband could be having an affair with her sister. An impoverished stranger wanders into town with an old photo of the biological mother she has never met. Our macho hero uncovers a boardroom plot to overthrow his father's corporation. And on and on it goes. Viewers can miss days, weeks, months—even years—and still pick up the show pretty much where it left off. The reason they can do this is because the scripts rarely change. The speeches of outrage, infatuated love, jealousy, and revelation are recycled and recycled until they lose any real sense of contextual meaning.

But your life is not a soap opera, even if some days' events make you feel like it is. Each day a new story is scripted, a new adventure in which our Lord has cast you as His shining star. Every day He affords you the opportunity to make your mark, impact your world, and take yourself to the next level. Don't get stuck in reruns when a new episode of your life awaits you each and every day.

Unfortunately, many women do not let the Lord's light shine through them. Oh, they're anxious to step out into the spotlight and take their place at center stage—they're just waiting for their cue. The problem is they were waiting so intently for some specific signal that they've missed the call completely, and are still waiting for the right time to make their entrance and Act III is almost over.

I hear these women say, "I'll go back to school when the children are older." "I'll start my own business when the economy is better." "I'll become more active in my church community when I get to know my neighbors better." "I'll go out on a date when the right man asks me." They're waiting for the perfect man, the perfect environment, the perfect set of circumstances before they make a move. But the truth is, earthly perfection is an illusion, manufactured by our impossible expectations and limited grasp of reality. When are circumstances perfect? We don't know what's in store for us in the next moment. What's the perfect time for us to move forward when we don't know what's waiting for us as we step around the corner? And what man is perfect? Men are just as imperfect as women.

You have to let go of your expectations and self-prescribed goals. You have to learn to fly on wings crafted from whatever materials you have at hand instead of waiting until the perfect gossamer white feathers have been tied to your shoulders. You can't wait until you have a perfect destination mapped out before you take the reins of your life's journey and give it direction. You don't need to know exactly the right thing to say to someone in need in order to bless them.

Certainly, I'm not advising you to take foolish risks in business or entrust your heart to a man who has proven untrustworthy. Nor am I recommending impulsive behavior fueled by impatience and a desire to determine your own agenda. But you must not wait for perfection before you flap your wings and let the Lord breathe His Spirit's gentle breezes beneath them. Wait on God and His timing instead, keeping your wings aloft on the wind of His love for you.

But those who wait on the LORD
Shall renew their strength;
They shall mount up with wings like eagles,
They shall run and not be weary,
They shall walk and not faint.

ISAIAH 40:31

Change on a Dime

MOST SERIOUS ACTORS often undergo specific training in the art of improvisation—the ability to invent your part unscripted, to come alive with the necessary lines and actions to bring your role to life, to create a unique role that only you can fulfill. The hardest part, of course, is that you haven't rehearsed, don't have a script, and don't know how your co-stars may respond. But that is the way real life works. Our circumstances shift and turn like driftwood on the churning tide, buffeted by the pounding storms one minute and then the next minute basking in the sunlit sands on the golden edge of a tropical beach. If you make your life choices conditional on what you perceive to be perfection, then you're in for a ride that will rival any roller coaster you can imagine.

As a boy I used to hear old folks say, "Life can change on a dime," and I never really understood what they meant until I was older. When I was a young child, most days seemed alike as I went to school, came home, did my chores, and played with my friends. Then suddenly my father was taken ill. As a teenager I watched my father's lifeblood pour out of him to be filtered by a dialysis machine hooked up beside his bed because his own kidneys slowly refused to do their job. A few years later I watched my father die from that disease, and I grieved that loss even as I wondered how my mother would manage our family without him. Suddenly that dime from the old saying glinted its silver spin of heads or tails. I went from the familiar, carefree days of childhood to the painful assault of sudden adulthood.

On the other side of this dime, I have seen hard times flip into blessings more times than I can count. As a young man I experienced times when God blessed my fledgling ministry beyond my wildest dreams, giving me more and more opportunities to unleash His power in my life and be blessed by His generous provision and mercy. As I've passed a newsstand and seen my face stare back at me from the cover of national magazines, I could understand what it means that life can change on a dime.

You must leave room for God to surprise you even amid the unexpected losses of life. "I would have lost heart, unless I had believed that I would see the goodness of the LORD in the land of the living," says the Psalmist (27:13). God always has something in mind down the road a stretch that He wants to give you. Don't presume you can always know what He's up to or how He will carry out His plans for your life. You can't anticipate and protect yourself from every imagined disaster and trial around the bend. Similarly, you can't even imagine the blessings in store for you waiting at the top of the next hill.

I believe that greatness is released when you seek God to make you effective. Seeking new heights is not as important as mastering your current challenge. As you master what has been given to you, He offers more challenging ways to extend your dominion and grants you more to subdue. Trudge forward if you can. Move forward, sometimes clumsily, sometimes gracefully, but always forward. Remember that it is not the speed of the runner but the relentless pacing of her well-timed rhythm that enables her to reach her goal. Sometimes it is the stumbling forward that breaks the ribbon at the finish line. Just don't quit!

Bitter or Better

OFTEN LIFE EVENTS rip the script we had prepared for ourselves right out of our hands. We are forced to improvise whether we like it or not. Have you ever seen a sudden turn of events leave your plans in shambles and your well-rehearsed ideas shredded like yesterday's newspaper? Life then writes a scene that you never thought imaginable. Who would have thought you would come home and find your husband dead or your daughter moved away? No one knows with the turning of a page which direction our story will take us. And occasionally life turns in such an unfathomable way that we feel the entire story has been derailed.

Such was the case for two leading ladies who were handed a painful script to read. Two extraordinary examples of the improvisational art are found in one amazing story. A woman and her mother-in-law, both widowed, both impoverished, bereft in a foreign land, strike out for the old woman's homeland. As we are about to see, both were tempted to become bitter because their life's script had gone awry. Events had not transpired as they had imagined or hoped. However, each discovered the ultimate source of improvisational power—faith in the goodness and sovereignty of God.

Their story starts with a twist. A once-wealthy and successful landowner is forced out of his comfortable nest by circumstances beyond his control. A famine had descended and decimated the crops and food supply of Elimelech and his family so severely that he was willing to transplant them to a foreign country. Times were so hard that in order to survive, this family packed up, left Israel, and moved into Moab, a land originally settled by the descendants of Lot and a nation that had cursed Israel in the past. Now, moving your family across country is never easy, but moving into a once-hostile territory where prejudice against your people continued was even harder. Nonetheless, Elimelech and his wife, Naomi, moved to Moab with their two sons. It wasn't long, though, before the patriarch died in this strange land, leaving behind his widow and grown boys, who had fallen in love with Moabite women. We're not told explicitly, but Naomi had to be wondering at this point why she had been uprooted just to see her husband die and her sons marry outside of their own people.

Now, as if things weren't bad enough, life throws another curve ball at Naomi. Not one but *both* her sons die as well. It is every momma's nightmare to outlive her babies, and Naomi must lay not one but two of her children to eternal rest. She was the wife of a wealthy landowner who most likely envisioned a happy and prosperous life for herself as a wife and mother. But in a cruel twist of fate, she becomes homeless and a widow, loses both her children, and is left in a foreign land with two foreign daughters-in-law and not much else. I am not sure what is hardest for a woman to face, the trouble in life or the powerless feeling of vulnerability that envelops her soul when life goes off the chart of predictability.

There are some things in life that we just can't understand, no matter how hard we try. And even the most faithful sometimes have trouble imagining how God will restore them with His future blessings after tragedy has struck. But Naomi, though beaten down by life's assaults on her, still retains a slight ray of hope that God will sustain her. She hears that God has provided food for His people back in Israel and sets out to retire there and survive as best she can. She gives her sons' widows, Orpah and Ruth, her blessing and wishes them well and dismisses them from any obligation they may feel toward her. "Go, return each to her mother's house. The LORD deal kindly with you, as you have dealt with the dead and with me. The LORD grant that you may find rest, each in the house of her husband" (Ruth 1:8–9).

When Orpah and Ruth object and reveal their intentions to accompany their mother-in-law back to Bethlehem, Naomi warns them off. Here's where the poison of bitterness creeps in and pollutes her soul until whatever reserve of faith remaining now teems with germs of anger and fear. The older woman presents an eloquent rhetorical argument for why they should stay in Moab. For one thing, she's too old to have any more sons for them to marry even if she were able to find a second husband for herself. And even if she could bear children, Orpah and Ruth would be old women by the time Naomi's new sons could wed them. So she concludes, "No, my daughters; for it grieves me very much for your sakes that the hand of the LORD has gone out against me!" (Ruth 1:13). It's almost as if she views herself as a kind of bad-luck charm, a female Job, and she blames herself for the girls' misfortune. She believes God has gone against her and no good can ever touch her life, and all those who associate with her will be plagued by adversity as well. Naomi is starting down the road to victimhood, to believing that she will always be destined to tragedy. There is a sense of resignation in her words, a weariness, and she doesn't argue further when Ruth insists on sticking by her.

Naomi continues her self-pity party when she and Ruth arrive back in Bethlehem. All her old friends and neighbors come running and ask, "Is this Naomi?" Many years have passed since she had last been in her homeland, and her hardship and grief likely took a physical toll. Perhaps Naomi is thinner, more haggard, has a bit more gray in her hair. Without a doubt, the years have not been kind to this woman, and her appearance may well reflect her misfortune. But this simple question pierces Naomi's heart and shatters her pride, for she has changed so much—lost so much. This question calls her to confront how far her life has gone off its assumed course. It is more than she can bear, and she replies, "Do not call me Naomi; call me Mara" (Ruth 1:20). This is confirmation not only that she is definitely not the woman she used to be, but that her life has changed so much that her very identity has been altered. For you see, Naomi literally translates to pleasant or joy, while Mara means bitter. Yes, she is bitter. Her life's script has been radically revised, and she resents it. "I went out full, and the LORD has brought me home again empty. Why do you call me Naomi, since the LORD has testified against me, and the Almighty has afflicted me?" (Ruth 1:21).

Have you experienced this kind of name-altering bitterness and heartache? If you live long enough, chances are that you will suffer loss. Now I pray that none of you reading this has undergone the devastation of losing your spouse, let alone your children on top of it. But I've been around long enough and lost enough myself to know that we all experience loss. Loss of innocence from the hands of abusers, loss of comfort from parents who abandoned you, loss of hope from children who rebel and reject you, loss of security from men who used your trust as an ATM card to finance their own selfish needs and desires. If you live long enough, life's losses snowball into an avalanche of despair and hopelessness. Perhaps you've lost your own child to a drive-by or to AIDS, or maybe just to the silence of estrangement that grows like weeds in the vacant lot of relationship between parents and their grown children. Maybe you've found yourself starving in a foreign land, one that you chose like the Prodigal Son because of its illusion of good times and cheap fulfillment. You were lured by the catalogue pictures of a flawless life of sensual pleasure, but now you find your belly rumbling at the pig trough. The reality of loneliness and the remorse of promiscuity cut through your fantasy. Or maybe you have had to return home to live with your parents or return to the place where you grew up and swallow whatever crusts of pride remained from your once large loaf of hope. Maybe there are some faithful friends who love you enough to stick by you like Ruth stuck by Naomi, but sometimes their faithfulness only compounds our self-pity. They knew you when and know how far you've fallen. They remind you of the life you could have had, the Eden that could have been yours, if only your script hadn't been ripped up and thrown in the air like confetti on New Year's Eve, leaving your hopes and dreams to be carried away by the harsh winds of fate.

Naomi had spent her life rushing through a wilderness of tragedy, aware of the Eden it could have been. Today as you read this, you, too, may feel like you could have been far greater if life didn't have you on the run. It is not the poverty, or loneliness, the moving backward that makes women the most bitter. It is living with the memories of what could have been, should have been, and even would have been, had this or that not happened. The briny taste of regret makes anyone swallow the gall of despair, and when you drink of it for so long, it embitters your soul. Have you shaken your head at God and rolled your eyes when others have tried to offer you hope or remind you of better times? Have you changed your name to Mara?

Sweetarts and Apple Pie

BUT THE STORY doesn't end in bitterness for Naomi. Despite her feelings that the Lord has afflicted her, she doesn't give up. As she watches the faithful perseverance of her daughter-in-law (we'll get to her momentarily), Naomi does not allow her bitterness and anger to consume her fully. Yes, she expresses and vents herself as we all do during the harsh storms of life, but she does not give up. When Ruth returns from Boaz's fields with her leftover bread and picked-over barley sheaves, Naomi tastes a mouthful of grainy hope. "It is good, my daughter, that you go out with his [Boaz's] young women, and that people do not meet you in any other field," she says (Ruth 2:22). This goodness glimmers like the first iridescent rays of the morning sun piercing the opaque, gray-dappled dawn, like the blackness of Good Friday, the day of our Lord's crucifixion, turns into the blinding bright light of a new dawn on Easter morning. Hope is on its way if you just don't give up.

Do you allow the kindness of others to give you hope? When a stranger opens a door for you, offers you a seat on the bus, or flashes the gift of a smile, do you receive it and let it offer you hope? Like manna fallen from the sky and waiting on the dew-kissed ground, gifts of hope appear to us from the Lord every day. It may be a song or a hymn of encouragement heard on the car radio or playing in an elevator. It could be a verse from God's word that darts straight to the need of your heart with its succulent comfort. It could even be reading this book right now in this particular season of your life!

Naomi seizes her hope and dresses it up for a night on the town. In other words, she marries her hope to action, doing what she knows needs doing for the hope to grow like leaven in a mound of dough. She advises her daughter-in-law in the fine art of modest flirtation, encouraging her to clean up and dress up before going to see Boaz in the threshing room that night. She even goes so far as to instruct Ruth on how to behave and what to do. Uncovering a man's feet while he lay asleep may seem inconsequential to us today, but in this Jewish culture such an act conveyed an intimacy leading to lovemaking. Yes, Naomi basically instructs her daughter-in-law to seduce this man!

Before you think something is amiss or immoral here, realize that in the Israeli culture at this time the ties of family were the backbone of its unity and strength. The young widow is not merely trying to pick up her benefactor like some sugar daddy in a juke joint. As Ruth informs Boaz, he is "a close relative" (Ruth 3:9). In this patriarchal culture, if a married man died, his nearest relatives became responsible for redeeming the potential in the seeds of life he had planted during his lifetime. This included bringing crops to harvest, land to fruition, and even widows to motherhood. While

Boaz has already shown Ruth protection and provision by allowing her to glean in his fields, he now accepts the intimate ultimatum resulting from their night together on the threshing floor. He knows that another kinsman falls ahead of him in the line of succession in redeeming the legacy of Elimelech, Naomi's dead husband. So, like the man of integrity he is, Boaz squares away the traditional customary procedure required before he can restore Naomi to family and prosperity, and before he can marry Ruth and consummate their relationship.

In the end, Ruth—now Mrs. Boaz and a new mother—blesses Naomi with these words: "Blessed be the LORD, who has not left you this day without a close relative; and may his name be famous in Israel! And may he be to you a restorer of life and a nourisher of your old age; for your daughter-in-law, who loves you, who is better to you than seven sons, has borne him" (Ruth 4:14–15). Indeed, the Lord had not abandoned or afflicted Naomi in her hardships—He becomes the supreme redeemer kinsman, generous and kindly, compassionate and comforting, eager to fulfill the seeds of potential greatness that seemed to have withered in the drought. The son Ruth bears and speaks of to his grandmother here is Obed, who grows up to father Jesse, the father of David, the lineage of our Messiah, Jesus.

How could Naomi have known during her season of coldest winter that a spring of hope was thawing just beneath the glaze of ice? How could she have known that this spring would burst into this world as the Water of Life offering hope for any and all of us who thirst for His goodness? How could she have known that she would have a new family, a new son, and the time-tested loyal love of a woman like Ruth? She didn't know, but she never gave up.

Let me say it again, a little louder. She never gave up! If she had abandoned all hope and refused the little sparks of comfort and love God offered her through Ruth, then the tinder of her soul would never have seen the glorious blaze of her old age. If Naomi had given in to the temptation to withdraw, withhold, and withstand the possibility for God to restore and bless her, then she would have missed a joy richer and deeper than the losses she suffered. Her bitterness made the sweetness of those final years richer and juicier than she could have ever imagined. What she had once viewed as a liability—a widowed daughter-in-law from an alien land—becomes the vehicle for her transformation of blessing. As Ruth rightfully tells her, "I'm better than seven sons!" What had once been unbearably bitter has become oh so sweet.

It reminds me of Sweetarts candy and my mother's apple pie. Each one starts out with a tart tang that makes your mouth pucker and your eyes water just a little at the corners. But then the sweetness sets in and relaxes your taste buds and makes you appreciate the sugary goodness of its sharp flavor even more. The tart edge of the apples meets the sweet sugar and cinnamon nestled in the crust. It's the combination that makes it so delicious. God wants to redeem our past losses and our bitterness the same way. Like a kinsman redeemer, He wants us to act in faith, to seduce the hope just ahead of us, and to celebrate the joy and power of His restoration.

Take comfort from the example of Naomi's life, dear sister. You are never too old, and it is never too late! While we may never understand the timing of our Lord and His purposes, we must trust in His goodness for us and in His Hope. Too often women who've tasted the tartness of life become embittered and give up. If they will only hold onto their faith and wield the power of their prayers, they will see mighty changes. "Wait on the LORD; be of good courage, and He shall strengthen your heart; wait, I say, on the LORD!" (Psalm 27:14).

Bringing in the Sheaves

AS RUTH WITNESSED the transformation of her beloved mother-in-law's losses into a legacy, what might she have been thinking? Here she was a Moabite woman, not a Jew, married into a family beset with the tragic deaths of its patriarch and two sons. She loved her husband, and it must have been devastating to put him in the ground after such a short time together. The life she had envisioned as a wife and mother was suddenly snatched from her like a warm blanket ripped away on a frigid, starless night. And there she was, left to breathe the cold, bitter air of loss, even as it stung her lungs with its burning fear of uncertainty. Did she give up and give in to the cold? No. Like a single candle burning its lone flame in the darkness of a winter's night, she kept the tiny flicker of her hope alive through the care bestowed on her mother-in-law.

Although it's likely she loved her own parents, Ruth's devotion to Naomi certainly gets our attention. It's clear that she's a good, kindhearted woman by the way her mother-in-law blesses her and tries to send her back to her own family and culture. However, Ruth reveals her commitment to stand by the older woman and accompany her to the strange land that Naomi called home.

Entreat me not to leave you,
Or to turn back from following after you;
For wherever you go, I will go;
And wherever you lodge, I will lodge;

Your people shall be my people,
And your God, my God.
Where you die, I will die,
And there will I be buried.
The LORD do so to me, and more also,
If anything but death parts you and me.

RUTH 1:16–17

Perhaps there was something about Naomi's kind blessing that touched the young widow. Or maybe she had observed the older woman's faith—even as her own troubles eclipsed this faith for Naomi herself—and became inspired by the God her mother-in-law served. Regardless of what led up to this moment, it's clear that Ruth has discovered a courage and innocent boldness that lifts her beyond the present storm clouds of loss and grief. She is willing to commit herself to someone she loves and knows she can learn from. Although Naomi may have been tempted to give up on herself and her faith, Ruth never did.

Have you committed your loyalty to the right people in your life? As a leading lady learns and grows into her role, it's vital that she have an older, more mature role model from which she can learn and whom she can emulate, someone who embodies the dignity, wisdom, and beauty befitting a queen who has been around the theater long enough to know hard times get better. Leading ladies often learn from their mothers how to grow into their womanhood and how to find their places onstage. Some young ladies may not have had loving mothers in their lives, or even maternal figures whom they respected, so they react against their mothers and feel contempt toward them through most of adolescence. Many women, however, learn that it's often much easier to hear words of counsel and advice from older women whom they meet as adults. There's not the same baggage and "I told you so" attitude that these young women often perceive when they share with their moms. If you already have a mentor, then thank God for her presence in your life—run and call her and tell her how much her support and encouragement and faith in you mean. If you're still searching for one, pray and ask your Father to send the right woman across your path. Look around you and see if there's a wise woman who has escaped your notice, and ask her to lunch.

Alongside Ruth's loyalty is her diligence. Her life's script has been ripped from her hands. She's agreed to traipse to some unknown land with her mother-in-law—two women with no man to protect or provide for them. So what does Ruth do? She asks Naomi's permission (showing her respect and allegiance to the old woman) to work in the fields and pick up the straggling leftover sheaves of barley discarded by the maidservants and male workers in the field. "Then she left, and went and gleaned in the field after the reapers" (Ruth 2:3). Ruth may never have worked in the fields a day in her life prior to this. She may have been terrified by the prospect of being perceived as an outsider forced to scramble for scraps of grain. But she didn't let her inexperience or fears keep her from improvising.

As you can imagine, it wasn't easy being a single woman at this time, but Ruth was resourceful. She saw the handful of barley heads that had been spilt in the rows of grain and knew that she could collect enough to feed herself and Naomi. Perhaps she even had a glimmer of hope, as we see in her first encounter with Boaz, that there was more waiting for her in this place than her next meal. But she's not afraid of the hard work of bringing in the sheaves.

So often we let our perfectionism, or our shock at the unexpected turn of events, or the ongoing grief of a past loss, keep us out of the grain fields where we should be gleaning. It's so much easier to stay at home in bed and collect unemployment and pretend that you're going to win the lottery than to put on your work clothes, hold your head high, and walk through the fields of job interviews. Like some Pharisees who fasted as a sign of their self-righteousness and went unkempt and dirty, it's easier to play the part of victim and stay in your scruffy nightgown and watch Jerry Springer and feel sorry for yourself. But you must not give up on the day-to-day business that needs doing. You may not feel like it, but you must trust that you will feel better if you treat yourself with respect and give of yourself in the service of others. Clean up your act when hard times come. Keep your appearance neat and clean so that your dignity and self-respect will fuel your perseverance and stamina. Volunteer to give to others even when you know that you yourself are in need. Make it clear to those around you that you are willing to work hard and get your hands dirty in the fields.

Ruth displays this kind of resourcefulness and respect as she walks further and further into the fields of this new relationship with Boaz. She knows enough to ask her trusted and beloved mother-in-law for advice, and then she takes it. So often women come to me for advice and then get mad when I tell them the truth that God has already revealed in their hearts. They know that they should sever the abusive relationship with their boyfriend or get help for their prescription drug habit, but they don't want to hear it out loud. Or sometimes I hear about mothers giving wise counsel to their daughters with the same results. The young women know that they need to quit smoking or to be a better mother to their children by disciplining them rather than spoiling them. But then these women ask their mothers or the mother figures in their lives for advice just so they can pout and rebel and feel justified as they continue on their road of bitterness and self-destruction. If you truly trust the woman who mentors or mothers you, then ask her advice only if you intend to follow it.

Brazen Is Better Than Bitter

RUTH TAKES NAOMI'S advice, even when it might seem to risk Ruth's very reputation. As we've seen, the implications of her uncovering Boaz's feet in the threshing room leave little room for doubt regarding her intentions toward this man. She had humbled herself when the time was right, both with Naomi and with Boaz, but now the time has come to be bold, and Ruth seizes the opportunity. She is not manipulative and exploitative of the situation, she is not a whore or blackmailer of this man. All that she has been through has brought her to this moment, this one turning point in her life. Her loveliness had been put on hold by the painful way she had to survive for a while. But now, like a woman pulling out beads that she thought she might never wear again, Ruth rambles through the storage of her soul, dusting off her sensuality and polishing up her once-radiant beauty. As she brings it to full luster, she knows in her deepest being that life has not left her bankrupt. Indeed not. She has something to give yet. Beneath her wilted dress and rumpled hair lies a woman filled with passion and warmth. Though stored in moth balls and packed away in past pain, she now brings her heart out for one final encore. She will perform for Boaz with the intensity of a woman whose lonely losses have given her the courage and tenacity to be sensually open and passionately alive. She is not threatened or intimidated by her self-willed piety. She knows that opportunities are rare for love in life, and it has knocked at her door again. She will not allow her insecurity to whisk away this final moment to vindicate her femininity and retrieve her failed dreams. No, she uses her sensuality and beauty to yield herself to this man's redemption as her near kinsman.

When you know the timing is right, you must act boldly. As the old folks used to sing back in West Virginia, "It may be the last time, I don't know." When you know that life has given you another chance and that this could be your last time, you seize it, like a contestant on a game show who slams the buzzer trying to get the correct answer in on time and win the prize. Yes, timing is important, and who can tell what time it is for you? Others who judge your radical moves at this juncture in your life neither understand your past nor glimpse your destiny. They see you now, don't know much about "then," and fail to realize that there is a someday still humming down in your soul. They will not tell time by the same life clock that God has revealed to you. They're still running on Eastern Standard Time while you're set to a new future on Divine Saving Time. Ruth didn't ask herself, "What time is it?" and keep looking at her sundial. She felt it in her bones and attuned her rhythm to the movement of God working in her.

Her acute sense of timing allowed Ruth to risk the ignorant judgment of others. She makes it unquestionably clear that she is not trying to trap a husband but to pursue a relationship, to obey her trusted mother-in-law as well as her God. Now certainly in acting this way, Ruth left her behavior open for misinterpretation. Some of the other maidservants present might have regarded Ruth as a hussy out to steal their provider. Some of the other workmen in the threshing room might have mistaken Ruth for a sexual predator or a gold digger out to exploit the kindness of a good man. But

Ruth knows it is better to be called brazen and achieve her goal than to win all of their approval and secretly be reduced to the bitterness that once threatened to destroy her mentor. Which would you be willing to risk, being called brazen by some or left bitter inside? Too many women have chosen bitter to avoid public ridicule. But you must know and trust in the Lord's goodness enough to risk these misinterpretations.

Criticism is a natural part of achieving greatness. It is often laced with jealousy and misjudgments. Any who criticize you have never been where you are and are never going where you will go. If you dare to be a woman who turns to the next page of her life, then you cannot let the critics rob you of your destiny. They will seduce you into living by their standards, only because misery so enjoys your company. Ignore your critics and step out onstage!

What risks has the Lord called you to act on? Certainly you must be attuned to the voice of His Spirit in the timing of your endeavors, but once you receive the calling and the opportunity lies ripe before you, then you must not hesitate. Make haste, my sister, and move ahead, even in the midst of criticism. Courage must be your companion, as you do not have the luxury to linger with the fearful. Not when you are called to receive the ransomed reward of a faithful woman. There is only a split second between the winner and the loser. Move ahead now! The Scriptures are clear on this matter; God takes no pleasure in those who draw back.

Time to Improvise

YES, MUCH OF the art of improvisation is about timing, about knowing when to act in obedience and when to wait in silence.

Timing is everything. If you resist the Lord's timing and continue to muzzle the voice of the Spirit, then don't complain about your dreams not coming to life.

Has He shown you the perfect vacant storefront for you to open the restaurant you've always dreamed of? Has He provided some unexpected money in your life to invest? Have you awakened in the early morning hours and felt a nagging to write down the song lyrics burning through your latest dream? Maybe it's the Divine coincidence of God's provision in your life of a mentor or prayer partner to whom you can confide your worries. Perhaps it means letting go of the life script to which you've been clinging like a river raft even though you've known in your heart for some time that it's dragging you under the falls. Is there a relationship that needs to end before you can begin to improvise God's special role for you?

Only you know the answers to these questions, but do not ignore them, dear woman, if you expect to become a master of improvisation. Face the answers of your heart and God's Spirit and boldly step forward and loudly and proudly say your lines. You may need to throw away old scripts of defeat, defiance, and deflating fear. You may need to reset your watch to the Timing of your Creator. But take these risks and you will see a new stage spread out before you in a theater of self-confidence and growing faith.

Within this change of scene you will come to know that you are as unique and unforgettable as any leading lady He has ever created. You will believe that you will be unleashed to give your greatest performance as you become focused on the present moment, right now. Dare to be an authentic leading lady who creates and offers the performance of her lifetime. Dare to improvise!

CHAPTER FOUR

Method Acting

IN ONE MOVIE a grizzled older woman sits in a smoky bar and toasts her past, lamenting the husband who abandoned her decades ago. In the next film the same woman becomes a fresh-faced farm girl whose singing talent catapults her from the church choir to the Top Ten. In yet another, this woman emerges as a warm, nurturing mother desperately seeking to keep her faith alive in the midst of her eight-year-old son's battle with leukemia.

In each respective movie, the same actress portrays wildly disparate characters. Certainly her makeup, props, and costumes help create the distinct look for each of these vastly different women. But it is the woman underneath all the roles, the woman inside the eyes of each character, who convinces us of the unique sufferings and triumphs of each film heroine. Whether she's portraying a prostitute or a pristine matron, a struggling waitress or a drug smuggler, a Colonial wife and mother or a suburban lounge singer, this actress manages to make us forget who she is in real life and invites us into the special world of each respective character. She lifts the words off the page and conveys the nuances of emotion, motivation, and psychology that help convince us of the authenticity of the screen woman's life. She is not just an actress delivering another performance; it is as if she has become another person. And yet there's something, the essence of who she is, that permeates her performance no matter what the role.

Who is this gifted lady? She could be a number of talented actresses currently working in our motion-picture industry today. We tend to reward actresses like Meryl Streep, Alfre Woodard, Angela Bassett, and Susan Sarandon with our box-office loyalty as well as our Academy Award nominations, as much for their diversity on screen as for their integrity to their talent in choosing such intriguing roles. But this ability to remain grounded and vitally connected to your core self even as you juggle a dozen roles is not reserved for Hollywood's elite. If you are committed to becoming God's Leading Lady by focusing your energies and His blessings into the performance of a lifetime, then you know what I'm talking about.

Your roles are many and varied. You awaken to the sound of a child's electrified cries, and instantly you're there in her room. Whether trained as a nurse or not, you have an ability to respond and treat the ailment with the expertise of a pharmacist, using home remedies and over-the-counter aids. You are the Florence Nightingale of your house. Or perhaps you awaken to the brutal drone of the alarm clock piercing your brain like a jackhammer, only to find your mind instantly consumed by and your stomach knotted over the report at work that you need to have finished by noon. Maybe you awaken to the big strong hands of your husband touching you in that distinctive way that suggests the momma role will not be needed just yet. His warm, rapid breathing touches the nape of your neck and needed sleep fades, not for the anxious thoughts of work, nor for baby aspirins down the hall, but for a few inflamed moments before you have to costume up and head downtown for another day at the office. Yet in another radical scene shift, you might find yourself drowsing in dawn's early light in a rocking chair nestled next to the bed of a dying parent, your body weary and stiff, and your spirit even more exhausted from the night's vigil. Ah, such is life, my sister. As my mother would say, "A woman's work is never done."

You know the roles, dear woman, and those listed above are just scratching the surface of your many performances. The lady and the leader, the mommy and the martyr, the seductress and the saint—it's almost as if the pages of a dozen different plays were shuffled together and then tossed into a wind tunnel. You scramble to be them all, confusing one cue for another, uncertain of which audience you are performing for. That essence of solid character and secure confidence in yourself drains out of you quicker than wine at a wedding reception.

Much of what motivates such scrambling and scratching is the lie that you can have it all. The upwardly mobile career, the satisfaction of mommyhood, the red-hot passion of a wonderful marriage, the sacrificial contentment of a relevant ministry, the secure foundational relationships with your parents and siblings, the joyful soul sisterhood of best friends and confidantes. Somehow all this can exist at one point and time in your life according to the images we see in our television shows, movies, and advertisements. If you know where to shop, what to wear, who to be seen with, why, it should all fall into place at your feet.

This isn't a pressure reserved for women caught up in materialism, either. It's tempting to read a passage such as Proverbs 31 and feel pressured that God expects you to have it all, too. Maybe in church circles there's even more pressure to live up to a standard that gets misinterpreted as a yardstick of womanhood rather than an ideal model of wisdom. No woman feels more insecure than when she walks into a room of Christian women who think they have it all together and expect you to as well. Let's examine some of their expectations from this particular passage.

Who can find a virtuous wife?
For her worth is far above rubies.
The heart of her husband safely trusts her;
So he will have no lack of gain.
She does him good and not evil
All the days of her life.

PROVERBS 31:10–12

If you read the rest of this passage through the end of chapter 31, you discover that this wonder woman brings in food from afar (v. 14), rises in the middle of the night to feed her household and take care of her servants (v. 15), trades in real estate and farming (v. 16) as a savvy businesswoman (v. 17–18), gives to the poor (v. 20), clothes herself and her family in beautiful modest fashions (v. 21–24), and counsels those in need with her wisdom and compassion (v. 26). Talk about your impossible standards. It's an exhausting passage just to read, let alone live out! So how do you face such a daunting challenge? It's all in your method.

Minding Your Method

IN TODAY'S MICROWAVEABLE, digitalized, hyper-tech world, it feels impossible to avoid the multiplicity of roles that we all face. True enough, we all have a variety of roles commanding our attention throughout each day as well as each season of our lives. But how you face them and go about living your life can provide an anchor to hold you secure and steady through the winds of change and the demands of each day. So how do you stabilize and ground your performance as a leading lady with an impassable grace constant throughout the myriad changes of props, costumes, and other actors in your life's theater?

Most successful actresses are familiar with the great acting teacher Konstantin Stanislavsky, the director of the Moscow Art Theater during the first half of the twentieth century. Stanislavsky developed the actors' training known as "method acting," in which performers worked to saturate themselves not just with the character on the page of a script but with all the unsaid, unwritten aspects of that character imaginable. Actors were trained to devise histories for their characters as needed to inform the motivation for particular scenes. According to Stanislavsky, an actor may need to experience the labor of apple picking simply to have a specific memory to draw from when she plays a worker from the orchard. The great director wanted to infuse his actors' emotions with concrete memories, perceptions, and sensual data so that their performances would reek of authenticity.

For him, the success of an actor's performance emanated from the method the actor chose to fulfill the role, hence method acting.

I want to appropriate this great drama teacher's philosophy of acting for the way you must fuel your performance as a leading lady. He would say, "Lights! Cameras! Action!" But I will say, "Get ready. Get ready! *Get ready!*" As the demands of each relationship and each season bring new roles and responsibilities, you must concentrate on the method by which you fulfill them rather than trying to measure your success by the world's approval. You must extricate yourself from the trappings of success heaped upon women in our culture today—the right house in the right neighborhood, the charming husband and the well-behaved kids, the successful career and the right image. Quit comparing yourself to everyone around you and forcing yourself to do what they're doing, wear what they're wearing, be who they're being. You must be a success in your own eyes—regardless of where you are in life right now—rather than compare yourself to those women with more clothes, more men, or more ministry success. It doesn't matter if you're working the register at Target or working as a registered nurse, you must mind your method if you are to carry yourself with the dignity befitting a leading lady. What is this method that will sustain you throughout the diverse roles of your lifetime? Read on, dear sister, and prepare to put your method in motion.

Method to Move Mountains

IF WE RETURN to the passage in Proverbs 31 for a moment, we see that its conclusion offers us the secret of a leading lady's method for success. You must not get lost in the catalogue of accomplishments here, for this amazing woman's power source is revealed at the end of the passage.

Charm is deceitful and beauty is passing,
But a woman who fears the LORD, she shall be praised.
Give her of the fruit of her hands,
And let her own works praise her in the gates.

PROVERBS 31:30–31

It's not that you have to be the perfect wife and mother, businesswoman and philanthropist, friend and family member to discover success in who you are. No, if you fear the Lord and work hard, your accomplishments will spill forth out of you like fresh water from a mountain spring.

"Charm is deceitful!" says the wise one. Like effervescent champagne bubbles rising to tickle your nose, charm can dizzy your world momentarily, but the sobriety test of reality descends sooner or later. No matter how good you are at juggling all your roles (let alone how exhausted you may be), if you empower yourself on charm—on your own ability to enchant others by your goodness, glamour, or giftedness—you will be deceiving yourself and others. Sooner or later you will collapse, because the charade demands too much from you. No one is perfect. No one can do it all.

Similarly, the wise writer of Proverbs tells us, "Beauty is passing!" If you construct your life's performance around giving the right impression and maintaining a certain look, then you are in for a rude awakening by the cold fingers of time etching its subtle tattoos into your body. Every single one of us ages. The fine lines appear around your eyes and mouth, your chin droops a little, your cheeks sag into jowls, your hair fades to a silver sheen. No matter how much makeup you use, no matter how much plastic surgery you can afford, no matter how well the custom-blended shade of your hair coloring matches, no matter how many vitamins or aerobics classes you take—you will get older. And, ironically enough, it is the women who embrace their aging with the wisdom it affords them who maintain their beauty with a graceful dignity that doesn't come in any perfume or powder.

No, charm and beauty are by-products of a leading lady's performance, not the fuel propelling it across life's stage. Proverbs 31 concludes with a reflection of a woman succeeding in her method. She fears and she works. So if fearing the Lord and working hard are the secrets to true success, then how do you appropriate this rocket fuel? What does it mean to "fear" the Lord? This word usually carries a negative connotation. If you're afraid of something, then you fear its power over you, distrust its appearance because you know the potential for danger lurking beneath, distance yourself from it so you can protect and defend yourself. I think of the way a child encounters a wild mutt in a back alley. Snarling and growling, the beast is larger than the child, and maybe faster. Most kids don't have to stop and think, "Oh, I should be scared and run!"—they just do it.

However, the fear that's due our Lord is not the same. In Scripture, godly fear is distinguished from natural fear, that anxiety caused by the impending teeth of a junkyard dog in hot pursuit. Godly fear results from respect, reverence, and repentance.

> *Therefore, my beloved, as you have always obeyed, not as in my presence only, but now much more in my absence, work out your own salvation with fear and trembling.*
>
> PHILIPPIANS 2:12

As Paul indicates in this admonition to the Church at Philippi, godly fear can facilitate your faith, can serve as a tool by which you stay grounded to what matters most. Encountering God and his goodness leaves you with an awe-inspiring respect that transcends your imagination. Such awe provokes you to appreciate God's holiness through worship—the reverence that is due One who is so perfect and so sacred through and through. And an encounter with such holiness inspires you to change your life, change your behavior, change your allegiances so that you might live out of the depth of this newfound love and devotion.

Instead of the junkyard dog, this kind of fear reminds me of what I felt when I saw the African Motherland for the first time. I cannot explain with words the impact of my excursion to the beautiful and mysterious continent. The experience was unbelievably moving and fulfilling. There at night I listened with enchantment to the tribal drums beating beneath the windows of my hotel. The primal rhythm pounded out the proud cadence of a culture to which I was deeply related but unfamiliar. Like a twin separated from his sibling at birth and restored in adulthood, I was bewildered by how emotional my reunion felt. Though a proud American, I now knew why Alex Haley had to write *Roots.* For my roots go through Plymouth Rock, but they don't stop there, extending all the way to Table Mountain in Cape Town.

When my plane landed in South Africa, the first stop on my continental visit, the sounds and smells seemed strangely familiar to me. I watched with fascination as I went through wildlife camps and saw animals, familiar from American zoos and television, roaming proud and free. Signs cautioned us to beware the potential danger of these beasts in their natural habitat (a warning that I really didn't need, incidentally). The land with its hardy wind-sculpted shrubs and the people with their broad smiles and intense styles of expressive dress left me deeply moved, reflective, and intrigued by this culture to which I had no prior exposure. That feeling of respect and, yes, even admiration, was a life-changing experience that I consider one of the greatest adventures of my life. And now, even though I've traveled to many different countries in Africa and experienced the uniqueness of each one, from the bush in Ghana to the resorts in Cape Town to the Nigerian Palace where I dined with President Obosanjo, I find one constant. My abiding respect and awe for the continent and its varied beauties only grows richer and deeper.

On a much larger scale, but with the same intensification of respect and awe, fearing the Lord is a lifelong process of knowing and growing in love with Him. As you experience His mercies and goodness in the blessings upon your life, you begin to venture off the well-worn trail and climb further and deeper into the vast continent of His adventure for your life. Your faith, activated in this great exploration, yields you an integrity and a solid awareness of who He created you to be that can never be found in any of the roles or costumes that you must don for a season.

Unleash yourself—your true self—by fearing the Lord and working hard from the resources that He entrusts to you. That is how you become an Academy Award–winning leading lady—by performing life's many roles from the inside out, not the outside in. If you do not know who you are with a vision for who you're becoming as you answer His call, then you will work too hard and hurt too much, only to discover that no single role can define you, no single achievement fulfill you enough to feed your soul for a lifetime.

Giving, Giving, Gone

WHILE GOD'S REVELATION of your unique identity as His beloved daughter will vary from woman to woman, one common characteristic unites all of his children in a sisterhood of success. This shared trait is the plutonium in the nuclear reactor of every leading lady's method of acting. Are you giving life to those around you? Are you loving and nurturing your relationships with all you've got? Are you giving life as only a woman secure in herself can give? The common trait that virtually all successful leading ladies share is their willingness to give. Giving is the method to their means. Giving is the means to their end.

So many examples of giving abound from the pages of God's Word, but several women are known foremost by what they give of themselves to our Lord and His ministry. One of the most striking to me is Joanna, a woman mentioned only a couple of times, on both occasions as one of a group.

> *Now it came to pass, afterward, that He went through every city and village, preaching and bringing the glad tidings of the kingdom of God. And the twelve were with Him,*
>
> *and certain women who had been healed of evil spirits and infirmities—Mary called Magdalene, out of whom had come seven demons, and Joanna the wife of Chuza, Herod's steward, and Susanna, and many others who provided for Him from their substance.*
>
> LUKE 8:1–3

This passage makes two important statements concerning the role of women in Jesus' ministry. First, that those who had experienced His healing power in their lives—like Mary Magdalene and the exorcism of her seven demons and Joanna with her infirmity—committed themselves to following their Lord. It wasn't just the twelve disciples following in His footsteps—these women wanted to be there and give all they had to their Master's cause. They wanted to share in the excitement of other lives transformed and other weaknesses healed. They wanted to participate in comforting His suffering and in meeting His needs. And this is where we see the second great truth jump off the page. These women "provided for Him from their substance"! Either from a position of wealth or through the sacrificial service of the impoverished, these women supported Jesus' ministry.

Regardless of your income level, are you giving of your resources to further the Lord's purposes? Have you experienced His healing in a way that inspires you to bless others? It is important that as God blesses you, you help support the ministries that carry the cool water of redemption like a pipe tunnel to your thirsty soul. No, the ministry is not the water. Christ is that alone. But the ministry is the pipe it comes through. If we who are blessed by it do not support it, then who will? The Bible says, "Let the redeemed of the Lord say so," and these women knew that their support was a loud way of saying so.

But I'm not just talking about giving to the Church, although that is a vital arena to which God calls all of us to give. No, I'm talking about giving to those right under your nose who need what you have to give—a shopping excursion with your daughter to discuss the changes going on in her pubescent body; a listening ear for the elderly neighbor whose own family has abandoned her to the ravages of her body's demise; an open heart to the husband who needs to be held by you as much as you need his strong arms around you. You are powerful and gifted, you enhance and bring life to everything you touch. As a woman, you are by nature a life-giver, and whatever you give life to will increase and grow. Whether it is birthing a child, loving a man, leading a company, or propelling a cause, you are a life-giver, a force to be reckoned with. When a woman knows what she has and knows how to use it, she influences everything she touches, and she touches everything that she wants to live. Touch it, my sister, and it will live. Support it and it will grow and grow. You are the life-givers of ministries, companies, and relationships. Are you giving before what you have to give is gone?

Joanna, whose name means "Jehovah has been gracious," received the Lord's blessing and reciprocates gratefully to Jesus and to others. It was her nature to serve as a conduit of grace and goodness to those around her. Even as she follows our Lord unto His death, she is still giving.

> *And the women who had come with Him from Galilee followed after, and they observed the tomb and how His body was laid.*
>
> *Then they returned and prepared spices and fragrant oils. And they rested on the Sabbath according to the commandment.*
>
> *Now on the first day of the week, very early in the morning, they, and certain other women with them, came to the tomb bringing the spices which they had prepared. But they found the stone rolled away from the tomb.*
>
> *Then they went in and did not find the body of the Lord Jesus.*
>
> LUKE 23:55–56; 24:1–3

It was Mary Magdalene, Joanna, Mary the mother of James, and the other women with them, who told these things to the apostles.

LUKE 24:10

Joanna and the other women were surely devastated with grief at the death of their Healer, their friend, their Lord and Master. Perhaps they never expected Him to have to endure a physical death, let alone a demise of such cruel and scandalous proportions, His death like a petty criminal on two beams of rough-hewn wood. But they didn't lose their hope or their willingness to give. They gathered together their balsam oil and their myrrh, their hyssop and eucalyptus, and prepared to tender their love and service to His lifeless body. I believe it's important that their act reflected both of these—love and service—and that the two components work together as to be indistinguishable.

If you've ever lost someone you love, you know how important it can be that you see that their body is prepared with dignity and respect as befitting their cherished place in your life. You want their physical body, although now lifeless and cold, to become a receptacle for your love for them. It's why we want to dress our dead in their most beautiful dresses and handsome suits. Though I must admit that I have seen a few of us carry that premise to extremes, still it gives us comfort to know that we have done what we could for those we love. So these women come to express their love, their respect, their devotion to their entombed Master.

But they come not just to toss a flower at the grave but to do something that needed doing. As a body decayed, it would foul the air surrounding it with its smell. There were no embalmers as we know them today, so the women were planning to eradicate the smell of decay from Jesus' body. It was not an easy job, but one that needed doing. While their love does not make this job effortless, it does empower them with the strength, fortitude, and courage needed to make the journey to His tomb. You must remember that Jesus had been regarded as a criminal. Guards had been posted at His tomb to ensure that no one stole the body to generate political power for this self-revealed Messiah. So these women were risking arrest and persecution by their willingness even to visit the tomb, let alone attend the body.

But they cannot be stopped and persuaded not to go. They honor the Jewish Sabbath but go as soon as they can to their Lord's tomb. And what an incredibly rewarding sight awaits them! He's not there! The stone has been rolled away and the cave-like tomb echoes their voices like a hollow tunnel. His shroud lies crumpled like the outgrown cocoon of the most beautiful butterfly. Jesus reveals His resurrection to these faithful women, and they are the ones who announce it to the apostles. He could have sent a host of angels with fanfare, he could have sent a marching band from ten countries, he could have sent an army brigade in brightest raiment, but he sends women. Jesus knows their hearts, knows how much they have given and want to give still, and He delights in revealing the power of His resurrection to their disbelieving eyes and ears.

He still does this today! He will always honor the woman who gives—amazingly she never runs out. These women who are often criticized for their giving hearts somehow rebound time after time. The principle remains to this day. Give and it shall be given to you again. Whatever one gives always comes back, and when it does, it is always more than its original form. If you want it to live, then you have to give!

Method or Madness

IT'S IMPORTANT TO remember that Joanna did not come from a mountaintop place of perfection before she gave of herself and her resources. Neither do most women who are willing to risk everything they have in order to fulfill their gift of giving. If we look to the Scriptures, two women in particular stand out, both with shady pasts and both with tear-filled eyes.

Mary Magdalene has traditionally been portrayed as a prostitute or a kept woman, a woman with a shady past tinged with the smoke of illicit passion. Regardless of her former life, her deliverance from seven demons at the hands of Christ informs us at the very least that her life was divided, dispossessed, and debilitated. It's no surprise then that she commits herself to following after this glorious stranger claiming to be the Messiah—she had experienced his extraordinary healing presence firsthand. Instead of the bickering voices haunting the ears of her soul, she became free to hear the Master's voice. "I am the good shepherd; and I know My sheep, and am known by My own," He says (John 10:14). He spoke into her life, and she heard him with a clarity shattering the chatter of all other distractions.

Mary Magdalene experienced a reunification of self that is essential for any woman attempting to find out who she really is beneath all the rotating roles, juggled responsibilities, and fragmented feelings. You don't have to be demon-possessed to know what it feels like to be divided and at loose ends. Simply follow yourself around for a day and take note of the times when you're merely going through the motions: preparing your family's breakfast; ironing something last-minute for work; filing reports; sending e-mails; taking a call from a girlfriend with man problems; following up on your parents' Medicaid bills; picking up the kids at ball practice; stopping to shop for the dinner you don't have time to fix. Round and round you go. When will it stop? Nobody knows.

Leading ladies may be forced to juggle many of these same items, but the difference is that they don't lose themselves in them. They don't feel the pressure to be everything to everybody. They don't have that desperate need to live up to others' expectations in order to feel good about themselves. Down that path lies madness, not a method for fueling your one and only true role. Instead, leading ladies possess the calm, inner strength of a feminine identity forged in the image of their glorious Creator. Instead of the voices of seven demons, or seventy unreturned e-mails and phone calls, they hear the quiet tone of the Holy Spirit resonating in the chambers of their heart.

And like Mary Magdalene, leading ladies remain in pursuit of their Savior. As we have seen, after her healing, Mary supports Christ's ministry with her resources and follows His ministry until His death and resurrection. In fact, she is not only one of the women who has mixed her spices and oils to prepare His body, she is the first woman to encounter the risen Lord.

> *But Mary stood outside by the tomb weeping, and as she wept she stooped down and looked into the tomb.*
>
> *And she saw two angels in white sitting, one at the head and the other at the feet, where the body of Jesus had lain.*
>
> *Then they said to her, "Woman, why are you weeping?" She said to them, "Because they have taken away my Lord, and I do not know where they have laid Him."*

Now when she had said this, she turned around and saw Jesus standing there, and did not know that it was Jesus.

Jesus said to her, "Woman, why are you weeping? Whom are you seeking?" She, supposing Him to be the gardener, said to Him, "Sir, if You have carried Him away, tell me where You have laid Him, and I will take Him away."

Jesus said to her, "Mary!" She turned and said to Him, "Rabboni!" (which is to say, Teacher).

Jesus said to her, "Do not cling to Me, for I have not yet ascended to My Father; but go to My brethren and say to them, 'I am ascending to My Father and your Father, and to My God and your God.' "

Mary Magdalene came and told the disciples that she had seen the Lord, and that He had spoken these things to her.

JOHN 20:11–18

Mary presumed that she had lost the most precious person in the world to her. Even when confronted with the empty tomb and the bookend pair of angels at the head and feet of the death shroud, Mary presumed that Jesus' body had been stolen. Even when confronted with the living Son of God returned from the dead before her very eyes, Mary did not recognize Him. He had to call her by her name before she realized who He was, and consequently, who she was as well.

What do you expect to find when you peer into the tombs of life? Have you resigned yourself to find only the cold, lifeless body of a dream that was once as warm and rhythmic as a child skipping rope on a sidewalk? Even when the body of the dream is missing, do you immediately assume that someone else has stolen your hope, robbed you of your dream? Or do you dare imagine that somehow your dream is still alive, invisible to your eyes, maybe, but resuscitated by the power of a miracle?

Life is full of tombs, my sister. The tombs of fear when the policeman calls from the hospital emergency room and tells you your baby's been shot, the tombs of heartache when your little girl shows up on your doorstep as a young woman about to birth her own little girl, the tombs of betrayal when your husband says he loves someone else, the tombs of bitter disappointment when you don't get the job because you're a woman, the tombs of loss swallowing up the bodies of loved ones into the cold earth. These tombs lie hidden like land mines waiting to send you sprawling to your knees against life's pavement. How will you respond when you enter a tomb? How will you keep going?

In these times, your method must become the power of a mountain-moving faith. You must defy all odds and dare believe with whatever mustard seed of faith you can muster that this is not the end of the story. Jesus said, ". . . If you have faith as a mustard seed, you will say to this mountain, 'Move from here to there,' and it will move; and nothing will be impossible for you" (Matthew 17:20). There's more to come. The Savior rose from the dead to defeat death and all its life-draining power. He rose so that you might know hope even as you pass through the valleys of the shadow and the tombs of your dreams.

For Mary, her spell of fear, disappointment, and frustration melts with one word from Jesus' lips. "Mary!" He says, and despite whatever confusion and turmoil roiled within her heart, Mary knew her name. She knows her name, the sound of it from her Savior's lips, and she calls him with affection and incredulity and relief all rolled into one exclamation—"Teacher!" Yes, He is her teacher, the ultimate Director of her performance, her Guide to the true method her life requires. Their eyes lock and she knows that His power and love are larger and stronger than even she, His most devoted, had imagined. He has cheated death and defused its sting!

Do you know your name when you hear it roll across you from your Lord's voice? He knows you through and through, the number of hairs on your head and the collected tears from your pillow, and He alone knows your identity unlike any other. If you listen and learn your name from Him, then you will never lose yourself in the many roles life requires you to juggle.

Alabaster and Obsession

THE OTHER WOMAN who gives of herself as a model from which we can learn also brought a sweet-smelling gift with which to anoint the Savior's body, but she didn't meet Jesus at the empty tomb. She encounters her Lord at the home of a Pharisee.

It's one of the most intimate, sensual, even erotic scenes in all of Scripture. An unnamed woman seeks out Jesus while He is dining at the home of a Pharisee. She is identified only as a woman "who was a sinner," who brought with her an alabaster jar filled with perfume. Although some biblical scholars think she may have been Mary Magdalene, it seems important that her name is not given so that she is every woman. She is every woman who has ever failed, who has ever given in to her own weakness for the wrong man, who has ever charged over her limit, medicated over the prescribed dosage, drank herself into the bed of a stranger. She's every woman who has ever been slapped with the label of a reputation. In some versions of Scripture, this woman's label is interpreted as a "notorious" sinner. Do you know what it means to be notorious? What are the labels that follow you around like a pack of wild dogs chewing at your heels? What are the mistakes that would send the old ladies into new rounds of gossip and the men into shameful thoughts of their own?

You can imagine what it must have felt like for this woman when this kind of woman with this kind of past encounters the Lord in the presence of a Pharisee, a teacher of the Law of Moses. At the risk of being humiliated and shamed, scoffed and ridiculed, this woman begins to sob uncontrollably. The years of heartache and guilt, of regret and several hundred second chances, all converge in this moment before the Messiah. As an act of repentance, submission, and gratitude, she falls at His feet. It was the least she could do. Words became unnecessary, and so she let her tears sing out in a chorus of thank-yous and her tender kisses punctuate their song with genuine affection untainted by sexual motives. She recognized Jesus for Who He really is and didn't want to miss this incredible opportunity to give from her heart, to give the only thing that any of us has to offer the Creator of the Universe—our worship.

True worship frees us to let our hair down and stand naked and vulnerable before our Lord. In His presence we feel compelled to be real about our past mistakes and tarnished attempts. We can't hide, and we don't have to. He loves us and forgives us because He knows we are created for so much more than a sordid reputation and a low-cut dress. He knows you are His Leading Lady and uses everything, especially your regrets and lost opportunities, to mold you into His masterpiece.

This awareness permeated into the heart and soul of the woman with the alabaster jar like the perfume it contained seeped into the skin of her Lord. And the fragrance was just as sweet. Her gratitude could not be contained inside herself any more than the costly perfume could remain locked within the stone bottle. Do you know what happens to perfume that goes unused? Go look in your bathroom cabinet or on your vanity table or nightstand. I'll bet somewhere in your home right now you have a bottle of perfume that's never or rarely been used. Once an intoxicating scent designed to titillate and entice, if you open it now, what do you find? Colored water mixed with a little alcohol. This rare perfume in its beautifully colored bottle loses its potency if it's not used.

Now, most women have a favorite fragrance, whether it's Obsession or Eternity, Happy or Beautiful, White Shoulders or Red, Chanel No. 5 or love potion number 9. It's her signature scent, and to leave a bottle unopened and unused would be a crime. So it is with the scent distilled in our hearts from our awareness of God's goodness and mercy toward us. Are you willing to pour out this perfume of gratitude before it goes stale?

Our mystery lady with the alabaster jar was willing to pour herself out before the Lord without regard for what others thought of her. With her flask of fragrant oil, she stands behind Jesus and begins weeping until she suddenly bends down and washes His feet with those tears. She wipes them dry with the hair of her head and then uses the precious oil to anoint her beloved Savior. It's a shocking sight for the Pharisees and other religious leaders there for a dinner party. They say, "This man, if He were a prophet, would know who and what manner of woman this is who is touching Him, for she is a sinner" (Luke 7:39).

But Jesus refuses to let these men with their judgmental attitudes contaminate the purity and beauty of this woman's sacrifice. He recognizes and accepts the worship she gives so freely and completely, and He forgives her for all her sins. Certainly He is aware of the sensual nature of her gift, its intimacy, but because of her bold willingness to give the most by humbling herself, Jesus silences those around Him. He tells them of the parable of the two debtors.

> *There was a certain creditor who had two debtors. One owed five hundred denarii, and the other fifty.*
>
> *And when they had nothing with which to repay, he freely forgave them both. Tell Me, therefore, which of them will love him more?*
>
> *Simon answered and said, "I suppose the one whom he forgave more." And He said to him, "You have rightly judged."*
>
> LUKE 7:41–43

Jesus is letting them know that He fully acknowledges this woman's past, but He has forgiven her, and the woman, recognizing the enormity of the blessing the Lord has bestowed upon her, gives all that she has in gratitude. But Jesus goes a step further, pointing out that this woman, uninvited and risking wrath and shame, gives everything she has, while His host has given Him nothing.

> *Do you see this woman? I entered your house; you gave Me no water for My feet, but she has washed My feet with her tears and wiped them with the hair of her head.*
>
> *You gave Me no kiss, but this woman has not ceased to kiss My feet since the time I came in.*

You did not anoint My head with oil, but this woman has anointed My feet with fragrant oil.

Therefore I say to you, her sins, which are many, are forgiven, for she loved much. But to whom little is forgiven, the same loves little.

LUKE 7:44–47

It would be customary hospitality to offer a guest in a Jewish home at this time a basin of clean water to wash his feet, perhaps even to have a servant cleanse them for him. Simon the Pharisee overlooked this courtesy, but the sinful woman used her own tears to clean the Master's feet of the dirt, sand, and grime of the city streets. It would be considered a gracious warm welcome to kiss the cheek of your guest when he arrived, something not far removed from our own casual greetings today. The Pharisee kept his distance from Jesus even as this mystery woman kissed His feet. Regardless of how clean they may have been after her foot-washing, we're still talking about the dirty, callused feet of a grown man. But she kissed them as if they were the clean, sweet little feet of a newborn. Finally, it would have been a special recognition to anoint your guest of honor with a dab of oil in the presence of your dinner party. Simon blew this one, too. But the lady with the alabaster jar didn't—she released her rare, costly perfume in its entirety, soothing the feet as well as the senses with its pungent spicy odor.

Are you giving your most precious resources to your most prized priorities? As I mentioned at the beginning of this story, it may be easy to identify with the sinfulness of this woman. You may know what it's like to have a reputation for any number of scandalous acts, whether it is a reputation that's rightfully deserved or one that's the product of vicious gossip and half-truths. Or you may end up developing a reputation when others observe the beauty of a woman yielding herself before the Lord's calling on her life. Are you willing to be misunderstood by others who can't fathom the cost of what you've been given by your God? Are you willing to risk their condemnation and attempts to silence and shame you back into your past on the other side of town? Will you let your hair down and open the jar of your heart so that the sweetest essence of who you are will bless those around you? As the song says, "No one knows the cost of the oil in your Alabaster box."

Your Cycle Starts Today

BECAUSE GIVERS KNOW how much they've been given—like the woman anointing Jesus' feet or the debtors in His parable—they are motivated to give more. I believe it is part of the unique identity of each woman that she reflects the generosity and benevolence of God in ways that men are not always capable. That certainly doesn't let men off the hook as givers, but it means they often learn by the examples of their mother's sacrifices, their sister's generosity, their wife's openness, and their daughter's gratitude.

There are cycles of giving in a woman's life. She starts out coloring stick figures and rainbows with her tiny fingers clutching the crayons so that she can give her construction-paper masterpiece away. As she ages, she learns what it means to give to her family, to pitch in and play on the team so that those she loves can enjoy her talents. As a teenager, a woman learns to give of her beauty, to be seen and appreciated for the potential life blossoming within her. In her studies and in her career, a young woman discovers the power of her mind and its ability to enrich the world around her as she designs new buildings, opens new businesses, and writes new books. As a new mother, a woman experiences her giving taken to new heights as she endures the sleepless nights and aches of her exhausted body. Later she endures two or three jobs so that her baby can one day have a college education. Or maybe she forgoes her successful career or puts her dreams on slow-simmer so she can give all of her attention to her children. As she reaches middle age, a woman realizes the cost of a successful marriage and the price required to hold it together. She realizes that she must give to other women around her: those younger in search of guidance and mentors, and those older in need of a loving daughter's hug or listening ear. At the end of her life, a woman is still giving—to her church, her neighbors, her grandchildren, her adult children, her community.

This is the hallmark of a true leading lady. Not that she's wealthy or famous, not that she's mothered children or maintained a forty-year marriage, not that her business or career has thrived, but that's she's given life to everyone around her. Whether it's the perfume of her grateful heart or the news that the Savior has risen, whether it's a wayward smile to a downcast stranger on the corner or a check for $100,000 to the local women's shelter, women's gifts serve as catalysts and heartbeats of life. The gift of giving is the lifeblood of woman's vitality and energy. It empowers the method of living that will sustain you over the long haul of life's bumps and spills.

Are you giving all you can to become the leading lady you were called to be? If not, what's holding you back? There's someone right now who needs the rare gift of your time, beauty, energy, or material resources. Bring all your roles into focus by igniting the bonfire of compassion and generosity inside your heart. Undergird your strength by remembering what your Savior has done for you. Rain down a shower of blessings on those you find yourself face-to-face with each day and be prepared to receive what they will give in return. Remember, a leading lady is known by the gift of her giving.

PART TWO

Dress Rehearsals:
Trials of a Leading Lady

CHAPTER FIVE

Life's Outtakes

As glittering snowflakes dance in the glow of the streetlights, an amazing reunion takes place. The lovely ingenue recognizes her long-lost love across the bustling street. He stops in his tracks, pulls his leather jacket closer around his muscular body, and then he hears her voice. Could it be? Their eyes meet, and emotion swells up in the hearts of every viewer in the theater. All obstacles have been overcome, and the tenderhearted heroine has been reunited with her dark-eyed leading man in the last reel of the film. Rustling in the rows of darkened seats, women dig out tissues to dab at the tears brimming in their eyes, as do their men, only more discreetly. As popcorn buckets are gathered and the house lights shimmer to a dull glow, the credits begin to roll. Instead of romantic music from the movie soundtrack, however, the theater speakers resound with unexpected laughter and the stammer of a stuttering star. Instead of a darkened screen listing the many names of the individuals responsible for bringing this film through production, these credits run over various clips known as "outtakes." Like the name implies, these are scenes taken out of the final edited film for various reasons. The most common of these is that the actors in the particular scene made a mistake—they flubbed their lines, broke the intended mood of the scene with a burst of laughter, or missed their position facing the camera. These bloopers often make for very entertaining and amusing scenes, where we see the flawless starlet with spinach in her teeth or the brilliant English actor becoming tongue-tied by his intended lines. Allegedly, some outtakes cast such a negative light on an individual actor and her struggle to perfect her performance that no one is ever allowed to see them.

Perhaps you can relate. For most of us, our outtakes are displayed on life's screen every day of our lives, either before an extended audience or known only to the critic within. These outtakes range from a night of giving in to an old sexual indulgence to a failure to speak to the sorrow of a co-worker who's lost her spouse to cancer, to a portfolio conveniently dropped into the trash to make another employee look bad in the boss's eyes. Maybe it was a cruel and often unsubstantiated rumor mentioned over dinner under the guise of a prayer request. And wouldn't you like to forget the indulgence in the chat room, veiled in the anonymity of an alias, as you gave in to unbridled lust in a carnal communication? It may be an outtake as simple as merely pretending to listen to your husband. Or maybe a call to your girlfriend with the latest unmitigated news about another's scandalous behavior at the party last weekend. Or perhaps the way you make note of who is and isn't at church each Sunday.

If we're honest, most of us have as many, if not more, outtakes than we do shining moments when we get things right! What do you do with your life's outtakes? Attempt to edit them out of your memories, or make light of them as nothing more than moments of lost concentration? Surely there's a better use for these less-than-stellar moments of self-revelation.

Putting It Together

I SAW A bumper sticker recently that read "Life isn't a dress rehearsal." I nodded and smiled at its reminder that today, right now, is the only moment we've got for sure. We can't make our life conditional on some future event or benchmark—there's not some "opening night" for our life's performance scheduled in advance. We can't wait until everything in our lives is perfectly in order to be fully present in the moment and give ourselves away. The curtain opens every morning when you wake up.

However, I also realized that I don't entirely agree with this sticker's clichéd wisdom. While life isn't a dress rehearsal, we certainly experience enough mistakes and miscues as any inexperienced actress must when she first crosses the stage. But a real leading lady doesn't assume that she's doomed to flub the same lines and miss her cue every time the curtain goes up. No, part of the power of a genuine leading lady is her ability to learn from past mistakes and her growing awareness of her own flaws. As she seeks to give her all to this lifetime performance, she knows that knowledge of her past errors, even those with the devastating consequences, can be transformed into golden nuggets of wisdom that enrich her presence onstage.

I know I've certainly learned from my errors before the cameras.

On my daily show "The Potter's Touch," my guests and I have the luxury of post-editing our show before it airs. The crooked tie can be adjusted, the static-cling skirt can be sprayed, the guest who needs to relieve himself can make the necessary visit down the hall. It is amazing how blunders can be fixed quickly in post-editing. Perhaps because I have the security blanket of post-editing, I've jokingly earned the nickname of "One-Take" Jakes by the staff and production crew. They seem amazed that most times I can tape an opening or a sequence in just one take, but without the pressure of having to get it right the first time, I'm more relaxed and able to easily do what needs to get done.

This can spoil you, however, for far different is the scenario of a live broadcast. When I am asked to do an interview on CNN's "Larry King Live" or even TBN's "Praise the Lord" show, I have no opportunity for alteration or clarification of a remark poorly articulated or an obscured idea. Faced with the pressure of live, unedited broadcasts, I've been known to get nervous and have left the set more than once wishing I could edit a statement or clarify my position on an issue. Particularly when I'm interviewed on a sensitive subject, when I share the program with other guests, or when there's only a limited amount of time for my response, I long for the luxury of post-editing. In these moments I must humbly admit that ole One-Take could use another take sometimes.

In live theater there are no retakes or post-editing, either. All the bugs must be ferreted out and corrected in the dress rehearsals. If you've ever been part of a theater production and experienced a dress rehearsal firsthand, then you know how essential these bumpy performances are if all the details and dynamics are to fall into place before opening night. These run-throughs help everyone, from the actors and director to lighting and sound crew, to identify what aspects of the performance need fine-tuning or even a complete overhaul so that everything is perfect when the show opens. In the dress rehearsals that I've witnessed, there has always been something that needed a little work. But that's okay, that's what rehearsal is for.

Likewise, the first time we enter into new experiences or risk ourselves in new venues, we should not expect to get everything right. We mustn't be too hard on ourselves; we are venturing into new areas, trying new things, drawing on talents and skills that have not yet been tapped. However, we mustn't resign ourselves to a choppy performance with a patchwork of mistakes and distractions. No, we must fully concentrate and notice what needs attention in order to perfect our technique and polish our performance.

Dress rehearsals usually involve some awkward silences in which lines—or even entire scenes—are dropped because someone forgot her cue or misspoke his line. Even the actors' movements onstage may seem awkward and stiff at first, as they find themselves concentrating on so many nuances of their performance at once. They have to remember their lines, consider their positions onstage, recall their characters' motivation in the scene, get used to the glaring lights, wait on the musical interlude, and take notice of the director's cues. Costumes may be ill-fitting and claustrophobically uncomfortable. Often the props and special effects don't work in synchronicity with the storyline—the school bell rings five minutes after the character pulls the rope from the bell tower or the knock at the door drags behind the leading man's entrance.

Amid this three-ring circus of details and drama, a good director scrambles during dress rehearsals with two things in mind: (1) to keep the show running as best he can despite the numerous mishaps, and (2) to make sure he makes note of each flaw so that later he can go back and correct every error, rehearse every scene in need, and rectify each imperfection in his actors, props, and sets. Regarding the first objective, a novice director may not have learned how important it is to keep any and all momentum progressing in a production's dress rehearsal; she wants to stop with each mistake and go over it again until it's flawless. However, such time-consuming perfectionism loses sight of the show in its entirety, the end goal of a smooth, unified performance. A veteran director knows that she must keep things moving even when her players trip through their lines as much as they do across the stage.

The second goal seems a little easier to understand. The director must take note of the problems and discern which ones are correctable. A thoughtful director keeps track and then develops a strategy for overcoming those obstacles that would obscure the shining brilliance of her production. Like a master jeweler refining a raw gemstone, this director knows which flaws in the stone can never be polished away and which ones simply need a delicate marquis cut to reveal a stunning sparkle of clarity. She works to find the right combination to maximize the potential and minimize the distractions.

These two objectives provide us all with some sage advice about how to manage life's outtakes. You must keep going no matter how terrible the mistake or how devastating the loss. Don't stop and try to fix and analyze every glitch as it occurs. Such self-consciousness tends to lead to self-absorption, and when you're only absorbing yourself and your mistakes, you lose sight of God's larger stage for your life, your audience, and your other players under the lights. When you focus on yourself and your self-perceived imperfections, you get trapped in a dark, miserable world where nothing is right and nothing is good. You lose sight of God's great magnificence, the awesome light that shines through you and the rest of the world. You become so intent on what's wrong and how you can fix it, that the rest of life just slips away. Don't become paralyzed with a critical spirit, a perfectionism that's unattainable, or a cynicism based on what you see from your limited view.

I realize, dear lady, that this is hard to live out when you're faced with the loss of your nephew atop the Twin Towers. It's hard to keep the show going when you discover a lump in your breast and you're awaiting test results. It's painful to keep moving when your children don't call or come home for the holidays, when your spouse rolls over with his back to you in a sullen stupor of detached disinterest in your relationship, when your unpaid bills and empty purses keep you awake at night. Realize that I'm not advocating denial—don't pretend that these moments aren't awkward, painful, anguished, or numbing. But don't you dare believe for a moment, even in the midst of your darkest moments, that this is all there is. Don't believe that you are alone onstage no matter how desolate and bare your life's theater feels. Don't accept that your life will be consumed by the ravenous jaws of this momentary affliction. ". . . Count it all joy when you fall into various trials, knowing that the testing of your faith produces patience. But let patience have its perfect work, that you may be perfect and complete, lacking nothing" (James 1:2–4).

Regardless of your age and life circumstances, God has brought you too far to leave you in this dark cloud of downcast depression. Jesus bolsters us with his promise, "I am with you always, even to the end of the age" (Matthew 28:20). He has not and will not abandon you, even as your temper flares and your patience wears threadbare in the cloak of your spirit. Hold on, and keep the show going as best you can.

The other focal point of a good drama director is her list of mistakes from the production's dress rehearsal. Sometimes they pile up faster than leaves falling from a tree in autumn, but she keeps track of them, studies them, reflects on the shortcomings, and identifies what went wrong and why. If an actor needs to learn her lines better, an attentive director will spend hours coaching her until the words spring effortlessly from her lips. If the lighting bears down harshly on a tender scene, she will work with the technicians to ensure a softer, mellower mood. If a prop malfunctions during a tense confrontation, then the director will reconfigure the irksome object until it works right.

In the same way we must study our mistakes and motives from the past and identify what is in our power to change and let go of those things that are not. Turn those areas over to the Lord and pack away the worries obscuring your vision. Focus on what you have some control over, the areas that can improve with some hard work, disciplined attention, and consistent practice. Attend to the details within your grasp as best you can and leave the rest to your ultimate Director. He delights in transforming even the gravest tragedy into the happy ending of a romance. Let's consider the first leading lady to experience this Cinderella transformation.

All About Eve

IN THE HISTORY of storytelling and leading ladies, Eve sets an unparalleled standard for tragic scenes. She is the first woman to have it all and lose it all—not once, but twice. Can you relate to such a steep path through the hills and valleys of your faith journey?

Imagine the glorious splendor of a gentle rain spilling down on the fertile earth, watering the myriad of colorful blooms and burgeoning blossoms. Pink and red, yellow and blue, orange and white burst forth from rosebushes and the uneven margins of wildflowers. Fields and trees dance in green dresses. Azure blue skies kiss the horizon, and a bright sun bathes the faces of the first man and the first woman with an amber glow. They bask in the loving presence of their Parent like children discovering the toys of their playpen beneath their caring mother's watchful eyes. The moment is timeless, ethereal, limitless in its innocence and depth of beauty.

Only one thing nags in the consciousness of this first couple, only one site serves as a sign of separation from their loving Creator. It's called the tree of the knowledge of good and evil, and its fruit, luscious and blushed red as a sunburned cheek, must not touch their lips. Eve is troubled by the tree's pull on her attention and finds herself standing before it even though she is committed to obeying her Director's instruction. But one day she stands before it when her enemy takes his cue and hisses his venomous lies into her eager ears. "Has God indeed said, 'You shall not eat of every tree of the garden'?" he slyly asks, targeting her vulnerability.

Eve plays the scene just as her enemy had hoped—she mouths the rules that she only halfheartedly believes. Like a little girl mimicking the sophisticated lines of an adult woman, Eve doesn't fully understand the motives behind the rule. Perhaps she intuitively knows it is for her own good, but without the harsh reality of pain and loss, this must have been a tough concept to grasp. Consequently, the sneaky snake is as ready as a vaudeville villain twirling his handlebar mustache with the ultimate comeback line: "You will not surely die. For God knows that in the day you eat of it your eyes will be opened, and you will be like God, knowing good and evil" (Genesis 3:4–5). Basically he says that God has misled her about the power of this tree; He's misinformed her because He's afraid of sharing peer status with anyone who eats the special fruit and sees the way He sees.

How many times have you found yourself standing in front of the tree that grows the forbidden fruit with your name on it? You have good intentions but find yourself driving past an old flame's apartment, walking past the liquor store on your way home, or stopping just to socialize at Ruby's Club. You have good intentions but find yourself caught up in a swirling wreath of hypnotic memories from your past, from your desire to feel and forget, from your ache to communicate and connect. The fruit looks so good dangling there right in front of you and would taste so sweet. You're tired, you're hungry, you're longing for something that you haven't found elsewhere. And along comes a snake.

He may be dressed in an Armani suit or she may be slithering along in a pair of high heels. Snakes show up next to fruit that's both forbidden and good-looking. They provide the voice urging you, convincing you to give in to your temptations. "Come on, woman, has God *really* forbidden you to see that old boyfriend again? Has He *really* said that you can't walk into that place for one little drink? Did He *really* mean that you shouldn't feel good with a few friends?" And like most daughters of Eve, you parrot the good girl's response: "Yes, He's protecting me for my own good. He's given me all these other things to enjoy. But this one here will kill me." You know in your head that forbidden fruit never nourishes your ultimate good. But in your heart and the heat of the moment, the fires of passion inflame your longing, pushing you to give in. "I really shouldn't, but maybe this once . . ."

The snakes in life are just waiting to hear you repeat the good girl's mantra, for then they know that you're weak, that your attempts to stay on the right path are halfhearted. "You're not gonna die!" they laugh. "Are you kidding me, sister? This is the good stuff right here—eat this and your eyes will open to a whole new world. You'll be able to see things like God does. He's holding out on you, baby."

Inside many of us is the elusive hope that somehow we can be more than who we are. I believe this is due in part to the many messages we receive daily—from magazines, television, advertisements—that we are not good enough as we are and can be better if only we had the right clothes, man, house, job, or other accoutrements of success as they define it. It is also partly due to our self-centered pride that we believe that we alone know what's best for us. We know what we want, who we want to be, and we set our own goals and agendas based solely on our desires. We are so certain of our superiority that we think we transcend rules—"That is a good rule for most people, but I can manage things on my own. I'm the exception"—and even convince ourselves that we know better than the One who created us.

It reminds me of when I was growing up and my dear mother would lay down the rules in our house. "You can't stay out past ten—you're too young and there's too much trouble to get into with a pack of boys late at night," she'd say. I would try to talk her into bending the rules, but she wouldn't budge. One night, however, the temptation and urgent need to be with my friends superseded my desire to obey her rules. So I sneaked out of the house after she had gone to bed early, certain not to make a sound. I even stuffed a half-dozen pillows under my covers to make it look like I was fast asleep should she look in on me before I returned. The next morning at breakfast I sat at the kitchen table with my red eyes and guilty conscience, suddenly aware of how bad my body felt. It dawned on me then that somehow my momma actually knew what I needed more than I did. Her rules were not about her authority or power nearly as much as they were about protecting her children from harm's way and heartache, from rage and regret.

Similarly, the Lord's commandments and His prescription for how you should lead your life are grounded in the intense love He has for you. He created you—He created each one of us—to fulfill a Divine Plan. He wants us to experience glory in this life and in the Kingdom of Heaven, and daily He affords us the opportunity to walk the path He has laid before us.

Unfortunately, when the road seems difficult to follow or when we are deceived into believing a greener pasture lies elsewhere, we are tempted to veer off track, to set our own direction. This is exactly what Eve does.

> *So when the woman saw that the tree was good for food, that it was pleasant to the eyes, and a tree desirable to make one wise, she took of its fruit and ate. She also gave to her husband with her, and he ate.*
>
> *Then the eyes of both of them were opened, and they knew that they were naked; and they sewed fig leaves together and made themselves coverings.*
>
> GENESIS 3:6–7

The Bible says that all that is in the world is the lust of the flesh, the lust of the eyes, and the pride of life (1 John 2:16). All three are represented in Eve's temptation. She saw that the tree was good (the lust of the flesh), pleasant to her sight (the lust of the eyes), and desirous to make one wise (the pride of life). The tree produces delicious fruit that appeals to the senses. Imbued with the power of wisdom, to discern good and evil, the tree's attraction becomes irresistibly magnetic for the susceptible Eve.

This combination of power sources provides us with the anatomy of most every temptation that you may face. Yes, you have only three things to fight in all the world. Three old temptations that have been around for years. But what a trilogy of misery they are to us when we allow them to sting us with their venomous seductions.

We all crave comfort and pleasure, from the tiniest infant eager to nurse at its mother's breast to the wealthiest CEO pursuing another BMW for her collection of luxurious status symbols. We want what feels good and we want it now. As someone once told me, "If sin didn't feel so good, then it wouldn't be a problem!" No kidding, sister; if the fruit didn't look so beautiful and smell so good, if that man hadn't been so handsome or the moment hadn't seemed so magical, then you wouldn't have an issue. You'd walk on by such fruit as if it were a discarded apple with soft spots and brown wormholes.

One way to combat this aspect of temptation is to treat yourself well with the good things that God provides for you. I've said it before, but it's worth saying again. Too many women nurture what they should neuter in their lives and neuter what they should nurture. You have a hard time pampering yourself with healthy, soul-healing gifts to yourself but then rush headlong into some soul-numbing, feel-good moment that's going to bite you the next morning, if not before. You skip a meal thinking that will help you lose weight and look better, only to find yourself bingeing on an entire cheesecake before the day is done. You overextend yourself trying to be everything to everybody and then wonder why you can't resist falling into bed with the first man to seduce you with smooth compliments and empty promises. You're too busy to make it to church—there are too many things that have to get done—but you don't understand why you keep turning to narcotics in an attempt to fill the emptiness you feel inside. You must learn to take good care of your body, mind, and spirit without feeling any sense of guilt or apology. If you don't love yourself first, how can you expect to love others? How can you expect your weak flesh to resist the juicy apple in the store window when all it has to look forward to is a dried prune at home? Don't get me wrong. Treating yourself well will not make all temptations go away, but it will deflate the power of many unexpected moments when you find yourself at the base of a tree with a snake hissing smooth lines to you.

Now, I'd like to focus again on Eve's temptation. The Scripture reads: "So when the woman saw that the tree was good for food, that it was pleasant to the eyes, and a tree *desirable to make one wise,* she took of its fruit and ate." That the tree was good for food is easy enough to understand; the tree was full of luscious fruit that could nourish them and satisfy their hunger. It was also pleasant to the eyes—it looked good. Have you ever seen a picture of a piece of homemade cherry pie in a cookbook and your mouth just starts to water? Have you ever walked by the window of a bakery and just seeing those delectable confections of chocolate and cream gets your appetite all revved up? Well, that's exactly what Eve was facing. The fruit was ripe and red and she knew just by looking at it that it would be juicy. Ah yes, it was tempting, all right. But what does it mean that the tree was "desirable to make one wise"? I believe it simply attaches the one thing Eve was aware of not having in her life—wisdom to discern good from evil—to a concrete, tangible thing. It's not just that the fruit looks good and tastes good, it's not just that she needs to resist eating it like you might resist a cookie after dinner. No, this fruit has power! It can nourish her heart with an ability that she so longs for. It's not just any old fruit—she could resist that. It's *special* fruit.

When you find yourself tempted, you need to stop and ask yourself about the power at the core of the fruit. It's similar to the powerful way advertising marries its products to concepts and lifestyles of success. "Choosy mothers choose Jif" peanut butter. The insinuation is that careless mothers—those who aren't choosy—pick some other brand. You want to think of yourself as a good mom, don't you? Well then, simply buy this brand. And ads only escalate from there. Want to be sexy and seductive? Use this special kind of perfume. Want to be successful and intelligent? Then use this brand of office products. Want to portray an image of sophistication and mystery? Then drive this kind of luxury sedan. It's not necessarily the car or the product that is so tempting, but the promise that it offers. Of course you can buy whatever peanut butter or nice car that you want, but you should be aware of your motivation behind the purchase.

When forbidden fruit is dangling there before your hungry eyes and salivating tongue, ask yourself, what is it promising? What is it that you hope, expect, need to happen by eating your apple of aspirations? Will it make you happier with yourself because it gives you the approval of a man? Does it make you feel attractive and desirable? Does it make you feel like you belong to something or someone that matters more than you do by yourself? Does this fruit promise to empower you and make it easier to be strong and courageous? If you aren't willing to ask yourself these questions, dear lady, then I'm afraid you're going to be doing a lot of apple picking.

And I'm here to remind you of what you already know: This kind of fruit is rotten to the core.

Eyes Wide Shut

AS EVE DISCOVERED, such fruit creates a massive case of indigestion. The pleasure is momentary at best, fleeting, before harsh reality comes crashing down: "Then the eyes of both of them were opened, and they knew that they were naked; and they sewed fig leaves together and made themselves coverings" (Genesis 3:7).

Yes, after you've bitten into the juicy fruit of bad choices, it comes back to bite you with an awareness of both your need—it's still there, it hasn't been filled by that apple—and your folly—did you really think this time would be different? Your eyes are now open, at least momentarily, you see yourself more naked and vulnerable than ever before, and you have a greater awareness of your own neediness. It's like stepping out of the shower and catching sight of yourself in the mirror and realizing how much weight you've put on or how tired you look. The truth hurts. And much of the time we don't handle it well. So, like Eve and Adam, we scurry around like squirrels in winter and sew a handful of fig leaves to shield ourselves from ourselves. Long before there was a film by this title, I thought of this paradox—our eyes are open but we don't want to see so we cover ourselves—as a case of having our "eyes wide shut."

What sights have your eyes been opened to that you didn't want to see? What are the fig leaves you've been sewing in your life? Certainly, denial is the tree with the biggest fig leaves that I know of. You simply tell yourself over and over again that red is white until you've bleached the color right out of your shame. You grab some fig leaves at the department store or the shopping mall and "reinvent" your image—I'll spend a lot of money to dress conservatively and minimize my beauty so there's no way anyone can think I'm promiscuous. Or you surround yourself with other people who wear the same kind of fig leaves you wear. You all suffer from the same weaknesses and can reassure one another that you're okay. It's like a roomful of drinkers sitting in a bar at closing time telling each other that none of them needs AA.

But if you've sewed enough fig leaves, then you know that they only last for a while. Eventually, the Lord seeks you out and asks you what in the world you're doing behind those scrawny little leaves. "Why are you hiding your light under a bushel? Why are you ashamed of the beautiful creation I fashioned from My own hands?" He asks. Then, like red-faced kids with their hands caught in the cookie jar, Eve and Adam fess up to their fears. "I heard Your voice in the garden, and I was afraid because I was naked; and I hid myself." The line of questions culminates with Eve's admission, "The serpent deceived me, and I ate" (see Genesis 3:8–13). While she indicts the serpent for his role in the fruit transaction, Eve knows that she has been deceived. Funny how close that is to dis-Eved. She is no longer innocent. She ate of the fruit, even when she knew better. The snake might have charmed her, but ultimately she made the decision to eat the fruit and she must face the consequences.

So the LORD GOD said to the serpent:
"Because you have done this,
You are cursed more than all cattle,
And more than every beast of the field;

On your belly you shall go,
And you shall eat dust
All the days of your life.
And I will put enmity
Between you and the woman,
And between your seed and her Seed;
He shall bruise your head,
And you shall bruise His heel."
To the woman He said:
"I will greatly multiply your sorrow and your conception;
In pain you shall bring forth children;
Your desire shall be for your husband,
And he shall rule over you."

GENESIS 3:14–16

I include the Lord's punishment for both the serpent and the woman here because too often women act as if they're condemned to the serpent's curse instead of realizing the promise of blessing hidden in the consequences of Eve's mistake. It's the serpent, the enemy with his fiery darts trying to take down God's children, who receives the brunt of God's anger. Notice he gets addressed first. And he's not a scapegoat. He is the antithesis of a kind and loving Creator; the serpent is a malevolent and hateful destroyer. Therefore, he is doomed to crawl on his belly and eat dust. I see far too many talented, gifted, beautiful women who act as if they can make penance for their sins by crawling around on their bellies and eating the dust of life's leftovers. They feel guilty and ashamed of the fruit they've eaten, and continue to eat, and believe that they're no better than the snake that tempted them. They have failed, so they buy into another of the serpent's lies and choose to believe that they deserve the worst. They shy away from anything remotely resembling success or health or balance, let alone grace and mercy.

But you are not the serpent, sister, and you must not think that God regards you as such. You are a leading lady set apart for greatness. But you're never going to discover the spotlighted place He has for you on the stage of life if you don't stop punishing yourself for your mistakes. So you've messed up in life—we all have. Being human doesn't excuse it, but it does infuse it with the power of God's grace. God's forgiveness and loving mercy must become embedded in the heart of every leading lady who wants to move on to the next level of her potential.

This is why the second half of God's edict to the serpent and its relationship to what He places on the woman are so important. Eve may be the first woman to fail, but she is also the first woman to be uplifted by her Creator. Yes, she and Adam have blown it big time—they have chosen to go against the perfect plan that God had set up for them in Eden. But they are not without hope, for two reasons. The first is that God tells the snake that there is enmity between him and the woman, and that her offspring will crush his head while he will merely bruise the heel of her children. God promises that the serpent will not triumph, even though he will still be allowed to crawl around. The second is just as bittersweet. Eve will give birth and bear children even though it will cost her great pain. Because she is created as a woman in the image of her Maker, she will create life and produce fruit. Because she has sinned and chosen to disobey, it will be painful, both literally in the physical labor of childbirth and figuratively in the heartache of suffering that every parent experiences. Even though she has failed, God still loves her and wants to bless her. Similarly, He can't erase your acts of yielding to the harmful fruits of addiction, gossip, lust, and envy as if they never happened, but He can redeem them and transform them into blessings for your life and into emblems of His glory and mercy.

Then Came Seth

EVE FULFILLS GOD'S words to her as she gives birth to two sons with her husband, Adam. As you likely know, they are famous for more than just being the first children of God's children. Out of his jealousy and anger, Cain murders his brother Abel after God prefers the latter's sacrifice for its spirit of excellence. Cain offers a token and Abel gives his very best. God doesn't respect Cain's offering, and He receives Abel's with respect (see Genesis 4:3–8). So Cain lures his only brother out into the fields and murders him, and he deludes himself—like his parents before him with their fig leaves—that God won't notice. But of course He does, and Cain is cursed and exiled to roam the earth as a vagabond.

Can you imagine being the mother of such sorrow and heartbreak? One of your babies kills the other and then is sent away from you forever? Sadly enough, I'm afraid some of you may have experienced such a twin tragedy. You may know what it feels like to have salt poured into the wound of one tragic loss after another. Eve had experienced the unspeakable delights of paradise, a world of sensual beauty and unfettered innocence that she didn't even fully recognize until she was on her way out the door. Then she experienced the uncomfortable pregnancies and deliveries that are part of her new status as a mortal woman exiled to a fallen world. Ah, but the joy of a new mother surely soothed her weary and disappointed soul—the tiny baby sons, cooing and nursing at her breast, totally dependent upon her in their shriveled forms of innocence. She watched them grow to manhood and become hard workers, like their father, one a shepherd and one a farmer.

And then she experienced the unexpected horror of one spilling the other's blood in a senseless plot of jealous resentment. I'm sure she felt a sense of responsibility, that somehow she could have stopped the crime from taking her baby's life. If only she could have stepped in and broken up the childish fights that spark between all boys who are brothers. But it was too late, and Eve was forced to mourn her lost Abel before lamenting the loss of her son Cain as well. Even if she understood and respected the Lord's punishment upon Cain, he was still her baby just as much as Abel. No matter what your children do in life—steal, smoke crack, get pregnant, rape, even murder—they're still you're babies and you love them.

While I'm sure Eve struggled and wrestled through this rocky salt mine of grief, her story doesn't end with the bitterness of tragedy. "And Adam knew his wife again, and she bore a son and named him Seth, 'For God has appointed another seed for me instead of Abel, whom Cain killed' " (Genesis 4:25). Like his promise that new life would spring from her pain, God had another surprise in store for His beloved daughter. Seth, whose name means "appointed," serves as the lineage bearer of Christ Himself. From Eve's wounds and the scars of consistent loss comes the birth of a Hope she can only dream about. But the gift of her son is more than enough to sustain her and remind her of God's goodness. There's no way to compensate for the losses in her life, but the sweetness of new life soothes her soul. Despite her losses, Eve discovered that God wasn't finished with her yet. He had Seth waiting for her, a son who would bear children and grandchildren leading down to the birth of the Messiah. God did not forget her or abandon her.

And He has not abandoned you either. No matter what "outtakes" of life you may have hidden away in the back of some dark closet, God has something special in store for you. Seth is just ahead. You may think that all your "good old days" are behind you and that you've lost all sense of purpose and hope in your life, but the very fact that you are alive right now and reading this indicates that God is not finished with you. No matter how barren, how broken, or how bombarded you feel in the present, you must set your heart's watch on hope for the appointment ahead of you. Leading ladies know that the show ain't over until the Lord says it's over, and He can reverse the darkest tragedy into a brilliant prism of light-bearing glory. So don't try to bring the curtain down yourself when God still has an appointed Seth-experience for you in the next act of life's drama. The enemy knows that God has an appointed seed of greatness in you and is committed to snaking you away from it. The devil knows God's planning good things for you and wants to undermine it every way he can. So he dangles out the forbidden fruits. He sends roadblocks and trials, red lights and tribulations, losses and disappointments so that he can sidetrack you from the road leading to your appointment with God's goodness. If he can deal you and your faith a deathblow of despair, then you will give up and die without realizing the incredible future waiting just ahead.

So you must confront the Prince of Lies with the Lord of Truth's promises and move on with your life so that you may bring the appointed seed of greatness in you to life. You must start looking ahead and dare to dream again. You must believe that there's something wonderful—maybe not what you would choose, but something Divine nonetheless—coming up on God's calendar for you. Over the horizon of the future lies a Seth-experience in your relationships, your marriage, your family, your finances, your ministry, your career. For everything you have loved and lost, there's another appointed seed. Where you are right this minute is not your next destination, let alone your final one. You have an eternal purpose intertwined with your identity as God's Leading Lady, and He will not abandon you. Satan may try to drag down your performance with his critical reviews and brutal mockery, but you must attune your ears to your true Director and the applause of heaven if you want to fulfill His destiny for you.

Rearview Mirrors

IF YOU AREN'T willing to hope in the future our Lord has for you, it becomes far too easy to get lost in your rearview mirror. Have you ever tried to drive without looking through your windshield at what's in front of you? What would happen if you drove your car by focusing only on what you could see in your rearview mirror? Silly, isn't it, even to consider such a feat? It wouldn't take five minutes before you hit the curb, the lamppost, or the car in front of you.

No, we mustn't look behind us if we want to move ahead into the future of possibilities. Faith's history gives us this warning in the story of Lot's wife, a woman we see transformed into a pillar of salt (see Genesis 19). Due to the consistent lack of repentance for its wicked standard of living, the cities of Sodom and Gomorrah are destroyed by the Lord. Lot and his household escape with the warning not to look back at the smoking heaps of brimstone and fire. "But his wife looked back behind him, and she became a pillar of salt" (Genesis 19:26). What in the world could possess her to look back even as she flees for her life? Certainly not the rampant sexual immorality or even the dangers to her daughters. Likely not the relationships or family that she was taking with her. While we can't know for sure, I suspect Lot's wife had trouble letting go of the only successful home she had ever known. In a nomadic culture of extreme desert climates and impoverished, makeshift tent dwellings, Lot and his wife had established a respectable, comfortable home, thanks to the wealth of Uncle Abraham. It probably wasn't even the particular features of her abode dwelling or the special items she had used to decorate and make the place comfortable that caused her to look back. Those could be replaced. No, I believe it was the idea, the concept of a solid, respectable home that was vanishing like sand through her fingers.

The Lord had warned her not to hold on too tightly, not to look back and risk losing the future appointment with His goodness. But this woman could not turn her head away. She was terrified that the best was behind her, and she could not bear to let it go. As a result, she lost her humanity, her faith, her ability to birth new life. She dried up into the bitterness of salt, the salt of her tears of loss.

We all have those things that we just can't leave behind us: past lovers, abusive husbands, nice homes, hard-fought successes, fair-weather friends. We know in our heads that they no longer have any place in our present, but still we insist on twisting our heads until we're contorted in the wrong direction. But if you don't let go of them and leave them in the past, they will turn us into our own pillars of salt, into the bitterness of brine as we drink our own tears instead of the living water of our Lord. Even if the past has held rich moments of success—and I hope it has for you—we must not hold onto past trappings of success and refuse to face the risks of the future and what God has in store for us. We must believe that regardless of the cost, He has something better for us ahead. Lot's wife chose not to believe that the path ahead of her was better than the path behind her. But sometimes, you just have to let go. You just have to keep your eyes on the road in front of you and trust that the journey the Lord has mapped out for you will lead you to greater things.

Date with Destiny

LIFE'S OUTTAKES HAVE the potential to embarrass, humiliate, disappoint, and stagnate us all. But as we see from comparing Eve to Lot's wife, how you handle the moments of crisis in your role as a leading lady sets the stage for your next scene. Like Eve, you can choose to grieve yet continue giving birth to hope, or you can lock your neck like a whiplash victim around the pillar of the past. Keep in mind, however, that other leading ladies have had to make the same choices.

Consider the awkward, shy girl desperately hungry for attention and affection growing up. From a prominent family in New York, her parents' wealth and status could not prevent their untimely deaths. When their daughter was eight, her mother died, followed by her father's passing two years later. Forced to endure a boarding-school education and entrance into staunch society as a debutante, the gangly young woman caught the eye of her distant cousin, an up-and-coming public servant. They became engaged and were married two years later, just as her new husband's political career was taking off. After several successful years in the Senate and as Assistant Secretary of the Navy, her husband leapfrogged to the governor's office and on to the White House.

Despite the numerous critics who mocked the plain looks and keen intelligence of this First Lady, Eleanor Roosevelt served tirelessly even as she overcame setback after setback. Early in his career, her husband had contracted polio, and her role as his helpmeet was only reinforced by his physical limitations. Early in their marriage, their first child, a son, had died. In the chaos of the Great Depression and the shadow of World War II, this lively First Lady dared to speak her mind through radio addresses, public lectures, and her own syndicated newspaper column. She championed human rights on every level and used her grounding in life's sorrows—losing her parents at a young age, not being a conventional "beauty," her husband's disability, her child's death—to reinforce her commitment to the welfare of children around the world. Her tireless efforts enhanced the United Nations, helped found UNICEF, and led to the Universal Declaration of Human Rights. Even after she had established a chain of successes that any person, male or female, could rest their reputation upon, she continued to greet the future with new fruits of greatness.

Consider another young girl, also from a wealthy family, this time in the South during the close of the nineteenth century. Surviving meningitis before her second birthday, this baby girl suffered the side effects of "brain fever," as it was called then, and lost her hearing and her sight. Since she couldn't hear from that point on, she couldn't learn to speak. Her prison of silence and darkness often enraged the young girl into tantrums when her keen mind could not communicate. Doctors and teachers recommended that the wild child be institutionalized permanently, but her mother could not bear the thought. Finally, her parents found a teacher who broke through the chasm of inexpression by teaching their daughter sign language through finger and hand movements. Patience and perseverance harnessed themselves to the girl's intelligence, and she began to flourish.

Helen Keller, and her teacher, Anne Sullivan, went on to become household names for their inspiring story of courage and patience. As a college student at Radcliffe, Helen wrote her autobiography, *The Story of My Life,* and it began the process that continued until her death of changing the general public's perception of people with physical challenges. As you may know, Helen continued to be a prolific writer, poet, and humanitarian, embracing controversial issues of her day, like women's rights and the need for public assistance for the handicapped. She has become a world-renowned model of a leading lady who turned her life's outtakes into an award-winning performance of a truly inspired life.

Finally, consider someone you've seen on your television screen countless times. Unlike these other two great overcomers, this young girl was born African-American, impoverished, to unwed teenagers, in the racially charged backwoods of Mississippi in the middle of the twentieth century. She was abused by male relatives and got pregnant out of wedlock at age fourteen. This woman wouldn't seem to have many choices about her future and its potential successes. But through the losses, she learned to succeed by working hard, by being true to herself, and by communicating with candor and compassion.

Oprah is now one of the most influential women on the planet. With her syndicated show, *O* magazine, and production of such films as *Beloved* and *The Women of Brewster Place,* she commands the public eye. She has explicitly described her own battles with depression, her weight, and her relationships. She has made numerous connections between her past struggles and poor choices to the "aha!" moments that awakened her to new levels of integrity and success. She's the first to admit that her successful career may look like a fairy tale, but that her life's tragic foundation helped establish her commitment to persevere with excellence.

There are countless other women who have their own places in the Leading Lady Hall of Fame as overcomers, women who didn't let the odds intimidate them, who refused to look back and dehumanize themselves as a block of salt. It's not too late for you to join them. We all have our outtakes, but how we use them makes all the difference in our performances. Are you willing to turn your life around, to wait on God's appointed seeds of greatness, to keep your date with destiny? My hope and prayer is that you are.

CHAPTER SIX

Fatal Attractions

NESTLED IN THE bougainvillea-covered hillside of Hollywood Hills sits a grand mansion. A security fence and twelve-foot hedgerow sequester the elegant estate away from the bustle of traffic and tour buses. Nevertheless, when the handsome actor and owner of this fine property walks into his kitchen one morning, he discovers a stranger waiting for him with a look that's equal parts desperation and devotion.

Hardly a week goes by that we don't hear about some fan going overboard in her zealous devotion to a movie star, sports figure, or political leader. It may have started as an innocent hobby in which she enjoyed the actor's performances, the athlete's abilities, or the senator's rhetorical savvy. But somehow the secret infatuation with this person and his lifestyle grows into an obsession with being a part of the star's galaxy. The fan resolutely believes that this figure serves as a catalyst to fulfilling all her dreams. If only they can meet in person, the star will shine his elusive solar light onto the ordinary girl next door and transform her into a celestial goddess.

I don't have any direct experience with stalkers breaking into my home or following my ministry when it travels around the world, but I've encountered many performers from television and the movies, many recording artists and well-known athletes, who have told me of their own frightening confrontations with such people. And I can relate on both sides.

No, I'm not inclined to be a stalker myself, but I do enjoy meeting interesting people and have been blessed to know and work with a diverse array of talented and world-renowned singers, actors, and athletes. In most cases, I've formed some impression of the person's substance prior to meeting them. I've watched their films, enjoyed their music, or cheered their ball games. So when I meet them in person, even though I may not show it on the outside, on the inside I feel like the freshman kid sharing a cafeteria table with the senior quarterback. They have charisma, a fascinating personality, extraordinary athletic prowess, and if these people all have anything in common, perhaps it is a commitment to excellence without compromise in their respective fields. Unless they are incredibly stuck on themselves or surprisingly shallow compared to their public persona (and I've met a few of these), most of the celebrities I've encountered exude an energy that's inspiring and enticing, and I count myself fortunate to know them.

On the other side of the coin, I have encountered some curious fans of my own. Most weeks I receive hundreds of letters and e-mails from people who have been blessed by my ministry or who want to share their testimonies of God's faithfulness with me. A handful of these letters each week are what I call "fan letters," from viewers of my television programs or from readers of my books. Some of them are sincere epistles of appreciation and respect for how God has used my teaching in their lives. Others are a bit more questionable in that they never specify a particular blessing they've received from a particular book or program. Instead they compliment me on my dapper wardrobe or on the way my voice sounds or on the kind of glasses I wear. As you can tell from my tone, I have trouble trusting in the intentions of such strangers even though they may be well intended. Perhaps I am leery of those compliments, though I appreciate them if sincere, because I am occasionally sent hideous, hateful letters filled with odious remarks. I am sure you are surprised. So was I. I thought if a person went about helping others, all people would love them or at least respect them for their contribution. But the Holy Spirit reminded me that no one loved people like Jesus and they killed him!

I get letters from angry racists, extremist groups, and anonymous sources threatening death as well as marriage, which can also be dangerous. It is amazing what happens when a person goes into millions of homes through television around the world. Most sane and credible people enjoy their talents, ministry, or contribution. But I had to learn that there will always be a certain number of people who seek your harm when you are in the public.

Therefore, you see, in our age of celebrity stalkers and media-obsessed viewers, I am as wary as the next person who works in the public eye. A couple of letters in the course of my ministry have clearly been from people who imagined me to be some larger-than-life hero and wanted to attach themselves to me in some fashion. My guess is that either through mental illness or through a myriad of stresses, these people were simply looking for someone or something to give them life and hope. Certainly, I'm committed to being used by the Lord to bless others and bring His messages of transformation, redemption, and blessing to all His people. And I have many wonderful committed ministry partners who, though many are strangers to me personally, write and soon become like friends exchanging concerns, prayer requests, and testimonies that can even be very personal in nature. That is not a problem—in fact, it is so gratifying to be trusted. But when a letter takes on a tone to suggest I am some kind of savior and have the power and sole responsibility to give a person's life meaning, one does get a little disturbed. When a viewer writes in to say that she perceives that I must get lonely traveling all the time and she feels called to keep me company, that's a problem. Or when a woman writes in to describe her dream in which something happens to my wife and she steps in to comfort me, I know I am confronted with an unstable and misguided individual who suffers from delusions and obsessive fantasies.

Star Power

ALTHOUGH CELEBRITY STALKERS are extreme examples of how people get fixated on another and imagine them to have life-changing powers, I believe this tendency is in all of us to some degree. We all, at some time and in some form, generate what I call fatal attractions. I am sure you remember the movie in which casual admiration turns into flirtatious attraction before crossing the line into a suspense thriller culminating with death and disgusting tragedy. Fatal attractions are the irresistible, magnetic relationships, often with people who are unavailable and inaccessible, that we invest with too much power and too much of our self-worth.

Instead of simply admiring the talent, perseverance, and successful careers of these performers in the public's spotlight, when you succumb to a fatal attraction, you are searching for an external source of your personal power.

While we may shake our heads and wonder how some "crazy" people could be so foolish as to stalk a total stranger, don't be so sure that you're immune. You don't have to fixate on a particular celebrity to be considered a stalker. Many people stalk romance and the illusion of love in their lives by the way they dress, by the places they hang out, and by the company they keep. They find themselves desperate to keep up an ultra-sexy appearance, to be admitted to the exclusive clubs, to be seen with the beautiful "in crowd" of the moment because they believe this gives them worth. These people are still feeding into a fatal attraction and abdicating the responsibility every leading lady has for her own performance's power source.

Some ladies become addicted to romance novels so that they can perpetuate the fantasy of the dashing and dark mystery man who sweeps them off their feet and carries them to an awaiting bedroom. Some psychologists have said that romance novels feed a woman's illicit desires the way pornography feeds a man's. Now this comparison seems a bit extreme, but I do know that women often want to attach themselves to a fantasy-based male power source. Whether it's romance novels, reliving the memories of a promiscuous past, multiple affairs, or the more socially acceptable half-dozen divorces and remarriages, women often look to leading men to fuel their purpose and nurture their dreams. A loving husband, a devoted father, and a caring brother can certainly inspire and support you in your endeavors, but ultimately, you must find your inner power source if you are to succeed as a leading lady. Before we discuss how to pursue this energy cycle, let's explore the minefield of fatal attractions and how to avoid them.

Somewhere Out There

AS WE HAVE seen in prior chapters and their examples, and as you know even better from your own life, so much of life is a struggle. The harsh teeth of a variety of stressors nip and cut at your heels like a blind seamstress trying to sew your hem. Even amid the blissful rest of slumber's blessed unconscious, there is no rest as your dreams betray the haunting images awaiting you the next day. You then awaken in the middle of the night and your mind spins lists and scenarios, worries and fears faster than a ticker-tape machine on Wall Street. You watch your husband become more distant and more stubborn as the years pass by, and you secretly wonder if the marriage will last—are you investing your heart in an enterprise that is doomed to fail once the kids are grown or he finds someone more passionate about his interests? Or maybe you're single or widowed, abandoned or jilted, and you lie awake and desperately fear that there's no man out there who will love you—a secret terror that frequently haunts the lonely chambers of your heart.

You watch your daughter entering puberty and struggling with her body image, trying on dress after dress, skirt after skirt, blouse after blouse in an attempt to find one that she thinks doesn't make her look fat. You wonder if she's developing an eating disorder because of the passive-aggressive attitude she displays in the dining room, one meal picking at her plate, the next one asking for third helpings. Your heart aches because you've been there, and part of you still is there, that awkward, heavyset young teen whom the boys teased and the thin girls snubbed and the relatives patronized as having a "pretty face."

Similarly, you watch your son's growing body stretch into teenaged manhood as he struts and preens and tries to prove how tough and cool he is. Beneath the Starter jacket and the Fubu T-shirt, beneath the baseball cap and the Nike basketball shoes, lies the same scared little boy you used to rock back to sleep after a bad dream. He's still frightened but now the bogeyman is the constant threat of drug addiction and sexual promiscuity, gang allegiance and profiling by the cops in your neighborhood.

Then there are your parents. Your momma has grown more stubborn and certain of her opinions about how to run your life than ever before. Your daddy's health continues to plummet like a once-bright comet streaking from the high heavens down toward the dark crease of the earth's horizon. He still doesn't approve of the man you married or the career you've chosen and likely never will. How much he could give you if only he would whisper, "You've done well, baby. I'm proud of you. I love you" just once when you hug him good-bye.

Your career, if it can even be called that, rolls along on the white-water rapids of corporate takeovers, layoffs, economic recessions, the whims of management, and office politics. You paddle and adjust the weight of your talents inside the frail raft of your ego-strength, but the rocks are jagged and puncture your dreams with each passing day. Your fantasy of commanding your own ship on smooth, safe waters lingers in your heart even as it fades in your mind. Could you start your own business from home? Not likely. It's hard enough to survive on two incomes as things are, and the kids have college coming up in the next few years, and the ten-year-old minivan has been resuscitated for the last time. Not to mention the roof needs to be replaced and the termites are feasting on the foundation's east side.

You pray, but it feels like the words get caught in your throat, or if you find the voice to articulate them, they seem to fall on deaf ears. You read self-help books and try to keep a positive outlook. You listen to the success stories of women like Rosa Parks and Cathy Hughes and Oprah and daydream that somehow you, too, are destined for success.

It's at this point that many are tempted to look for an outside power source. It's the fairy-godmother syndrome; we hope that someone will come along with a magic wand and solve all our problems. Only for most women I've spoken with, the daydream relies more on a handsome prince than a magical godmother. It's the belief that someone's out there to help you turn your life around. If you let the daydream crystallize into a clear snapshot of desire, like the resolution of a photograph emerging from the darkroom, you realize that your hero has strong arms, a winsome smile, and material resources beyond counting. His confidence and compassion combine to exude an air of hope and prosperity that is only reinforced by his powerful physical presence. If only you could find him, he would recognize your true potential immediately, awakening you from the mundane slumber of mediocrity with an electrifying kiss. He would venture unlimited capital to set you up in your own entrepreneurial business. He would know how to touch your soul in a massage of passionate devotion that would send your self-esteem tingling right off the charts.

Sleeping Beauty's Nightmare

IT'S TEMPTING TO think there's someone out there who could make it all better, isn't it? Even if you know in your head that there's no such man out there, your heart still aches for that kind of relationship, that kind of relief, that kind of rescue from the cascading boulders of your reality. But here's where you must make an important distinction. All of us long to be valued, to be loved, to be fully known and appreciated for no other reason than who we are. But there's no Prince Charming who's going to sweep you off your feet and make you happy with yourself. Even when the first part of the story seems to go well, Sleeping Beauty usually wakes up to discover her prince is just a common frog. He may be a good frog, a kind frog, but alas, he is only a frog. There is no man who is going to fulfill all of your needs. There is a certain love, a certain power, that only you can give yourself. Self-esteem doesn't come in a can, and it certainly doesn't come from a man. I don't care how complimentary he is or how good he makes you feel. Sure, sweet words are melodious music to your ears, and by all means, you deserve a man who lifts you up. But unless you recognize your own self-worth and stand on your own two feet, you're bound to fall flat on your face.

Similarly, you can't expect a man to give you what only your Father can provide. I don't care if your guy is six-foot-six and can bench-press 560 pounds, there are some things that are too large and too heavy for human arms to bear. The Lord's love and glory are mighty and awesome and truly life-transforming. Mere mortals, even with good intentions, can never come close to the Greatness of God. You can't expect your guy to have the power of a Superman when all he can ever be is Clark Kent.

When you pin all your hopes and dreams on someone else, you're bound to be disappointed. When you believe some superstar or idol, some illusion of imagined perfection, some pie-in-the-sky promise of prosperity is your winning lottery ticket, you become so desperate you'll likely bankrupt your spirit and sell your soul in an attempt to attain the unattainable at any cost. But let me tell you, dear lady, the cost is high and the potential for peril is steep. Don't let a fatal attraction be your fatal flaw; don't let obsessive desire lead you down a path of despair.

Spring Fling

LET'S EXAMINE ONE of the most famous fatal attractions in the pages of Scripture—the King and the Bathing Beauty, David and Bathsheba. The scene of our seduction begins with David tarrying at home in Jerusalem while his armies pillaged and plundered during the spring of the year. Harsh weather had broken, and now the soldiers, and usually their king, the commander in chief, were off on military excursions. But David, perhaps feeling his middle age, or perhaps bored with his career victories, lingers at home. And that's when the trouble starts, because his eyes linger where they shouldn't.

> *Then it happened one evening that David arose from his bed and walked on the roof of the king's house. And from the roof*

he saw a woman bathing, and the woman was very beautiful to behold.

So David sent and inquired about the woman. And someone said, "Is this not Bathsheba, the daughter of Eliam, the wife of Uriah the Hittite?"

Then David sent messengers, and took her; and she came to him, and he lay with her, for she was cleansed from her impurity; and she returned to her house.

And the woman conceived; so she sent and told David, and said, "I am with child."

2 SAMUEL 11:2–5

Like the sensational tabloid-style gossip about stalkers and celebrity-crazed fans, affairs of the royalty are nothing new. But what kind of women find themselves attracted to His Royal Highness? Certainly, powerful men exude an allure that many women find irresistible. It's a false correlation to believe that a royal nobleman will be a conquering knight in the bedroom, but many women want to believe this. They fantasize that the successful corporate raider must be a sensitive, attentive lover.

If there is one exception, however, it's likely King David. He's not just the giant-slayer and warrior-king of Israel, he's an accomplished poet and sensitive musician. And while the king is certainly to be held responsible for allowing the lust of his eyes to lead to the adultery in his heart and then of his flesh, there's no indication that he coerced his soldier's wife into lying with him. God's Word does not shy away from the topic of rape, as we will see with Tamar in the next chapter, so it seems that Bathsheba must bear some responsibility for what happened.

Now I'm not saying she shouldn't have been bathing in a place where others, especially the king, could see her. "And from the roof he saw a woman bathing, and the woman was very beautiful to behold." While it's tempting to accuse her of being an exhibitionist, a wily seductress just waiting for the right moment when there's someone on the roof above her, it seems more likely that in the crowded urban dwellings of ancient Jerusalem, the stair-step skyline made it hard to ever have total privacy.

"So David sent and inquired about the woman. And someone said, 'Is this not Bathsheba, the daughter of Eliam, the wife of Uriah the Hittite?' " The fact that she is immediately identified, both by her father's name and her husband's name, seems to indicate that she wasn't a prostitute with a sleazy reputation. She's a respectable woman from a decent family, married to an honorable man. She just happened to be splashing the intricate curves of her body at the wrong time in the wrong place.

Then the king sends for her. Should she have gone? Certainly there are some who would say she is obligated to go. There's a double bond of duty here, one that is personal, because her husband works directly for this man, and one that is national, because she is subject to this leader's authority. And perhaps there's another pull of attraction as well. Think about how important it might make her feel to know that such a dignitary wants to see her. Here is the king, the richest and most powerful man in the land, and he wants her. Such attention could be quite intoxicating. So, it seems hard to blame the young woman for obeying the king's summons.

But from there the storyline leaves so much unsaid about how the intricate transaction of human desire was negotiated between David and the woman he sent for. Like a silent film, all we're told about is their actions. David sent for her, she came, he lay with her, she returned home. The next thing you know, pregnant. Surely

Bathsheba isn't to blame here, is she? Isn't she just a victim of the powerful king? After all, he called for her. She was simply obeying her commander in chief. She couldn't refuse him, right?

Yes and no, ladies. As I've already mentioned, David certainly bears the sole responsibility for initiating this little tryst. Some people believe that Bathsheba's the temptress, out bathing for others to see like a flower blooming before a hive of bees. Maybe she was being immodest, maybe she bears more of the blame than we will ever know. But I believe the problem begins as David takes action to fulfill his lust. It's one thing to happen across the beautiful body of a young woman in her tub; it's another to find out who she is and send your messengers after her. But at this tricky point in the story, as we've also seen, Bathsheba yields mighty easily. It doesn't seem like she put up any type of argument. It doesn't even appear that she's hesitant, deliberating what she should do.

Certainly the scenario in which she finds herself is quite appealing. The king wants *her.* What a boost to her ego. And when we consider her circumstances, we note that her man, Uriah, had been out in the field for some time. She was bound to be lonely. When we see what a loyal and disciplined soldier Uriah is, we might also surmise that keeping his wife fulfilled was not what he considered his first priority. Not that he is to blame for her indiscretion. But it's easy enough to trace the lighting of the fuse in Bathsheba's mind that seems to have exploded in the powder keg of passion between her and the king. She is vulnerable, and David seems just the one to fulfill all her needs.

What is it that lights your fuse? Too often it's lamenting about what you don't have. When you focus on what's missing in your life, you enter into a place of need, which can quickly turn into obsession to obtain that one thing you think will fulfill your need.

Obsession is a powerful thing. It fuels fantasies and drives you to reckless behavior. It can generate enough power to transform ordinary encounters into opportunities to make your desires come true. Do you brush up against the good-looking newcomer at church in the guise of giving him a sisterly hug? Does the scent of your brother-in-law's musky cologne cause you to buy a bottle for yourself just so you can think about him? Do your eyes linger too long when that certain someone shakes your hand or kisses your cheek in a casual greeting? If you spend too much time lamenting what you don't have, you may be compelled to exploit an opportunity to actualize what you think you're missing.

Was this the case with Bathsheba? There's no way we can assess blame with any kind of percentage of accuracy. And because David proceeds to murder her husband in order to cover up his indiscretion, I think more blame rests on his shoulders. But it takes two to tango, and you're well aware of when you're getting swept off your feet. If you wait to say no until his hands are cradling the small of your back in search of a button or zipper, then it's too late. I don't want to shock you with my language, but let's be honest about the power of our emotions and how our bodies express them. The time to raise your defenses is not when your pulse is pounding in the exhilaration of his lips on your neck.

No, you must prepare your heart far in advance by thinking through your boundaries, knowing your weaknesses, and guarding the commitments you know are best for you. Deal with the conflicts as they come up in your marriage or your relationships. It has become a cliché, but only because it is so true: Couples need to communicate. You and your spouse must really understand each other. You have to overcome the tendencies of many men to keep silent and to withdraw from articulating their needs. You may have to overcome your tendency to criticize or to remain silent about the wrong things. When you talk to him, really listen to what he has to say in return, and expect the same of him. Otherwise, those little resentments and secret disappointments gain an incredible power to be toxic, to contaminate your commitments, and to detonate your fantasies and flirtations.

If you're willing to stay in touch with your heart's commitments, and not your heart's resentments, then your emotional and spiritual strength can bolster your proper boundaries. You may still be faced with temptations from men, but it won't have the same power and you won't be tempted to embellish it with Anita Baker singing in the background and a bottle of chilled wine by candlelight. If you want to succeed as a leading lady, then you must consider your relationship with your leading man. Pay attention, dear lady, before it's too late.

Casualties of "Love"

BY THE TIME Bathsheba finally seems to regain sobriety from the intoxication of her affair with the king, her husband is dead and she's carrying another man's child. To her credit, she is not involved in her lover's nefarious schemes to cover up her pregnancy. By calling Uriah home from the front and giving him a night's leave to be with his wife, David hoped to cover up the evidence of his indiscretion growing in Bathsheba's womb. But the dedicated soldier can't bear to luxuriate in the comforts of home when his fellow soldiers and General Joab are suffering in desert tents and makeshift camps. David then tries to get him drunk, but still Uriah does not go home to sleep with his wife. When all else fails, the king sends Uriah with a message back to Joab. Little did Uriah know that he was delivering his own death sentence. When placed unprotected on the front line as David instructed, Uriah is killed by the "friendly fire" of a jealous and frightened king.

When the wife of Uriah heard that Uriah was dead, she mourned for her husband.

> *And when her mourning was over, David sent and brought her to his house, and she became his wife and bore him a son. But the thing that David had done displeased the LORD.*
>
> 2 SAMUEL 11:27

Like the portrait we've gathered of her prior to this loss, Bathsheba walks the tightrope between victim and vixen, the ambiguity between princess and pawn. She mourns the death of her husband, but we're not told if she was totally surprised by his early demise. We're not told if her mourning was simply carrying out the proper ceremonial duty a wife owed her deceased spouse at the time, or if Bathsheba's grief was genuine. But her mourning is short-lived. As soon as the official grief season ends, she's whisked off again to marry her lover.

Other than the zigzagged path of illicit passion, deceit, and murder that got them to this point, things might have settled into the appearance of a fairy-tale ending from here on out. Only, God hadn't missed all the crooked steps that David took to get what he wanted. And whether Bathsheba blatantly stalked David and seduced him by letting him see her bathe, or if she simply yielded to temptation, when approached with this opportunity that she thought could fulfill her needs, she did commit adultery and must face the consequences. Are you hearing what I'm saying? Even if

Bathsheba had no evil intentions, if she is just portraying herself as the needy victim, she is responsible for her actions.

In my ministry, I constantly meet women who wear the mantle of victim. Even as they confess their sins, they're quick with the refrain, "But it wasn't my fault." "Yes, I slept with another woman's husband, but it wasn't my fault. He seduced me, made me feel like a woman for a change." "I know I shouldn't have been out at the bar all night, but my boss is a tyrant and my boyfriend's a dog, and the alcohol helps me escape my problems." Or "I know I shouldn't be so promiscuous, but I was abused as a child and I'm just looking for some love."

Now, I don't discount these women's problems. I realize and sympathize that life can be cruel and demanding. I pray for the women who struggle with low self-esteem, abusive relationships, and the burdens of being female in a society that still oftentimes degrades and dehumanizes women. But along with my prayers I advise them—no, admonish them—that they must take responsibility for their actions. They can't be looking for salvation in the arms of some man or at the bottom of a whiskey glass. They won't find love until they love and respect themselves enough to stop looking for someone or something outside of themselves to give them worth. Only you, working in tandem with the Lord, can propel you to greatness. When you turn to an external power source, no matter what it is, you're going to have to pay the price for your misguided actions.

Now, we know the punishment that was imposed on David. God responds that David will receive a whole lot of what he had wished for as punishment. "You wished for the sword to slay Uriah? Fine, then. The sword will never depart from your house. You want to take another man's wife? Great, but know that you'll experience a civil war in your own home and that your own wives will be taken out in front of everyone. Have it your way, big boy." Although it's not expressed directly, you might wonder if Bathsheba experiences a similar decree. "You want another man who's not your husband? You got him, sister. Along with the wrath of the Lord and a baby growing inside you. But it's going to cost you the life of the good man who was your husband. It's going to end up costing you the life of your baby. And it's going to cost you the price of your self-esteem that you compromised in the royal palace that night not so long ago."

You see, the thing about looking for your power in an outside source is that once you've attained it, you'll find it is powerless and likely more trouble than it's worth. Have you ever wanted someone so badly that you did anything to win him, and then once he was in your life you wondered what you ever saw in this guy who cost you your self-respect?

But Bathsheba loses more than her self-respect; she loses her baby. The death of her child seems like an especially steep punishment, but it illustrates the terrible, tragic loss of a dream borne out of hidden sin and secret shame. The fruit we try to produce on our own, out of the Divine script of our ultimate Director, is doomed to an early frost. When we attach ourselves to the wrong power source, our dreams don't have the right kind of fuel for our journeys. Misappropriated dreams leave us misguided and sputtering along our path in life. We must depend on God's love and guidance to propel us forward and sustain us for the long haul. We must let God be our road map and our source of fuel, and we must have enough faith to know that we can drive where He directs us.

The story of David and Bathsheba teaches us a bitter lesson, but what's heartening is that it also illustrates that even when we get lost searching for that elusive pot of gold that we mistakenly believe will change our lives, God does not abandon us. He allows us to redeem ourselves and He rights our paths. We see the impact of David's devastating punishment as he himself wrestles with God over his child's life. During the seven days that the baby lived, David fasted and wept, and lay on the ground pleading before his God. When the child dies, David gets up, anoints himself, and then goes to worship the very God that inflicted this terrible punishment on him. This is important, because it shows that David accepts the finality of his actions and the consequences they brought forth. He doesn't blame God for his suffering; he knows that was his own doing. And he goes to worship his Lord likely looking for redemption and direction.

We see that David is transformed. After he accepts the death of his child, he goes to comfort his wife. For the first time he treats Bathsheba not as an object of his physical desire but as a loving partner who shares in his grief. And together they become parents mourning a dead child, no longer accomplices in deception and shame.

The Lord rewards their new union. "Then David comforted Bathsheba his wife, and went in to her and lay with her. So she bore a son, and he called his name Solomon. Now the LORD loved him" (2 Samuel 12:24). God redeems them and in His forgiveness gives them a new baby who would grow to be the wisest king of Israel, who would accomplish magnificent feats and continue the lineage leading to Jesus' birth as the Messiah. Who could have imagined that out of the tangled mess of this affair, the Lord would unravel a knotted skein of personal desires and consequential mistakes and weave its threads into the beautiful tapestry of His plan?

Can you invite God into the secret dreams and future hopes that keep a leading lady's performance grounded and triumphant? No matter how you may have failed, no matter how many men or women you have attempted to attach to like a parasite, no matter how empty you feel on your own, it's not too late. If you're still alive, then God can turn the pattern of your mistakes inside out until a new pattern emerges, a design of intricate beauty and unimagined grace that only He can shape. Bathsheba aligned herself with the most powerful man in Israel, paid an unbearable price, but saw the Lord change her heart as well as her new husband until He restored them to new roles in His cosmic drama of love and redemption. He can do the same for you. It's never too late.

Well with Your Soul

JUST ASK ANOTHER leading lady who suffered the same proclivity to attach herself to men as her sister-in-need Bathsheba. Born on the other side of God's gift of Jesus to the world, this woman had survived the turmoil of a painful life by taking husband after husband after husband, until finally she no longer needed to play the legal name-game and she merely cohabited with the latest star to pass by her dreamcatcher. Until one day, all that changed in a simple but forever profound encounter with a stranger at Jacob's well.

> *So He [Jesus] came to a city of Samaria which is called Sychar, near the plot of ground that Jacob gave to his son Joseph.*
>
> *Now Jacob's well was there. Jesus therefore, being wearied from His journey, sat thus by the well. It was about the sixth hour.*
>
> *A woman of Samaria came to draw water. Jesus said to her, "Give Me a drink."*

For His disciples had gone away into the city to buy food.

Then the woman of Samaria said to Him, "How is it that You, being a Jew, ask a drink from me, a Samaritan woman?" For Jews have no dealings with Samaritans.

Jesus answered and said to her, "If you knew the gift of God, and who it is who says to you, 'Give Me a drink,' you would have asked Him, and He would have given you living water."

The woman said to Him, "Sir, You have nothing to draw with, and the well is deep. Where then do You get that living water?

"Are you greater than our father Jacob, who gave us the well, and drank from it himself, as well as his sons and his livestock?"

Jesus answered and said to her, "Whoever drinks of this water will thirst again,

"but whoever drinks of the water that I shall give him will never thirst. But the water that I shall give him will become in him a fountain of water springing up into everlasting life."

JOHN 4:5–14

Can you picture this strange encounter near the community watering hole? This scene always reminds me of those little mom-and-pop gas stations dotting the countryside just off the interstate throughout the Midwest. Every motorist needs fuel. Everyone needs to eat and drink. People stop because they have to, and such places are few and far between in many regions. The same is true with Jacob's well. Our Lord is taking a road trip with his disciples from Judea to Galilee, from the southern part of Israel straight up north to the Sea of Galilee. In between his departure and destination lies Samaria, and the city of Sychar lies dead center between

Jerusalem and Galilee. It's a halfway point, and being the desert country that it is, water was a scarce commodity to be valued. So when the traveling cadre stop for refreshment about noontime (the sixth hour, we're told), Jesus goes to the well while his disciples go in to town for the food. He has a Divine appointment to keep with a most unique leading lady.

We're not even told this woman's name; she's identified only by where's she's from. She's a Samaritan. Ever attuned to the men around her, this woman instantly notes the barriers between her and this stranger. He's a Jew and there was a cultural and political enmity between their nations. Jews considered Samaritans as less than holy people, hardly worth the time to engage in idle chitchat, let alone real conversation.

The Samaritan woman can't quite decide what to make of this stranger. It's likely that this woman had never met any man like Jesus before. But Jesus cuts right to the chase here. He lets her know that He knows who she is and what she thirsts for, and He implies Who He is and what He supplies to thirsty people.

She responds with an astute observation and more questions. "Sir, You have nothing to draw with, and the well is deep. Where then do You get that living water? Are You greater than our father Jacob . . . ?" This woman seems to ride the line here between calling this odd stranger's bluff and daring to hope that He might really be offering her the chance of a lifetime. On the one hand, He has nothing with which to draw water from the well—so He must be talking foolishness or something profound. On the other hand, who is this guy? This water has been good enough for our esteemed patriarchs before us, so why isn't it good enough for Him? Please remember that this was a place where few men would come. It was a place where women gathered to draw water. The presence of a man generally would suggest that he was looking more for a woman than for water. She couldn't be sure about Him, but she kept on talking.

Jesus then spells it out to her, the same way He does today. It's almost as if He's saying, "Look, there's a key difference between your body's thirst for water and your soul's thirst for Water. You can offer me the former, I can offer you the latter." Can you imagine such a strange encounter? How has the Lord spoken into the thirst of your soul as you attempted to quench it temporarily?

Whether it's with the solace of alcohol or shop-till-you-drop, the elixir of a powerful man's arms around you or the workaholic's fat bank account, what do you use to slake your thirst? And have you heard God when He told you that your soul will remain parched until you drink the Living Water of your Savior?

Here in Dallas where I live we experience some scorching heat during the summer. It's the kind of heat that makes 100 degrees in the shade feel cool, the kind of heat that requires remaining indoors if you don't want to be dehydrated into dust. I'll never forget driving down the highway one blistering August day and turning to see the woman in the car next to mine wearing oven mitts so that she could hold onto her steering wheel! In this kind of heat, staying hydrated is not just about comfort but about staying alive. What's interesting is that people will drink all kinds of things—iced tea, soda, beer, wine, milk shakes, Gatorade, lemonade, orange juice—to stay cool and quenched, but they forget about the beverage that works best: water. There's nothing like cold, sweet water on a hot day. Similarly, in the desert heat of life's sandstorms, there's nothing that will see you through but the Living Water of your Savior. The worst thirst is one that you attempt to assuage with drops of every liquid except the one it truly craves.

And the woman at the well recognized this instantly. This curious stranger wasn't playing games with her. He had something to offer her unlike any other man—and she'd known a lot of them—had ever offered her.

> *The woman said to Him, "Sir, give me this water, that I may not thirst, nor come here to draw."*
>
> *Jesus said to her, "Go, call your husband, and come here."*
>
> *The woman answered and said, "I have no husband." Jesus said to her, "You have well said, 'I have no husband,'*
>
> *"for you have had five husbands, and the one whom you now have is not your husband; in that you spoke truly."*
>
> *The woman said to Him, "Sir, I perceive that You are a prophet.*
>
> *"Our fathers worshiped on this mountain, and you Jews say that in Jerusalem is the place where one ought to worship."*
>
> *Jesus said to her, "Woman, believe Me, the hour is coming when you will neither on this mountain, nor in Jerusalem, worship the Father.*
>
> *"You worship what you do not know; we know what we worship, for salvation is of the Jews.*
>
> *"But the hour is coming, and now is, when the true worshipers will worship the Father in spirit and truth . . ."*
>
> *The woman said to Him, "I know that Messiah is coming" (who is called Christ). "When He comes, He will tell us all things."*
>
> *Jesus said to her, "I who speak to you am He."*
>
> JOHN 4:15–26

Whether she's playing coy with the stranger's offer or simply equating her spiritual thirst with her physical thirst, the woman's reply expresses a sincere interest in Jesus' invitation. So that there's no mistaking his offer for a come-on line, Jesus tells the woman to go and get her husband. It's a shrewd move on at least two levels. First, Jesus makes His intentions clear and honorable—what He offers is no sleazy proposition for a lonely woman dazed by the heat of the day. What he has to offer can be extended in the presence of her husband and even offered to her husband as well. On the second level, Jesus clearly knows the woman's history and uses this instruction to fetch her husband, not just as a sign of his honorable intentions, but as a springboard for addressing the polluted water that this woman was accustomed to drinking. When the woman admits that she has no husband, Jesus stuns her with His complete awareness of who she is and how she's lived her life.

Five husbands! While we might acknowledge that men's life spans were typically shorter than women's due to war, famine, and disease, it seems remarkable that this Samaritan woman has gone through five of them. We're not told if she has been widowed five times or weathered five divorces, or some combination of the two. We are told that the man she's currently with is not even her legal husband. Whether these relationships are tainted with shame and guilt in the mind of the woman, or whether she managed to justify her dependency on men as a cultural necessity during perilous times, we don't know. But it seems clear that this lady's lack of a name in the story is not just coincidence.

Name Game

DO YOU RECOGNIZE this kind of woman? She's the kind who needs to be Mrs. John Q. Somebody in order to feel like she has any kind of identity at all. She has no name of her own. She's the kind of lady we see in society circles leapfrogging from husband to husband amid the scions of wealth and power. She dates, marries, and divorces only to begin the cycle over again, like test-driving, buying, and then trading in her luxury sedan for a newer model with more options. She constantly tries to trade up, the Taurus for a Regal, the Regal for a Seville, the Seville for a Mercedes, and on and on. Apart from her attachment to a successful man, this kind of woman feels invisible, both to herself and to those around her. It's as if she is so accustomed to her reliance on automobiles that she can't imagine using her own two feet!

On the other end of the social spectrum, she's the kind of woman who moves from loser to loser, in a downward spiral of desperation and down-on-their-luck men. She's so terrified of being alone that she endures abuse, risks her children's safety, and accepts his lies about her self-worth. She may visit the local emergency room frequently with bruises and burns, lying to authorities about their real source of infliction. She may steal for him, lie for him, drink and drug with him, all because she thinks she's worthless without the attention of a man, any man, regardless of how dangerous or demented he may be.

And certainly there are many points of unhealthy codependence on men in between these extremes. Where would you locate your current position on this barometer? How do you relate to the leading men in your life? Do you compromise the standards of your performance, the dreams of destiny that God has appointed for you, in order to cling to a male character whose time on your stage has long since expired? Reflect honestly on the men you have related to in your lifetime. Is there a pattern there that resembles the relationships of the woman at the well?

Jesus' awareness of her situation must have startled the woman, but she grasps at the hope He offers her. Could it really be that she had an identity that didn't derive from her bedroom partner? Could this stranger really touch the deep aching thirst that no marriage or man's touch could quell?

Notice her first line of defense as these questions surely ran through her mind. "Sir, I perceive that You are a prophet. Our fathers worshiped on this mountain, and you Jews say that in Jerusalem is the place where one ought to worship." Very clever defense, dear sister. The Samaritan woman falls back on the generalizations and cultural stereotypes that all people have used and continue to use to defend themselves from the specific invitation the Savior extends. The geyser of living water springs up before her, and what does she do? She tries to unleash the dam of floodwaters gathered around cultural religious controversies. She hopes that by sidetracking the stranger into the tidal waves of religious disagreement buffeting their two societies, she can escape His up-close-and-personal scrutiny of her as an individual.

Be honest; you've used this defense yourself. When faced with the time to move on from your past and face up to your thirst and the only One who can quench it, you drag out the old religious smokescreen. You think you can't join the church because so many of the people there know who you are and what you've done. They know about the five husbands and the current boyfriends, about your rap sheet and parole hearings, about your welfare payments and backroom abortions, about your gold-hearted divorce settlements and your jobs gained through sexual extortion. And then you start to think about all the hypocrisy in the Church, all the divisive issues of doctrine and denomination, and you convince yourself that you're better off without it.

The Church is not flawless and neither are its individual members. But don't allow yourself to hide behind the smokescreen of your criticisms about religion. Don't pretend that you are so caught up in the tornado of controversy over issues that you don't even really care about—like the Samaritan woman's claim of wondering who's right, the Samaritans or the Jews, about where and how to worship. Your more contemporary arguments might range from denominational doctrinal disagreements to partisan issues and right-wing causes. While you're entitled to have an opinion about anything you choose, including these kinds of religious matters, you must stop using them as an excuse to run from the call of God on your life. There may always be differences of opinions among Christians. But that doesn't negate the fact that there is a deeper thirst in you, a thirst for much more than joining a sorority or a reader's club. There is a role that Christ and, yes, His Church, can play in bringing you to this place of peace. None of this will begin if you take the coward's way out and join the choir of complaining chorus girls whose criticisms and biases have blinded their eyes to the fact that the Church is like a well. It may be eroding, discolored, or inconveniently located, but it still has the coolest Water your soul ever tasted. Be real about where you are and what you're thirsty for.

When Loving You Is Wrong

WHAT'S GOING TO sustain your role as a leading lady over the course of a lifetime? What will have gotten you through the glare of the spotlight and into the applause of your eternal audience? While it's likely that you will have to share the stage, at least some of the time, with a leading man in your life, you must know that you will never fulfill your role by hiding behind him, mouthing his lines, and dressing in his costumes. In the absence of a leading man, a borrowed one will not suffice the need within.

Otherwise, you fall prey to fatal attractions, to the belief that "If loving you is wrong, I don't want to be right." It's a fine refrain for a country-western song, but living it out depletes you of your raw materials for greatness—your own talents and confidence—and sabotages your true power source—your God and His loving commitment to you and your wholeness.

Do not believe for one minute that you need a man to succeed. If a loving, supportive partner comes into your life, then receive him as God's gift and work to make the partnership thrive as a mutually beneficial enterprise of passionate love and enduring friendship. But do not devalue yourself and your role onstage by believing that men can affirm you, nurture you, or empower you in ways more potent than what you and God together can accomplish.

You must abolish the fatal attractions in your life. You must sever old ties and sticky webs of deceit and exploitation. You must realize your true worth in the eyes of your Creator and step proudly through the marks of your performance. If you haven't done so already, it's time to turn fatal attractions into faithful actions! When the Savior reveals Himself in your life and offers you drinks of His cool, sweet, life-giving Water, don't purse your lips and pretend you're not parched. When other leading ladies or godly men offer you sweet gulps of nectar that refresh your soul, don't turn back to the muddy water of your old ways.

And after you've tasted the Water of Life, give it to those you encounter as well. You'll recall that a leading lady is known by the gifts she gives, and there's nothing richer and simpler than her gift of a cool drink to another thirsting soul. This is what we see the

Samaritan woman doing after her encounter with the Wellspring of Life. "And many of the Samaritans of that city believed in Him because of the word of the woman who testified, 'He told me all that I *ever* did' " (John 4:39). She shared the news of this Waterbearer who had rocked her world and unplugged the respirator of her male-dependency problem.

Jesus knew all that this woman had done in her life but focused not on her sins but on her need. It's not that God doesn't judge us or want us to know our mistakes, but He sent His Son because He loves us and wants to see us whole. No matter where you are in your life, no matter how parched you may be, don't look to stagnant, polluted ponds to satisfy your thirst—you'll only thirst again. Drink from the water our Lord lovingly provides and be quenched and refreshed and satisfied forever.

CHAPTER SEVEN

Scarlet Letters

YOU SEE HER hiding along the frayed edges of the crowd, her ebony hair pulled away from her face, downcast eyes shadowed by the dark velvet cloak draping her neck and shoulders. In the bustling town square, mothers pull their children in tight as she walks by them. Older matrons whisper half-truths about her, pouring their vinegar tones into each other's ears. The men of the town regard her with an odd assortment of extremes: some judge her and condemn her sordid actions; others feel pity but don't want to be known as someone who condones her type; others tingle with curiosity and wonder if the rumors are true and if she would do the same with them.

Who is this mystery woman, the catalyst of so much emotive reaction in those around her? She is Hester Prynne, adulteress and mother of an illegitimate daughter named Pearl. She is the main character and bearer of the title in Nathaniel Hawthorne's classic

American novel, *The Scarlet Letter.* Set in the prim Puritan environment of New England during the dawning years of our country's settlement, this amazing tale tells how Hester is forced to cut the first letter of the alphabet from crimson fabric and sew it to her dress. In the repressed and often hypocritical Puritan communities, public shame over one's private sin was considered a lifelong penance. So as to forever brand her as an adulteress, Hester is sentenced to wear her big red *A* for the rest of her life.

The novel traces Hester's lifetime of coming to terms with her actions, the love of the man who fathered her baby, and the evil persecution of some community members with unexposed secrets of their own. I won't spoil the ending for you—check it out for yourself. But I do want us to consider the novel's central metaphor, one with which I'm sure you are probably familiar. The scarlet letter of the title, the big red *A* that this woman wears and transforms, has come to symbolize the way we identify and label each other's past sins and to influence the way we form our own self-identities.

Scarlet Alphabet

I BELIEVE THE battle with the scarlet letters of life is not just about adultery. I believe it reflects every woman's battle with self-esteem and self-worth. In my experience, I've found that most women don't know their true worth. They judge themselves against unrealistic standards set by advertisers and fashion magazines. They believe they can never be smart enough, pretty enough, rich enough, successful enough, good enough. They are their own harshest critics, panning every performance, calling themselves up short. They have so little confidence in their ability to succeed that it often leads to a critical case of stage fright. Unwilling to risk a negative review, they stay out of the spotlight and remain in the wings. Instead of venturing to step up and expose themselves to the hecklers they imagine are waiting to boo them offstage, they find it easier to hide behind a label—usually based on past wounds or previous mistakes—that justifies their inaction. They slap a scarlet letter on their chest and point to it whenever anyone challenges them to move forward. When guilt begins to bubble up, or else some gentle burning embers of hope urge them to trust in themselves, they simply look down and see that bright red emblem, glaring like a traffic light charging them to stop.

Are you aware of a scarlet letter on your dress? One that you've pasted there yourself? Maybe it's the secret abuse that deformed your precious childhood and left you incapable of seeing your own beauty or appreciating your lost innocence. Perhaps it's the shame you feel over your father's abandonment and your mother's addiction when you were growing up. Instead of braces and ballet lessons you suffered through the loneliness of your own tears and mothering your own momma instead of a baby doll. Maybe it's the way you've gotten to where you are now: by lying on your résumé, by retyping the letters of recommendation from old bosses to embellish their original words, by sleeping with the manager who interviewed you. It could be the haunting images of being raped while on a date with someone you thought you could trust, the violation trapped like a fossil in the amber of your memory. Or it could be your past as a prostitute, prescription-painkiller addict, or promiscuous party girl. Some women have told me they feel like they could sew the entire scarlet alphabet on their clothes!

We all have our mistakes and our sins that linger and surface in the otherwise placid shores of our minds. But once again, it's how you deal with them that determines the effectiveness and quality of your performance as a leading lady. In the last chapter we saw that some women deal with their insecurities and self-doubts by attaching to the wrong power source, an unhealthy relationship with the wrong man. Now I'd like to consider another couple of ways that I see women getting trapped in the confining envelopes of their own scarlet letters.

The first trap is one we hear a lot about and have already touched on briefly, but it continues to snare a leading lady's potential and needs to be fully explored. It is the bottomless swamp of quicksand known as victimhood, for lack of a better term. Now before you shake your head and say, "Bishop, I'm no victim!" (and I pray you're not), let's consider some of the slippery turf in this part of the woods. It's not just the welfare mothers and the single parents who are tempted by the escape-clause of being a victim to hard circumstances. It's not just the abused child or rape victim who struggles with the betrayal and distrust of those who claim to love them. It's not only the drug dealer or the paid escort who blame their present professions on their past deficiencies. No, I believe anytime you abdicate responsibility for any part of your life, any part of your commitment to fulfill your role as a leading lady of excellence, you're flashing your victim's license.

Only trouble is, you know and I know that your license expired a long time ago and, in fact, has been revoked by your Lord who rescues and redeems you. It's a frightening thing to turn in your victim's license and take full responsibility for yourself, for your womanhood, for your relationships, for your career, for your sexuality, for your ministry, for your family, for your life.

It's like a mountain climber strapped and harnessed to the top of the tallest mountain, making her way toward the summit. Every time she looks up, she thinks, "I'll never make it—the top is too far." Every time she looks down, she thinks, "I'm so scared—look how far off the ground I am. What if I fall?" So, trapped in between these two overwhelming perspectives, it's very tempting for the climber to close her eyes and wish she'd never started on this expedition. It's so tempting to think that Superman will spot her distress and come along and fly her to safety. It's so tempting to feel hopeless and blame the weather, your climbing partner, altitude sickness, or the unexpected avalanche of life's storms. But this is the time, dear sister, you must focus only on your present, while still aware of your past scars and your future hope, and take each foothold, each hand clasp as it comes. This is the time you must begin to transform your scarlet letter into a scarlet lifeline.

Vultures of Violation

AS WE'VE SEEN in the lives of several leading ladies, so much of their success revolves around how they handle the mistakes of their past. Often through perseverance, like Eve, or through overcoming their reliance on powerful men, like Bathsheba and the Woman at the Well, they are able to transcend the mistakes of their past and discover God's appointed greatness for their lives. However, I can imagine some of you out there reading this and wondering about how to overcome the mistakes that others have perpetrated *against you* in the past. It's one thing to admit your own mistakes, ask for forgiveness, and move on. It's another thing altogether to be haunted by the memories of abuse at the hands of another. One leading lady who suffered and survived such a violation is Tamar.

After this Absalom the son of David had a lovely sister, whose name was Tamar; and Amnon the son of David loved her.

Amnon was so distressed over his sister Tamar that he became sick; for she was a virgin. And it was improper for Amnon to do anything to her.

But Amnon had a friend whose name was Jonadab the son of Shimeah, David's brother. Now Jonadab was a very crafty man.

And he said to him, "Why are you, the king's son, becoming thinner day after day? Will you not tell me?" Amnon said to him, "I love Tamar, my brother Absalom's sister."

So Jonadab said to him, "Lie down on your bed and pretend to be ill. And when your father comes to see you, say to him, 'Please let my sister Tamar come and give me food, and prepare the food in my sight, that I may see it and eat it from her hand.' "

2 SAMUEL 13:1–5

The plot works: David comes to check in on his son and agrees to Amnon's request to be nurtured and nursed back to health by his sister. And the innocence of Tamar is reflected in her naive acquiescence to her brother's request to bring his food into his bedroom after he'd cleared the household of servants. There her brother's true appetite reveals itself, but she will have no part in satiating his desires. So the lust-sick man rapes his sister. In a matter of moments, Tamar's entire world is transformed. The young girl likely led a charmed, carefree life in the royal palace. She was beautiful, wore fine clothes—the brightly colored robes of the virgin princesses—and was kindhearted and good. She did nothing to bring on the evil deed perpetrated by her brother, and yet his actions tragically impact her life. Amnon betrays her, shames her, and strips her of her innocence. Tamar's perfect life is shattered; gray storm clouds darken the skies of her world and vultures circle, diving at her ravaged spirit.

These are the vultures of violation, the feelings of shame and guilt, of anger and fear, that accompany the nauseous memories of such a betrayal. They typically descend immediately after such a violation and may trail you for an entire lifetime if you don't banish them from your skies. These vultures circled Tamar even as she recoiled from the bedchamber where her brother's violence masqueraded as passion. She lay among the soiled and wrinkled linen of her brother's bed, wondering what went wrong, wondering if she was somehow to blame. She had just tried to help her brother in his need, had hoped to comfort him. Amnon looked so pale and seemed so sick, it appeared as if a little TLC would surely help him on the road to recovery. But the disease that plagued Amnon could not be cured by Tamar's food and attention. While she attempted to nurse her sick brother, he plotted the violation of her body. In the whiplash pivot of a moment, the helper became the prey and Amnon was upon her, leaving her bleeding and shocked in the wake of his rape.

Amnon does more than violate Tamar's body—although that is certainly wicked enough. No, Amnon's nefarious act is even worse than that, for he destroys her spirit. Wounds heal and bruises fade, but with violence against the spirit, the pain is deep and long-lasting. Amnon's deadliest blows are the ones that strike Tamar the hardest. First, he betrays her trust. Amnon played sick and asked Tamar to tend to him. She bakes for him, she feeds him with her hands, and in return her brother rapes her. Can you imagine how that feels? This is someone she cares about, a member of her family, and he violates her body, forcibly takes her against her will.

Unfortunately, I know some of you know exactly how she feels. Fathers, brothers, uncles, close family friends the world over perform sickening, sinful acts on the women in their lives. Innocent girls, faithful females, are violated every day by men they trust. Left with battered bodies and broken hearts, like Tamar, these women never thought a man they loved could hurt them so badly.

What's especially sad for Tamar is that she put off Amnon's initial advances, pleaded with him not to do it, and told him how much such action would hurt her. "But she answered him, 'No, my brother, do not force me, for no such thing should be done in Israel. Do not do this disgraceful thing! And I, where could I take my shame? And as for you, you would be like one of the fools in Israel. Now therefore, please speak to the king; for he will not withhold me from you' " (2 Samuel 13:12–13). Tamar tells Amnon that if he takes her virginity this way they will both be disgraced, and she will be subject to inescapable shame. And if you notice, Tamar doesn't really say no, she just says, "Not now." She basically tells him, "Look, don't do it this way. Ask the king first—he won't deny you—and then our union could be respectable." But Amnon doesn't listen; he doesn't care. Without regard to the consequences Tamar would bear, not willing to delay his own gratification, Amnon forces himself on her.

But even this is not the end of Tamar's suffering. It was bad enough that the brother she had trusted had betrayed her, but he rejected her as well. After Amnon defiles his sister, hatred for her consumes him. I am sure it is his own horrific actions that he loathes, but Tamar is the physical reminder of his depravity and he cannot bear to be in the same room with her. He throws her out of his chambers, and when she refuses to leave, he has his servants forcibly remove her. Amnon literally adds insult to injury, and this completely devastates Tamar. "This evil of sending me away is worse than the other that you did to me" (2 Samuel 13:16). She would never have believed her good intentions could yield such evil results, such a spiteful affliction compounded by hatred for her.

You must be careful, sister, even in the best and most secure relationships. You must watch out for the unexpected. Stay watchful because otherwise you may miss the moment when the tempo of a relationship changes. It can happen in the moment you take your eyes off him and he places his eyes on parts of you he has no business imagining. In the blink of an eye, a friend can become a foe with very little warning. Like Tamar, you could be left trembling and muttering to yourself, "Why didn't I see this coming?" You may have the best intentions, but that doesn't mean you won't suffer the heart-shattering blows of a selfish man. But thank goodness all men are not Amnons.

Overcoming Tamar-times

IT IS UNDERSTANDABLE that Tamar falls apart immediately after this shocking and brutal scene. "Then Tamar put ashes on her head, and tore her robe of many colors that was on her, and laid her hand on her head and went away crying bitterly" (2 Samuel 13:19). She put ashes on her head, which was a sign of repentance. Do you believe she actually thinks she needs to repent for what happened? So many women who suffer at the hands of another play the blame game, but blame themselves! In their grief they mistakenly believe that if they were somehow better, smarter, or if they could have seen this coming, they could have avoided this abuse. They suffer in sorrow, asking why this happened while at the same time looking in the mirror and blaming themselves. Tamar also tears at her clothes as a sign of her grief. She visibly marks herself—wears the costume of the repentant, literally wears her situation on her sleeve.

Now, I'm not condemning Tamar for her actions, not at all. It is perfectly okay to indulge your grief in the wake of tragedy. Certainly she should not blame herself for what happened; she has nothing to be ashamed about. She didn't bring this upon herself. But neither can she just walk away like nothing happened. You can't ignore the abuse inflicted upon you. That's denial, and your repressed emotions will only rise up and surface later in your life, with an intensity that is tenfold the original and so much more damaging. No, Tamar is right to express her devastation. She can't and shouldn't sweep the incident under the carpet. Nor should she endure the suffering alone. Pretending nothing happened would just protect Amnon, and feed fuel to the fire of her own shame. Sharing grief lightens its load and makes it easier to bear.

But what makes Tamar a leading lady to emulate is that she doesn't let that scarlet letter become a permanent emblem tattooed on her chest.

Just when it seemed as if Tamar could bear the disgrace and pain of shame no longer, another brother entered the scene. Absalom lifted her up from her disheveled state of shock and grief and told her to go to his house, where she could recover. Tamar had to realize that just because one man had violated her body and her trust, that not all men were this deceptive and exploitative. She had to learn to trust again, as most of us do after we have been betrayed by the harsh words and stunning blows of those around us. And she goes with Absalom, she lets herself trust him, and through her brother her honor is eventually restored.

You must take courage during Tamar-times, my sister. While you look for an Absalom to pick you up and comfort you, don't make your recovery dependent upon it. Pick yourself up and find the help you need from other sources. Lean on your sisterhood of support through the caring of good friends and family. Be willing to ask for help at the right time and be ministered to by the Church and its agencies. Banish the vultures of violation that will attempt to pick at you and destroy your body and mind. Their favorite target is your self-esteem and self-identity. They hiss their terrible lies from the enemy into your mind: "You're used goods, girl—no man will ever love you now." "If you're no stronger than that, then you deserve what you got." "You know those looks you gave him were more than innocent. You asked for this." On and on these lines swim and surface through your consciousness like oil slicks from the tanker of trauma contaminating your pristine waters. But you must recognize these for what they are: complete and absolute lies. This is the way the devil tries to take out the leading ladies from this world. If he can get you to believe falsehoods about your identity, then you won't be strutting the stage with greatness for God's glory.

Realize, too, that for issues as severe as rape and abuse, domestic violence and verbal abuse, you will need to get help. This will feel like the last thing you want to do—try to trust others again—but it is a shortcut through this valley of death into a healing meadow of wildflowers. Find a good counselor, seek out the domestic-abuse shelter, call the hotline, talk to an older woman or trusted girlfriend, start a recovery group in your church. The Amnons in life may have taken your power once, but now it's time to quit allowing them to continue to siphon away the power of who you truly are. It's time to take back your power, dear sister, and activate your potential for greatness. You may still be haunted by an occasional vulture looming overhead, but arise and fly on the wings of eagles away from this soul slayer's pursuit.

Many women often learn that as they work through their past issues of abuse, they become wounded healers, experienced ministers to those just coming to terms with their losses. Like the story of Joseph, a victim to his brothers' jealousy, violence, and greed, you reach a point where the scars of the past become the subtle beauty marks of your present. Joseph told his brothers, "Do not be afraid [of his retribution], for am I in the place of God? But as for you, you meant evil against me; but God meant it for good, in order to bring it about as it is this day, to save many people alive" (Genesis 50:19–20). It may seem like too much to believe that God can transform the evil intentions of others, but leave room for Him to work in your heart as you work through your emotions, your trust issues, and your image of yourself. Ask Him to bless you in miraculous ways because of what you've survived and endured. Ask His Spirit to reveal life-empowering glimpses and life-giving words to your true identity as His Leading Lady.

Rahab the CEO

GOD IS ALWAYS in the process of enhancing the performance of His Leading Ladies. Some of them lack in courage and confidence while others have the chutzpah and feistiness of a brass cannon. These latter leading ladies often do not lack courage as much as they lack faith and the ability to trust. They are strong, resourceful women who learned the lessons of life early. These women know how to manipulate the system to get what they want, to climb the corporate ladder, to get their education paid for, their checks delivered on time. These women often wear a scarlet letter as well, only they aren't known as victims as much as they are known as victimizers. Their reputations precede them wherever they go: "Oh yes, Mrs. Shrewd, I've heard all about you and know why you're here."

While these tough, often successful women may not act like it bothers them—their reputation is just another obstacle they hurdle in the pursuit of their goals—on the inside they often suffer from the same doubts and uncertainties as women with other scarlet letters. They are so used to taking care of their life circumstances—the bills, the mortgage, the groceries—and the needs of those around them that they seldom take time to appropriate and receive grace. They're such control freaks that they can't delegate or leave room to be surprised. But this place is often where the Lord intervenes and sends them a wake-up call, a life-saving opportunity that they can't turn down. Perhaps the most famous leading lady in this company is Rahab the prostitute, a woman like Hester Prynne whose scarlet letter always seems attached to her name and identity. Here's how her story begins:

> *Now Joshua the son of Nun sent out two men from Acacia Grove to spy secretly, saying, "Go, view the land, especially Jericho." So they went, and came to the house of a harlot named Rahab, and lodged there.*
>
> *And it was told the king of Jericho, saying, "Behold, men have come here tonight from the children of Israel to search out the country."*

So the king of Jericho sent to Rahab, saying, "Bring out the men who have come to you, who have entered your house, for they have come to search out all the country."

Then the woman took the two men and hid them. So she said, "Yes, the men came to me, but I did not know where they were from.

"And it happened as the gate was being shut, when it was dark, that the men went out. Where the men went I do not know; pursue them quickly, for you may overtake them."

(But she had brought them up to the roof and hidden them with the stalks of flax, which she had laid in order on the roof.)

Then the men pursued them by the road to the Jordan, to the fords. And as soon as those who pursued them had gone out, they shut the gate.

JOSHUA 2:1–7

There are several highly noteworthy moments in this breathtaking, action-packed encounter, a scene that plays more like something out of a James Bond movie than what we often expect from the Bible. First, as I've alluded to before, is Rahab's line of work and how this dogs her name to the point of reflecting her identity. In these ancient cultures, whether Canaanite, like the harlot Rahab in Jericho, or Jewish, like Joseph the Carpenter of Nazareth, people's professions became part of how others identified them. This tradition still plays out in our culture, especially in the older generations and smaller communities where what you do reveals something about who you are. Growing up in the countryside of West Virginia, I became accustomed to knowing whom my father meant when he referred to "Billy down at the garage," or when my momma referred to "Janice, the grocery clerk."

Rahab had made a name for herself all right. The word for prostitute here, *zoonah,* distinguishes what Rahab did—made money by selling her body for sexual services—as opposed to what the temple prostitutes did in the courts of Baal and Molech—offered sensual delights as part of pagan worship. So Rahab is a businesswoman, CEO of her own little cottage industry. Conveniently located near the city gates with a house built into the city walls, Rahab displays a shrewd business acumen. There was bound to be lots of traffic coming and going in and out of the city, and Rahab had a prime location from which to offer her services. I'm sure Rahab was successful in her enterprise, so successful that it defines who she is. She is not known by her place name, like the Samaritan woman at the well, or by her father's family name, like Bathsheba is identified. No, she is Rahab the harlot and runs her own one-woman show.

How would you be known if you lived in Rahab's day? Would you be Deborah the attorney who chases ambulances? Or maybe Angie the stay-at-home mother? What about Michelle the secretary? Perhaps you're Brenda the former stripper? Maybe you would be known as Marlene the makeover queen or as Janice the pediatrician with her nose in the air. Truth be told, we could all come up with our own labels that would cut to the heart of what we do and who we are when we do it. My title of "Bishop" makes it easy for most people to recognize who I am and what I do. It is not a self-imposed description, but rather the biblical reference in 1 Timothy 3:1 for one who oversees or leads others.

Maybe your title accurately describes what you do and is taken from Scripture or your company's job description. Or maybe your identifying phrase is the handiwork of clever gossips and the forwarded e-mail rumor mills. We might fight the urge to see ourselves this way, but others won't let us forget our pasts, our mistakes, or our place in society. Think for a moment whether or not your label is big enough to encompass all of who you are. My fear is that for most women they either settle for the lowest common denominator in their nomenclature or else accept the name stereotyped across their forehead by those who would keep them down. That's one reason I chose the identifying phrase of "leading lady" for this book—it's one of the few labels I can think of that does justice to the complexity, responsibilities, aspirations, and triumphs of where so many women are today. If you haven't already, are you willing to trade in your old name for a new identity worthy of your talents, time, and lifetime pursuit?

Losing the Labels

WHAT MAKES RAHAB so remarkable is that she refuses to be defined by her scarlet letter. She was ready to be known by more than her bedroom bordello. She's not only a shrewd businesswoman, she's a fast-on-her-feet catalyst for courageous change.

> *Now before they lay down, she came up to them on the roof,*
>
> *And said to the men: "I know that the LORD has given you the land, that the terror of you has fallen on us, and that all the inhabitants of the land are fainthearted because of you.*
>
> *"For we have heard how the LORD dried up the water of the Red Sea for you when you came out of Egypt, and what you did to the two kings of the Amorites who were on the other side of the Jordan, Sihon and Og, whom you utterly destroyed.*
>
> *"And as soon as we heard these things, our hearts melted;*

neither did there remain any more courage in anyone because of you, for the LORD your God, He is God in heaven above and on earth beneath.

"Now therefore, I beg you, swear to me by the LORD, since I have shown you kindness, that you also will show kindness to my father's house, and give me a true token,

"And spare my father, my mother, my brothers, my sisters, and all that they have, and deliver our lives from death."

So the men answered her, "Our lives for yours, if none of you tell this business of ours. And it shall be, when the LORD has given us the land, that we will deal kindly and truly with you."

JOSHUA 2:8–14

Rahab makes it unequivocally clear that many of her people there in the city of Jericho have heard about God's hand of protection and provision on the Israelites. The story of the departure from Egypt, with its plagues and bloodied doorposts, and the grand finale of the Red Sea parting, surely had reached epic proportions as it spread like a tall tale by word of mouth. But here Rahab transcends merely repeating the spine-tingling legends of the God of Israel—she believes in Him and fears Him and accepts that He will give her people's land to the Children of Israel. She lies to her own king's messengers—an act of treason punishable by death if her deceit is detected—to protect a couple of foreigners she's never met before. She doesn't have a lot of time to stew and think and reflect about what to do. She acts, decisively and dramatically, and has a plan in mind to reward her courage. She wants her kindness repaid with like kindness. She wants to make a deal. She's clear about what she wants, the terms of payment as well as delivery.

What a breath of fresh air she is! Women like Rahab are often looked down upon by society, labeled by her peers, and dismissed by the Church today. But these women are some of the brightest stars in leading-lady history. In their resilient, resourceful method of relating to their situations, they transform their scarlet letters into God's Word of Life for their souls and their households.

Two important principles leap out at us from Rahab's story that apply to all leading ladies. First, realize that you are not limited by your past, your reputation, or your present profession. Rahab emerges from the annals of history and Scripture as a woman known as a professional prostitute and transformed into a woman known by her faith. Out of all the people God could have chosen to use and save from Jericho, He honored the faith of this woman regardless of who she had been all her life up until that point. It would seem logical in our mind that God would choose some righteous little old lady who's prayed every day her entire life. But evidently, there weren't any around who possessed the kind of faith that the Lord found in Rahab. For you see, your past limits you, dear lady, only if you use it to barricade the path of faith. God doesn't limit Himself by what you've done or what others may think of you; He delights in the faith of His children.

And that spotlights Rahab's second fundamental principle of a leading lady—she acts on her faith, putting her belief in motion and risking the highest stakes possible for what she knows in her heart to be true. Are you willing to risk that kind of faith in action to see your dreams come true? Notice that Rahab is not asking for a large monetary reward, nor for something materially valuable but useless in the face of the impending Israeli siege. No, she's head-up and street-smart, and she asks for her life as well as the lives of those she loves—her parents and siblings and their households. She may be the original hooker with the heart of gold, willing to take an enormous chance on the promise of strangers, and an even greater chance on her newfound faith in the strangers' God. Do your dreams extend beyond yourself and your own selfish gain to include those around you, your loved ones and your household? True faith in action rarely risks without considering the needs of others in the equation.

Do you ask for what you want? Or do you remain silent, locked into passivity and mediocrity by your own unwillingness to give voice to your desires? I believe Rahab, and Tamar as well, demonstrate that women must give voice to their pain, voice to their violations, voice to their dreams, and voice to their terms of success. What dream keeps you up at night nagging at your consciousness, begging to be voiced and actualized? What vision do you have for your future and the futures of those you love and care for?

Scarlet Cords

SO RAHAB CUTS a deal with the Jewish spies. She will save them if they in turn save her and her family, and the spies agree.

> *Then she let them down by a rope through the window, for her house was on the city wall; she dwelt on the wall.*
>
> *And she said to them, "Get to the mountain, lest the pursuers meet you. Hide there three days, until the pursuers have returned. Afterward you may go your way."*
>
> *So the men said to her: "We will be blameless of this oath of yours which you have made us swear,*
>
> *"unless, when we come into the land, you bind this line of scarlet cord in the window through which you let us down, and*

unless you bring your father, your mother, your brothers, and all your father's household to your own home."

JOSHUA 2:15–18

Rahab asks boldly and receives the fruit of her faith. When the city is under siege from fire and rampaging soldiers, Rahab gathers her family members into her own home and transforms her scarlet letter into a scarlet cord of protection. Symbolically, the rope by which she lets the spies down from her window becomes a flare of hope when they return with their regiment to conquer the city. Rahab's red cord transforms her status as a lady in red into a lady in waiting to the King of Kings.

Legacy of Faith

WHILE WE'LL LOOK at the various legacies a leading lady leaves behind her in the third section, Rahab sees such an incredible harvest from her seeds of faith planted in the garden of her future that we must consider her legacy. First and foremost is her very life and the lives of her family—Joshua and the Israelites indeed keep their end of the bargain. She trusted God enough to trust that they would not forget her or the terms of their agreement. This affords life to her vision of the future in ways that she could never have imagined for herself.

"And Joshua spared Rahab the harlot, her father's household, and all that she had. So she dwells in Israel to this day, because she hid the messengers whom Joshua sent to spy out Jericho" (Joshua 6:25).

Notice that even at the time the Book of Joshua was written, well after the Children of Israel had settled this Promised Land, Rahab had become a legend in her own time and immediately afterward. Like the plagues, the death of the pagan kings in nearby lands, and the parting of the Red Sea, the faith of Rahab the prostitute establishes her place firmly in God's kingdom and in Jewish history.

For us looking back on her story, the happy ending seems a foregone conclusion. But don't minimize what this woman overcame. Whatever circumstances led Rahab into prostitution could have easily kept her there. But she finds the power to overcome her victimhood. In her past, Rahab had probably been hurt and betrayed enough times to extend the city walls around her heart. Yet as hardened as she appears, she lets the glory of God penetrate her defenses and lets herself believe that He will protect her. The key issue for her, like it was for Tamar, is one of trust, being used by men and coming to terms with her identity as a woman. Rahab and Tamar have been set up to see themselves as women closed off from the hope of the future. Their exit ramp of faith had been given a permanent detour. Then they dared to believe that maybe they were more than the abuse inflicted upon them. Faith in action, dear sister, removes the veil of your false self and your false identity. Faith in action sends the vultures of violation scattering away into the recesses of hell.

Fast-forward to the Future

USE THIS ACTIVATED faith to change the way you see yourself. Faith empowers you to let go of the hope that your past could ever be any different. Faith allows you to accept the stark realities of tragic blows and undeserved scars of others' selfishness. But even seeing these stark events and their consequences clearly does not ensure that you'll see yourself clearly in the present. Why? Because we buy into a worldly equation of success: born into the right family + good circumstances = $uccess. Why? Because it's a neat excuse for shrugging off the hard work and passionate anguish of giving your best, day in and day out. Why? Because it's so much easier to play a role that someone else has prescripted for you than a leading part that is self-motivated and directed by the One who knows and loves you best.

Scarlet letters come with a fill-in-the-blank script of labels and stereotypes. If you can hide behind the big red *A* plastered on your dress or embroidered into the shame of downcast eyes, then you don't have to redefine yourself and appropriate the courage needed to allow God to change your scarlet letter into a scarlet cord of rescue.

Quit hiding behind your own scarlet letters and look for the seeds of greatness God is sewing in your life. Fast-forward to your future and consider the faith legacy you want to leave behind. It's not surprising that Rahab became a favorite example throughout the New Testament. We see her mentioned in Matthew's lineage of Christ (1:5) as the wife of Salmon and mother of Boaz, who would grow up to marry Ruth. How wonderful to see her settling down with a good man and mothering a compassionate son. Her past ways did not preclude her future joys. And she is not alone. What is so striking about this genealogy is that Matthew includes any women at all in this patriarchal rundown, and that the women he includes are not pious old mothers of the faith when they started out. Rahab's sister of the scarlet alphabet, Tamar, is listed (1:3), and we saw what she had to overcome. Rahab is mentioned next, the legendary harlot who secured her future by dangling her faith on a scarlet thread. Then Ruth, a Moabite and one-time worshiper of idols, comes into the mix (1:5). Finally, Bathsheba is listed as she "who had been the wife of Uriah" (1:6). All these extraordinary women overcame remarkable obstacles to take their leading role on God's stage. They overcame rape and shame, loss and grief, alienation and adultery, murdered husbands and dead babies, past promiscuity and accompanying reputations.

The message here is a resounding reveille of hope for every one of you reading this right now. There is nothing so shameful, so heinous, so debilitating that your God cannot overcome. And don't be misled; it is only in rare cases that He transforms your past, your present, or your pain overnight. No, what fuels the transformation is your willingness to act in faith. To overcome those obstacles with a strident purpose and powerful faith that won't take no for an answer. To keep going when the sky looks darkest and the night closes in with a chill traveling up your spine. To persevere until your prayer power and hard work have actualized the dream your faith has harnessed and brought to life. It's a myth of success that women who have made it have perfect backgrounds, perfect educations, and perfect reputations. Most successful women have triumphed not because life has handed them perfection on a silver platter but because they never gave up. They learned to live with their pasts, their flaws, their circumstances, and to succeed nonetheless. Even someone we consider as saintly as Mother Teresa acknowledged that she had faults. In her memoirs she notes that someone once asked her if she had any regrets about the life she had led. She replied that she had many faults but no regrets that she could speak of. She had seen the Lord use her mistakes to build her character and strengthen her faith. She did not quit, and neither should you.

If you want to have a legacy like Rahab's or Mother Teresa's, then you must let the fuel of faith be your power source that propels you to transcend your labels and enables you to achieve your dreams. Act in faith, dear sister, and refuse to let your past hold you down. In the Letter to the Hebrews in which are catalogued so many great members of the Faith Hall of Fame, the author saves one of the best for last. "By faith the harlot Rahab did not perish with those who did not believe, when she had received the spies with peace" (Hebrews 11:31). Or consider the apostle James citing our girl as an example as well. "You see then that a man is justified by works, and not by faith only. Likewise, was not Rahab the harlot also justified by works when she received the messengers and sent them out another way?" (James 2:24–25). Have you married your works to your faith, dear sister? Are you taking the necessary steps to fulfill your appointed seed of greatness? If you're not, then consider what's holding you back and deterring your behavior from following through on what you believe. Take courage from the examples of Tamar and Rahab, from Ruth and Bathsheba. It's never too late, so don't hesitate!

If you are acting on your faith and pursuing your dream of destiny in concrete ways, then I commend you, dear lady. Be sustained in your journey and let nothing stand in the way of what God wants to accomplish in your life. Be encouraged by your sisters' examples. Transform your own scarlet letters into scarlet cords signaling your righteous rescue from who you used to be and your new ascent up the mountain of faith. Loose that woman and get out of her way!

CHAPTER EIGHT

Impossible Dreams

MEN ARE NOTORIOUS for doing it. Women, I suspect, are just as guilty of indulging this secret pleasure as their men. You sit in your favorite armchair or that comfort-worn spot on your couch. A cozy blanket drapes your lap and feet with its soothing caress. A cup of hot tea or piping cocoa steams its sweet aroma at your side. Electric-blue shadows flicker in the dimly lit room. In the palm of your hand rests the key to dozens of faraway portals. With each click of a button, you investigate the images and draw a conclusion about that story's appeal, much like an archaeologist interpreting hieroglyphics on ancient cave walls. With one click, you find two women hunched over their wineglasses as they share their heartaches over the men in their lives. You know if you linger you'll need your box of tissues before too long. With the next click, you're aboard a spaceship in the distant future with an alien and his human commander arguing over how best to colonize a newly discovered planet. Their dilemma is intriguing and imaginative, and you find yourself captivated by such a portrait of the future. Another click and you're alongside a young woman racing down a dark-shadowed alley alone. Ominous footsteps trail her every turn, accelerating along with the sound of her heartbeat. Even though you don't know who she is, you're already worried about what will happen to her if she's caught. Next click and you're in the safety of a familiar police precinct. Another and you find yourself caught up in laughter at the pratfall of a poorly coordinated young comedian. On and on the clicking goes, from A&E to QVC to HBO and BET, from CNN to TBN, ESPN to PBS, and the rest of the alphabet in between.

Channel-surfing. We all do it. It affords us a myriad of changing possibilities, all available with the flick of a button. And as we land for a few brief seconds on each station, notice how quickly we identify and assess the images before us. You can spot a tearjerker at ten paces; it's the same with an old black-and-white sitcom or a scary movie with its high-pitched violins screaming in the background. Whether it's a children's educational show or the latest installment of a soap opera, whether around-the-clock news or a classic western, you process the characters, costumes, and dialogues of each sound bite and determine if it's what you're in the mood for.

The main reason we are able to process each channel's offering so quickly is because we have watched enough television to know what to expect. We become so familiar with the respective genres that we immediately imagine what led up to the moment we're now witnessing and what will likely follow. If it's a love story, then we infer the conflicts keeping the young couple from complete bliss, nonetheless hoping for an exchange of wedding vows at the end. If it's an infomercial, then we can imagine the "real life" testimonials that preceded our viewing and the celebrity interview that's coming up. If we tune in to a courtroom drama, then we want to see what verdict the jury will return. Each genre—comedy, western, romance, action/adventure, sci-fi, soap opera, police drama, or cooking show, just to name a few—carries with it a set of expectations. If the shows are poorly done, then you've seen them all if you've seen one. How many episodes of the cute family sitcom do you have to watch to know that everything will be tied up with a neat bow by the end of thirty minutes? However, the shows we linger over tend to be ones that give us some surprises along with some fulfilled expectations. Yes, this is a celebrity talk show, but it features extraordinarily candid interviews with its all-star guests. Yes, the detective did catch the criminal by deducing his whereabouts from a set of clues, but the criminal turns out to be his brother, not the ex-con we expected. Good stories engage us by being familiar enough for us to recognize but surprising enough to be unpredictable.

Too often, I'm afraid, many women think they've identified their life story's genre and feel compelled to live it out without questioning the areas that they could change. They get stuck in a tragic mode, an ironic attitude, or a comic-relief frame of reference that takes nothing in their lives seriously. Consider this for a moment: What kind of show would your life be if it were on television? Melodrama or game show? The evening news or "Entertainment Tonight"? A wacky sitcom or a prairie heart-warmer? What do you expect to happen in your future? Have you already decided you know how the story ends?

Change the Channel

MANY WOMEN THINK they know the rest of their story when the plot suddenly swerves and changes the entire ending. They think they're watching one type of program when the channel is changed before their very eyes and it becomes an entirely different show. Consider Sarah, for example. Here's one of God's Leading Ladies who had basically resigned herself to a bittersweet drama, a saga of prophecy, thwarted hope, and disappointment. Throughout the ups and downs, the peaks and valleys of her life, she had been following God alongside her husband, Abraham. Despite the passage of time, God continued to promise them children, and not just any children, but a whole nation of descendants, scattered as far and as numerous as the stars blanketing the night sky. Certainly, this hope seemed dramatic and logic-defying, considering the fact that Sarah, or Sarai as she was known then, had been barren since their marriage began. "Then Abram and Nahor took wives: the name of Abram's wife was Sarai . . . But Sarai was barren; she had no child" (Genesis 11:29–30).

I've been blessed with children in my marriage to my wife, Serita. And I know that even after you've already had one child, when you want the Lord to bless you with another, your impatience gets the best of you. I remember a doctor telling us that it takes most couples an average of one year to conceive a child—that factors in those fortunate couples who conceive on the first try as well as those who've been trying for a decade. But even when you know you're still within the "normal" time required for conception, it's such a disappointment each month when no baby has been produced. I know from various friends' battles with infertility as well as a variety of women I've counseled how painful it can be to want children so desperately and not have them.

This is the anguish Sarah experienced for every day of her life. Maybe she harbored a small hope that God would miraculously enable her and her husband to conceive a child. But then the years slipped away, one after another until old age set in. Sarah ages well beyond childbearing years, and now the promise of the Lord seems like a cruel joke. It not only defied the odds, but it would defy the way life had always been known to work. A girl grows into a woman, reaches her childbearing years for several decades, then her body shifts and her reproductive potential is over.

How have you experienced the Lord's promises in your life? Are there areas where you find yourself still waiting—waiting for someone special to come into your life, waiting for your own miracle baby, waiting for the child you do have to come back home, waiting for your marriage to be restored, waiting for your ministry to be funded, waiting and waiting? Waiting has always been a part of a life of faith. We learn at an early age that the Lord's timing is not necessarily our timing and we must wait on Him. But if, like Sarah, you are continually reminded of God's promise even as you watch the years slip by, then it becomes harder and harder to hope.

What kinds of things do you allow yourself to hope for? Do you keep your hopes safe and predictable, like a familiar sitcom's ending, or do you dare believe that the impossible can happen, that God can work a miracle in your life? I believe every great leading lady must harbor at least one impossible dream, an area she feels led to pursue despite the odds. It may be with her job, or with her broken marriage, with her estranged children, or with her health, but I believe God wants us to expect the unexpected from Him. Too often, it feels like many people write off the end of the story before the show has ended. Leave room for Him to work in your life. Ask Him what impossible dreams He wants you to pursue. And when life's circumstances seem to block the path of your dreams, stay honest with Him about how you're feeling. You can express your disappointment and still cling to hope. In fact, it may be necessary to express those frustrations and sufferings so that they don't harden your heart with bitterness and rage. Or so that you don't decide to take matters into your own hands.

That is the point that Sarah reached in her journey of fragile hope. As we continue with her story, notice that it's not an overtly controlling decision she makes, but one that she spiritualizes and justifies through her rational understanding of her circumstances.

> *Now Sarai, Abram's wife, had borne him no children. And she had an Egyptian maidservant whose name was Hagar.*
>
> *So Sarai said to Abram, "See now, the LORD has restrained me from bearing children. Please, go in to my maid; perhaps I shall obtain children by her." And Abram heeded the voice of Sarai.*
>
> *Then Sarai, Abram's wife, took Hagar her maid, the Egyptian, and gave her to her husband Abram to be his wife, after Abram had dwelt ten years in the land of Canaan.*
>
> GENESIS 16:1–3

It seemed like such a good idea. Perhaps she had misunderstood the Lord or misinterpreted His method to produce Abraham's progeny. Maybe *she* wouldn't birth a child, but she could make it happen. It would require swallowing an incredible amount of pride and sorrow and relinquishing her husband to another, but maybe that's what God wanted her to sacrifice in order to fulfill the promise He had made. Maybe He wanted her humility. So Sarah convinces her husband to sleep with her maid.

But things don't work out exactly how Sarah planned. Oh sure, Abraham and Hagar come together and conceive a child, but the outcome is anything but ideal.

> *So he went in to Hagar, and she conceived. And when she saw that she had conceived, her mistress became despised in her eyes.*
>
> *Then Sarai said to Abram, "My wrong be upon you! I gave my maid into your embrace; and when she saw that she had conceived, I became despised in her eyes. The LORD judge between you and me."*
>
> *So Abram said to Sarai, "Indeed your maid is in your hand; do to her as you please." And when Sarai dealt harshly with her, she fled from her presence.*
>
> GENESIS 16:4–6

Sarah thought she had it all figured out. God promised her and Abraham a son, and Hagar would be the one to give it to them. But the Egyptian maidservant comes to resent her mistress. Perhaps she even has feelings for the father of her child, thinks that she could be Abraham's wife if only Sarah were out of the way. And Sarah, whose plan this was in the first place, treats Hagar harshly and runs her out of town. Funny how Sarah fails to recognize her own part in this situation. She was the one who orchestrated this union, but now that the results of her scheme are not what she had hoped for, she takes it out on her maid.

How many times and how many ways have you tried to force God's will to happen on your timetable? And how many times have you been disappointed with the results? Maybe it was the house you just had to buy even though it was out of your budget. Or maybe the job that you knew should be yours—even if you had to lie on your résumé to get it. Perhaps it was the Prince Charming you decided to marry, even though your parents insisted you were too young. Or, sadly, maybe it was the child you had out of wedlock. You wanted so much for your boyfriend to marry you, what did it matter if you had to drop out of school? And who did you blame when things didn't work out, when the bank repossessed the house because you couldn't make the payments, when you got fired for a job poorly done? Did you resent your husband for not making enough money? Did you complain that your boss was a tyrant and your company unfair? When passion fizzled out of your marriage and you started to grow apart, did your husband become the scapegoat? And what about that poor child? Do you scream and holler and hit when your frustration gets the best of you? You know how hard it is to be a single parent and try to support a family on minimum wage.

But the truth of the matter in all of these cases is that, like Sarah, you tried to deliver a dream before it was developed. You couldn't wait on God's timing, so you took the reins yourself. And when you try to push ahead without the Lord, you're bound to fail. It's not a matter of defying God; it's about not having enough faith to wait for His blessings.

So many women, with the best of intentions, work so hard to make their dreams come true. They set their sights on some goal, what they perceive to be their calling, and move ahead with diligence and determination. Certainly there is nothing wrong with this. On the contrary, one *must* put faith into action. You can't sit on your hands waiting for some magic moment for your dreams to come true. But it becomes a problem when you steamroll ahead because you're tired of waiting on God to fulfill His promise.

I recall a woman I counseled who was struggling with the bitter disappointment of her failed business. She had felt the Lord calling her to open a dress shop, a unique little boutique that would mix the work of young, sassy African-American designers with vintage accessories. So she scoured the city to find a location, put a second mortgage on the home she shared with her husband, and began buying inventory. Within six months she had opened her boutique in the cheapest location she could find: a strip mall housing a liquor store, a chiropractor, and a massage parlor. When I pointed out that this might not have been the right location for her shop, the woman looked at me and said, "Don't you believe the Lord wanted me to open my business? Don't you believe He really spoke into my heart about this dream of mine?"

I said, "Dear woman, that is not the question. I have no doubt or the authority to question what the Lord has called you to. But I also know that He calls us to wait on Him, not to get ahead of His timing for our dreams. Now He may miraculously bring in a lot of customers to your shop where it is located presently, but it's not likely. Perhaps you should scout out a site better suited to the young, upscale clientele you hope to attract."

This woman, though spiritually sincere and following God's calling for her, was not heeding His timing. What seemed common sense to me—to wait on the Lord to provide just the right spot for such a unique shop—had not occurred to this woman. She had the vision and felt compelled to run with it and make it happen in the first spot she came to. Like Sarah, who took things into her own hands when she masterminded a plan that she hoped would provide her with a surrogate son, this woman forced the birth of her dream prematurely.

Nothing Is Impossible

SARAH'S PLAN FAILS miserably and she treats Hagar so terribly that she causes the maid to run away. But Hagar is stopped in her tracks by the Angel of the Lord, who tells her that she must return and submit to Sarah. The Angel also informs her that she will bear a son, whom she should name Ishmael (God hears), and indeed this son is born to Hagar when the baby's father, Abraham, is eighty-six years old.

But the Lord doesn't break his promises, and He did promise Sarah that she would bear a child and become the mother of nations.

> *Then God said to Abraham, "As for Sarai your wife, you shall not call her name Sarai, but Sarah shall be her name.*
>
> *"And I will bless her and also give you a son by her; then I will bless her, and she shall be a mother of nations; kings of peoples shall be from her."*
>
> *Then Abraham fell on his face and laughed, and said in his heart, "Shall a child be born to a man who is one hundred years old? And shall Sarah, who is ninety years old, bear a child?"*
>
> *And Abraham said to God, "Oh, that Ishmael might live before You!"*
>
> *Then God said: "No, Sarah your wife shall bear you a son, and you shall call his name Isaac; I will establish My covenant with him for an everlasting covenant, and with his descendants after him."*
>
> GENESIS 17:15–19

Even Abraham can't believe what he's hearing. They've been waiting so long for this, he doubts it will ever happen. He thinks Ishmael is as close as they're going to get to God's gift. And besides, it's not humanly possible for a woman Sarah's age to have a child. But we know that all things are possible through the Lord, and He always delivers. Ishmael was a surrogate son, the child Sarah thought could fulfill God's promise for her. And while God had special blessings and a significant future in store for this baby, he was not the gift God intended to give Sarah. You see, Isaac was just ahead, but Sarah couldn't see that far. She didn't have faith that her promise was yet to come.

Not long after, three strangers arrive at Abraham and Sarah's place and are recognized as Divine messengers. Abraham affords them the best hospitality he can muster, and another prophecy of Sarah's impending pregnancy is delivered.

Then they said to him, "Where is Sarah your wife?" So he said, "Here, in the tent."

And He said, "I will certainly return to you according to the time of life, and behold, Sarah your wife shall have a son." (Sarah was listening in the tent door which was behind him.)

Now Abraham and Sarah were old, well advanced in age; and Sarah had passed the age of childbearing.

Therefore Sarah laughed within herself, saying, "After I have grown old, shall I have pleasure, my lord being old also?"

And the LORD said to Abraham, "Why did Sarah laugh, saying, 'Shall I surely bear a child since I am old?'

"Is anything too hard for the LORD? At the appointed time I will return to you, according to the time of life, and Sarah shall have a son."

But Sarah denied it, saying, "I did not laugh," for she was afraid.

And He said, "No, but you did laugh!"

GENESIS 21:1–6

Sarah is told yet again that she will bear Abraham a son, and she laughs. Can you believe that? She laughs at these messengers of the Lord. I suspect that her laughter contains the mixed emotions of a heart tormented by a dream yet to come true. I'm sure her laughter contains her disbelief in this prophecy. God has waited so long, it's hard to imagine that this will ever really happen. It is also likely the bitter laughter of irony and despair over her plight. Perhaps she is laughing to keep from crying. But I bet it is also a laugh tinged with hope from one who could still dare to dream that this absurdity could actually come true. For you see, when God challenges Sarah on her laughter, she denies it, and her laughter turns to fear. Why does she fear? Well, no matter how much disappointment she has suffered, no matter how skeptical she is, she still has faith in the power of God. She doesn't dare doubt His power.

Compare this scene to the one in which Gabriel announces to Mary, a virgin, that she will bear a child. Unlike Sarah, who laughs, Mary is taken aback. But in both cases, the refrain is the same, "Nothing is impossible with the Lord." Whether it is the incarnation of His Word in the womb of a virgin or the conception of a child in a ninety-year-old womb, nothing is impossible.

Think about the elusive dreams in your heart. When circumstances of life make the fulfillment of them seem impossible, when your goals seem out of reach, how do you react? Do you get angry? Do you rail against the people and things you think stand in your way? Do you blame yourself, your own inadequacy, for your apparent failure? Or do you take it out on God, accusing Him of abandoning you, breaking His promises and leaving you on your own? Perhaps you become a fighter, vowing that no matter what it takes, no matter what you have to do, you will succeed. With blind ambition and determination, you face your challenges, you forge ahead. But all the while fear of failure and silent self-doubt eat away at your spirit. You cry alone in darkened rooms and secretly wonder if your wishes will ever come true.

I know how difficult it is to wait on your dreams. I know how quickly excitement and anticipation can turn into impatience and uncertainty, before they spiral downward into an abyss of utter despair. But I pray that, like Sarah, you maintain some hope. Maybe it's buried under a pile of unmet expectations. Maybe it's been tarnished by your sorrowful tears. But I say to you, dig out that hope and shine it up, for as long as you have a grain of faith, your dreams will come true. Jesus said to his disciples, even if you have faith as small as a mustard seed, nothing is impossible. And I repeat it to you, with faith in the Lord, nothing is impossible.

God does fulfill His promise to Sarah.

And the LORD visited Sarah as He had said, and the LORD did for Sarah as He had spoken.

For Sarah conceived and bore Abraham a son in his old age, at the set time of which God had spoken to him.

And Abraham called the name of his son who was born to him—whom Sarah bore to him—Isaac.

Then Abraham circumcised his son Isaac when he was eight days old, as God had commanded him.

Now Abraham was one hundred years old when his son Isaac was born to him.

And Sarah said, "God has made me laugh, and all who hear will laugh with me."

GENESIS 21:1–6

Have you waited and prayed for years? Taken every action you know to take and stayed wide-eyed for opportunity, but still your dream has not come to pass? You've tried working and controlling and doing everything in your power to make the dream come to life, but still it languishes as a figment of your imagination. You've tried to "let go and let God," but still it feels like you're about to lose all hope that this dream will be realized in your lifetime. So many close calls, so many opportunities bottoming out, so much disappointment. You have no patience or you may even feel like time's run out. You feel like Sarah did. She never thought she'd hold her baby in her arms. Not her handmaiden's child—what a bad idea that turned out to be. No, a baby conceived in her own desolate womb by the seed of her lifelong husband, an old man himself.

Yet the "impossible" happens. The one thing Sarah had dreamed of, the promise she had been waiting for all of her life, finally comes to pass. She gives birth to a son and they name him Isaac, which means "he laughs." The bitter, ironic laughter that masked Sarah's tears has now become the joyful laughter of a newborn. Have you ever heard a baby laugh? It is a sound so pure, so full of life, it just makes you laugh, too. And Sarah, with her promise fulfilled, laughs out loud: "And Sarah said, 'God has made me laugh, and all who hear will laugh with me.' "

Laugh with Sarah. Hold on to your dreams, and with calm perseverance and faith in God, you, too, will see your promise fulfilled. Pray that God will not let you miss your destiny. Ask Him not to let you hope for things that are not part of His plan for your life. Listen to His voice and attune your heart to His Spirit so that when He speaks you will know it and know what you must do to see your own dream of laughter birthed into being. Ask Him for glimpses of hope along the way, signs to bolster your faith so that no matter how impossible the circumstances look—when doctors give up and accountants shake their heads—you do not give up. Ask Him to help you know the difference between what you must make happen yourself and what you must wait on Him to provide. When you are required to act on faith, then ask Him for the courage and the tenacity to stride forward with power and purpose undergirding your steps. When He wants you to wait on Him, ask that you will be granted the patience and peace needed to sustain the season. But never lose hope that He will present you with a perfectly timed gift. While God does not conform to our standards of timing, He is never ever late with His promises. He is always faithful and He asks us to be the same.

I believe that God gives us time to set the stage and prepare the way for the magnitude of blessing He has in store for us. Delayed does not mean denied. It may, in fact, mean that the blessing coming is so much bigger than the one lost, and that it will be worth the wait, worth the planning and the prayer expended to see the vision done right. If you have birthed an Ishmael in your business, if you have done the right thing at the wrong time, in the wrong place, or with the wrong partner, then hold on. God will bring you an Isaac in due time.

Provoked to Prayer

SOME OF OUR impossible dreams emerge from the provocation of others. We may not even know how much we desire something until we see someone else with it. But when that powerful grip on your heart closes in, you know that you won't be satisfied until you see that dream realized. It could be something as simple as seeing a beautiful bouquet of roses in the window of an elite florist. The blooms are so lovely, each pink petal gently prying itself from the tight-budded center of the stem. You can almost smell the soft fragrance like your grandmother's rose garden out behind her house. You're looking wistfully at the roses through the window when suddenly a large hand reaches down and pulls the arrangement into the shop. Two minutes later, a well-dressed matron strolls out like a beauty queen with your bouquet in hand. She looks at you contemptuously as if to say, "Don't you wish you could afford beautiful things like I can?" Your anger burns into shame in your cheeks.

It could be something even more precious to your heart that suddenly awakens and bridles your awareness of it. Perhaps you're lunching with a girlfriend who brings her new baby along. You find yourself envying the glow in your friend's eyes as she nurses the tiny child, cradles it and rocks it to sleep. Suddenly you realize how strong the maternal instinct blazes in your own woman's soul, but there's no man in your life, let alone the possibility for a baby.

Maybe you lost a promotion to someone less qualified but harder working. She's single and career minded and you have a husband and two kids. You're happy for her but resent yourself for not doing more to secure the approval of your supervisors. You know that you could accomplish so much more if you really gave yourself to the job. It's just so hard juggling work with the kids and your husband and church.

You're not alone, sister. Each of us has had a moment when we were tempted to covet the prize of someone next to us. Too often we chide ourselves for being envious and sink right back into the mediocrity that precipitated our jealousy to start with. The key is to transform that frustration, anger, resentment, or jealousy into the power of provocation.

When you allow others to provoke you because they have things that you want but don't have, then you have an important choice to make. You can hate those people and use them as a scapegoat for your life's ills. "I'm sure she had parents with money." "I'm sure she didn't have to work to put herself through school." "It's easy for her to climb the corporate ladder—she's not raising a family like I am." Or you can turn your provocation into prayer. Ask God for that raise, for that child, for that bouquet of roses in the window. That's what another leading lady did when, like Sarah, she found that she could not have a baby.

> *Now there was a certain man of Ramathaim Zophim, of the mountains of Ephraim, and his name was Elkanah the son of Jeroham, the son of Elihu, the son of Tohu, the son of Zuph, an Ephraimite.*
>
> *And he had two wives: the name of one was Hannah, and the name of the other Peninnah. Peninnah had children, but Hannah had no children.*
>
> *This man went up from his city yearly to worship and sacrifice to the LORD of hosts in Shiloh. Also the two sons of Eli, Hophni and Phinehas, the priests of the LORD, were there.*

And whenever the time came for Elkanah to make an offering, he would give portions to Peninnah his wife and to all her sons and daughters.

But to Hannah he would give a double portion, for he loved Hannah, although the LORD had closed her womb.

And her rival also provoked her severely, to make her miserable, because the LORD had closed her womb.

So it was, year by year, when she went up to the house of the LORD, that she provoked her; therefore she wept and did not eat.

1 SAMUEL 1:1–7

Notice that in Hannah's case, it's not just her inner desire for a child that fuels her provocation, it's the taunts and cruel jabs by her husband's other wife. What woman wouldn't feel provoked to misery? You must accept that there will always be people in your life who will taunt you and seek to keep you in your place. These are often insecure people who feel the need to put others down in order to elevate their own fragile egos. These are the women who show up at the party sporting the latest designer fashion and then proceed to coyly embarrass you because you're wearing last year's style. These are the competitive status players, parking their BMW next to your Escort in the church parking lot. These are the people who only seem to enjoy their success if they can rub it in the noses of those with less than they have.

If you are going to achieve your dreams, you must be prepared to use their insults for fuel and their treachery for inspiration. Yes, even those who chide us can be instrumental in assisting us to achieve the high-octane motivation needed to see the dormant vision come to pass. If any woman made it, then so can you. If any one woman was raised up, then why not you? My sister, you must use everything you have ever seen positively in the lives of others to provoke you to move ahead. Relentless and renewed, you will find that God has taken your ability beyond mediocrity and into the next dimension of your accomplishments.

Now you have a choice to either make something happen or be reduced to whimpering and complaining about others' attitudes and unwillingness to assist you. I have had to ignore some painful statements in my life, and I know from experience that before you get to the place God has ordained for you, you will have to thicken your skin and endure the hard ridicule of those who seek to intimidate you.

Sometimes it's easy to ignore them, to pity them, to laugh at them or pray for them. But every once in a while, they push the wrong button and you find yourself livid at their insinuations and comparative style of relating. You find yourself miserable because you feel powerless. But you are never powerless as long as you are still on speaking terms with the Lord. He will turn the pressure of your peers into the power of your purpose. That's what Hannah discovers.

> *So Hannah arose after they had finished eating and drinking in Shiloh. Now Eli the priest was sitting on the seat by the doorpost of the tabernacle of the LORD.*
>
> *And she was in bitterness of soul, and prayed to the LORD and wept in anguish.*
>
> *Then she made a vow and said, "O LORD of hosts, if You will indeed look on the affliction of your maidservant and remember me, and not forget Your maidservant, but will give Your maidservant a male child, then I will give him to the*

LORD all the days of his life, and no razor shall come upon his head."

And it happened, as she continued praying before the LORD, that Eli watched her mouth.

Now Hannah spoke in her heart; only her lips moved, but her voice was not heard. Therefore Eli thought she was drunk.

So Eli said to her, "How long will you be drunk? Put your wine away from you!"

And Hannah answered and said, "No, my lord, I am a woman of sorrowful spirit. I have drunk neither wine nor intoxicating drink, but have poured out my soul before the LORD.

"Do not consider your maidservant a wicked woman, for out of the abundance of my complaint and grief I have spoken until now."

Then Eli answered and said, "Go in peace, and the God of Israel grant your petition which you have asked of Him."

And she said, "Let your maidservant find favor in your sight." So the woman went her way and ate, and her face was no longer sad.

1 SAMUEL 1:9–18

Have you ever prayed so fervently that those around you mistook you for being drunk? Probably not, I'm guessing. But Eli the temple priest misinterprets the mumbling lips and silent ramblings of this anguished woman as the mannerism of a person drunk with wine. When he realizes his error, he blesses the poor woman and asks God to give her whatever it was that she was asking for so desperately. She leaves relieved, perhaps a bit more hopeful that her prayer would be heard and her wish granted. She is willing to break her fast and to change the expression on her face.

I believe God desires for us to share the birthing of our dreams with those close to us. I believe He wants to bless their faith by seeing us trust Him for our request. Have there been spiritual midwives and prayer partners in your life who helped you sustain the vision for your dream? Instead of allowing the provocation of others to isolate and insulate your faith, you must reach out and connect with your community members. So often the enemy squelches your dream by alienating you from God and from those who truly care about you. Your anger and resentment turn inward and refuse to find expression through prayer or sharing your heart with those meaningful others who want to help. So, when you find yourself troubled by the impossibility of a dream, by the provocation you feel by someone who has what you want, then speak out! Raise your voice in prayer and petition before the Lord. Share your dream with your spiritual leaders and family, with those who believe in you and desire your greatness. They will pray for you and be on the lookout for your destiny up ahead.

Stewards of Our Dreams

> *Then they rose early in the morning and worshiped before the LORD, and returned and came to their house at Ramah. And Elkanah knew Hannah his wife, and the LORD remembered her.*
>
> *So it came to pass in the process of time that Hannah conceived and bore a son, and called his name Samuel, saying, "Because I have asked for him from the LORD."*
>
> 1 Samuel 1:19–20

Hannah's request is granted and she is the proud mother of baby Samuel. What a glorious moment it must have been for her to look down upon her son and feel the heft of his swaddled body against her once-broken heart. But I wonder if somewhere inside, she wasn't regretting the condition she had offered to the Lord in making her request. She had promised the baby would be consecrated to the Lord and raised in His temple by the temple priests. But when the time comes to fulfill her end of the deal, she hesitates. We see that when the time comes the following year for the annual trip to the temple, she delays the giving of her son by deciding that he needs to be weaned first. There's enough tension in Hannah's reasoning to wonder if she will be able to follow through on her promise.

Can you relate to her dilemma? Have you ever wanted something so badly but promised to use it for God's glory once you attained it? Perhaps it was money that you so desired after growing up in hard times. You had always vowed that you would give generously to the Church, to missions, to the various ministries that had blessed you in your ascent. But suddenly the security of those numbers at the top of your bank statement seems mighty satisfying and it's hard to subtract and subtract some more, even if you did promise. Or maybe it was a leadership position that you wanted, and you promised God that you would seek His style of leading and not your own if you got the job. Now, however, with reports due to the board and risks to be taken, it's much harder to trust Him.

Yes, we all have moments when we cling too tightly to our babies. We want them to stay little and innocent for the rest of their lives. We want to hold them and protect them and keep them within the range of our control. But like the patter of little feet that grows into the footfalls of men and women, our dreams must grow and mature as well. If we hold them too tight, they will suffocate and wither. We must be willing to stay attuned to God's plan, even after He has given us what we asked for. Just because He has granted you a miracle to fulfill your impossible dream doesn't mean that more isn't required of you.

Sometimes His promise for us is so much more, so much bigger, than we could ever imagine. To limit ourselves to the aspirations of human musings is to obstruct the limitless potential that our Creator has instilled in us. We must trust that God knows how far to take us, and let Him carry us to that place that He ordains. We must be willing to let go of our dreams and remain open to receiving what our Lord chooses to give. God wants only the best for His ladies, and we must have faith that He will deliver it unto us. So, like Hannah yielding her son to Eli, give up your successes to the Lord so that He can bless them and grow them into larger visions of greatness.

> *Then they slaughtered a bull, and brought the child to Eli.*
>
> *And she said, "O my lord! As your soul lives, my lord, I am the woman who stood by you here, praying to the LORD.*
>
> *"For this child I prayed, and the LORD has granted me my petition which I asked of Him.*
>
> *"Therefore I also have lent him to the LORD; as long as he lives he shall be lent to the LORD." So they worshiped the LORD there.*
>
> 1 SAMUEL 1:25–28

Ideally, this continual process of relinquishing your dreams should involve worship. Because in the act of worshiping your Creator for His goodness and faithfulness to you, you realize that everything you have is just a gift He has loaned you. Everything in this world—children, money, jobs, houses, ministries, cars—all belong to Him and He gives them to us for a while in order that we might serve Him. But we cannot hold onto them nor take them with us when we leave this world for the next. So we must learn to be like Hannah and dedicate our offspring to the Lord's purposes.

Hope Floats

NO MATTER HOW impossible your dreams may seem, you must continue to hope. No matter how upset you become when you look around and see less deserving people with what your heart was built for, don't give up. It's been said that "hope floats," and I believe this is true, because believing in faith that you will see your dream come to fruition requires an ongoing buoyancy that never stays on the bottom of the pool for too long. Yes, you may have days when it feels like your hope has sunk to the dark recesses of the deepest ocean. You'll have moments when you can't muster enough hope to move a mustard seed. But don't leave it there—keep getting back on your feet every morning thinking that this could be the day when something amazing happens! It's not foolish or naive, even though it may feel that way. The Lord has brought you this far and protected you and nurtured you and placed dreams inside you that only you and He know about. Every leading lady, in pursuit of her appointed greatness, faces times when she feels overwhelmed and underwater. But her dream is actually God's Divine permission to do the impossible. The reason you have the dream in the first place is that God wouldn't allow you to settle for what you see with your eyes. So He gave you a vision of the unseen promises over your life. Your company may exist only in your own imagination initially. Your book may be nothing more than loose notes randomly scribbled and carelessly stored. But keep your dream alive. Eventually it will speak out of you and speak up for you.

This book is written for women who dare to dream. It is written for women whose water has broken and who have dilated to the degree that God can deliver something bigger through them than they would have ever thought possible. I challenge you to allow your faith to reach beyond the many breaches in life and climb up walls of impossibility.

Your dream is no more impossible than it was for a middle-aged housewife to build Mary Kay Cosmetics. Your dream is no more impossible than it was for a blind girl named Helen Keller to learn to read Braille. Your dream is no more impossible than it was for a woman like Susan Taylor to transform a company with very few resources, a company started by men, into a multimillion-dollar magazine empire called *Essence*. Who says dreams don't come true?

As a leading lady, you must dream big and trust Him to bring it to life. You must trust Him with your dream even after it's born. Share it with others so that you may nurture and bless their dreams as well. You are never too old to give birth to your dreams. The story ain't over till it's over. Like Sarah, you may become the mother of an entire nation of dreams and dreamers!

CHAPTER NINE

Dream Teams

Muscles ripple and glimmer with sweat as well-toned bodies stop and start across the sleek hardwood floor like human pinballs. Fans cheer and the orange ball zings from one player's hands to another. Dribbling down the court, each player knows his contribution matters in the timing of the shot, and ultimately their team's victory over a valiant opponent of equally talented athletes. With the return of Michael Jordan to basketball and the established excellence of masters like Shaquille O'Neal and Alan Houston, you don't have to understand the rules of the game to appreciate the physical prowess and exquisite athletic artistry displayed by the powerful players squaring off at center court. But superstars do not win championships alone. No matter how much skill a particular player has, no matter how superior his innate abilities, one man is not responsible for a team's victory. No, those in the playoffs, the men who can claim the title of the best in the league, can do so only when they all work together, when each man functions at peak performance and operates synergistically with his teammates. It's all about teamwork. It's like a complexly choreographed dance in which the athletes play off one another's strengths and minimize the weaknesses. They move with precision timing and synchronicity and share a commitment to put forth their best efforts, both individually and in concert with one another. These winning teams are often called "dream teams," because every player is a superstar in his own right and each gives 110 percent to the team. I repeat, it's all about teamwork. The high-paid salary and high-profile reputation are nice—compensation for the long hours of training and developing one's athletic gifts—but the true mark of a winner is the ability to do one's part to bring the team to victory.

Likewise, a good relationship between a leading lady and her leading man should reflect the same kind of shared commitment to each other and to the excellence in life to which you are both called, separately and as a couple. While we have alluded in past chapters to the relationships that a leading lady has with the costars in her life, it seems imperative to address the primary relationship she has with her leading man, and its implications. Your performance in your marriage has an effect on your pursuit of excellence in every other sector of your life. Conversely, whatever roles you fulfill outside of your matrimonial union will ultimately impact the bond you and your husband share.

How does a leading lady achieve an Oscar-winning performance in marriage? There are countless examples in Scripture that would serve to demonstrate both what to do and what not to do. However, although we touched on this example earlier, there's no better paradigm for fulfilling this starring role than the one we find in

Proverbs 31. Let's go through this passage together and explore the many aspects of a virtuous wife.

Who can find a virtuous wife?
For her worth is far above rubies.
The heart of her husband safely trusts her;
So he will have no lack of gain.
She does him good and not evil
All the days of her life.

PROVERBS 31:10–12

The wise man asks a rhetorical question, an open-ended query designed to provoke his listeners or readers to consider how they would define a "virtuous" wife. Before he lists the attributes he has in mind, the writer stresses her value; he says she is "far above rubies"—in other words, she is priceless gem. It is true, there is nothing more valuable to a man than a wife who is in every sense his partner and helpmeet. The Lord our God said, "It is not good that man should be alone" (Genesis 2:18), and so He created woman. God created every creature, every bird in the sky, and brought them all to Adam, but still he was missing something because none was "a helper comparable to him." Adam had everything. The Lord brought him every animal and bird to name—indicating Adam's sovereignty over all the creatures—but this wasn't enough. And that's when God created a woman, and then and only then was Eden, and Adam, complete.

Yes, a virtuous wife is invaluable, but as we all know, "virtuous" is the key word, and so the speaker goes on to catalog the characteristics that such a woman should possess. And at the top of this lengthy list, the first thing that is mentioned is that she must be someone that a man can trust. He must be secure in their relationship and know that she will do him good and not evil all the days of her life. Trust is an essential ingredient in any relationship, but especially so in a marriage. How can anyone focus on the fulfillment of their Divine calling when they are constantly worried that the person who stands by their side might stab them in the back? But with a secure foundation of trust, you can build your life to the greatest heights, confident that it won't be washed away like a castle built on sand. Throughout our time here on this earth, it is inevitable that we will experience the rains of misfortune at some time or another. Some of us may get caught in storms of tragedy and loss. And it is not uncommon that in trying to weather these difficult times, marriages are torn apart. But when your relationship is built on an impenetrable base of trust, you can buffet whatever conditions you face. Further, note that this trust between a wife and husband leads to "no lack of gain." When the trust is in place, the husband-and-wife team is destined for success!

A Woman's Work

A VIRTUOUS WIFE is also a provider. No, you don't necessarily have to have a job outside the home, but you must do your part to make your team—your family—a success.

She seeks wool and flax,
And willingly works with her hands.
She is like the merchant ships,

She brings her food from afar.
She also rises while it is yet night,
And provides food for her household,
And a portion for her maidservants.

PROVERBS 31:13–15

Here, the virtuous woman is portrayed as a domestic diva, taking care of the day-to-day needs of her family. While I admire and applaud women who excel in matters of business and have successful careers, I find it very disturbing when people look down upon women who choose to forgo opportunities for employment outside the home and instead devote themselves to the care and development of their families. How can anyone degrade the mighty contribution this type of woman makes? Is it more worthwhile to manage a Fortune 500 firm than to manage a family? Is there more importance in maintaining a business than there is in maintaining a safe and healthy home? Can we put more value on the production of products and profits than we do on producing children with strong bodies, strong minds, and strong morals? Should one receive higher commendation for growing a company or for growing children into adults who are productive, honorable, and give back to their communities?

The point I'm trying to make is that it doesn't matter whether you work outside or inside the home. What matters is that you contribute to the ultimate well-being of your team. Whether you're bringing home the bacon or frying it up with some eggs for breakfast, you are doing your part to bring home the victory.

But you working ladies aren't ignored in Proverbs. No, the virtuous wife can also be a shrewd businesswoman. Whether you hold a job out of necessity or the burning desire to pursue a career in the business field of your choice, there are guidelines here for you, too.

She considers a field and buys it;
From her profits she plants a vineyard.
She girds herself with strength,
And strengthens her arms.
She perceives that her merchandise is good,
And her lamp does not go out by night.

PROVERBS 31:16–18

This woman not only runs her business well, she is imaginative in her ability to see the potential in opportunities. She realizes that a field could produce enough to finance a vineyard, and grows her business from there.

I was fortunate enough to grow up around this kind of woman. My grandmother used to take in laundry from neighbors and wash it in a big iron pot before hanging it out to dry and then ironing it. She used the proceeds from her hard labor to finance her return to school, so that by age fifty she could begin her career as a schoolteacher. Her persistent efforts in the laundry room were not intended merely to make extra spending money but to provide the means to a lifelong dream. She may have inspired my mother, who entered Tuskegee when she was fifteen and completed her degree by the time she was eighteen. Throughout my lifetime I watched my mother purchase many "fields" and "vineyards," although in her case they were often rental houses or small businesses she could run from home. I learned to admire and appreciate the incredible combination of strength and creativity displayed by these resilient, resourceful women. They have both inspired me many times in my own pursuit of the opportunities God presents to me.

Strategies for Successful Women

AS WE DISCUSS the virtuous wife in her role as a businesswoman, I would like to take a moment to focus on an issue that has become much more prevalent in recent years. In my ministry I see many successful women who come to me with a whole new set of problems born out of the fact that they are reaching new heights in their careers.

With more and more opportunities opening up for women, and with the need for dual incomes to sustain a household, it is not uncommon now for women to be in the workforce. However, a new scenario is emerging in which women achieve a higher level of success than their husbands. They may be in a field where they advance rapidly, they may have a higher level of education, they may make more money and receive more acclaim. I congratulate and commend all women who have broken through the glass ceilings in corporate America or who have built up their own businesses. Their hard work and talent should be rightfully rewarded, and it is about time women have received their due.

But I am aware that this increased success comes with an increased potential for marital discord. It is important that a man and woman complement each other and not compete with each other. If one or both partners in a marriage uses career advancement and level of income as a measuring stick of contribution and importance in the relationship, then sadly that marriage is bound to be troubled.

This danger certainly exists when the man is the primary breadwinner and the woman stays at home or works in a job that isn't as well compensated. We can all understand how a housewife must feel when her husband comes home and she is eager to discuss what happened in her day. She immediately launches into a full-fledged description of the PTA meeting that night, the children's report cards, her suspicions that the delivery boy overcharged her, etc. As she shares the events of her day, she notices that her husband is not listening but merely grunting in all the wrong places. His feigned interest devalues not only her day but also her sense of importance. Or he may politely listen as his wife describes her difficulties in learning to use the new computer system her office has implemented, the petty jealousies that exist among the girls in the typing circle, or her excitement that she just got a raise of one dollar an hour. But when he smiles at her condescendingly and gently pats her hand, she feels inferior and insignificant, as if she is merely a bit player in their life together.

However, today this scene is often shifted. It is the high-powered, highly compensated woman whose workload is carried in a briefcase and not in a laundry basket who is guilty of not dignifying her partner and his concerns. This situation can be doubly devastating if your man has a fragile ego. I'm not condoning it, but it is a truth that in our society a man is oftentimes defined by what he does and how much money he makes. A man whose self-esteem is tied to his paycheck may have a hard time swallowing the fact that his wife makes more money than he does. He may resent her success or lament what he perceives to be his own failure. He may consider himself an underachiever. Simply stated, he may be insecure about what he brings to the relationship.

A woman need not give up her career, nor does her partner need to find a better-paying job. But there are a few things that a woman needs to understand and a few tips that may help her to achieve her goals as a leading lady professionally without sabotaging her dream team at home.

Balancing the Yoke

THE APOSTLE PAUL warned in his second letter to the Corinthians, "Do not be unequally yoked together with unbelievers. For what fellowship has righteousness with lawlessness? And what communion has light with darkness?" (2 Corinthians 6:14). Why this admonition? Because the faith that we live by is the measurement that we use as a guide, the counselor that we seek in a crisis, and the values that affect us sexually, emotionally, and spiritually. If we are not using the same measurement of faith, problems often become insurmountable because one doesn't respect the other's yardstick of beliefs. It creates a dynamic similar to the one you find in a marriage counseling session where one partner comes and the other refuses. While it may be helpful to the one attending, the session cannot restore the wholeness of the marriage without both partners' participation.

Shared Christian faith is so important to a marriage, but what many people fail to realize is that couples can be unequally yoked in areas besides faith. An unequal yoke just means that the relationship is out of balance. A couple could be imbalanced due to a disparity between their respective positions in the professional world. For instance, a woman could find herself the rising star in her field while her husband's job has reached a plateau, offering little excitement. Or a wife's career could offer more prestige than her husband's. It is not uncommon to see a professional woman married to a blue-collar worker. Both are hard workers, both could bring home handsome pay, but status attached to a doctor, a lawyer, or a business executive far exceeds that of a mechanic, a mailman, or a bus driver. Please know that I'm not in any way attaching more value to one job over another; I am simply pointing out that such perceived imbalances do exist.

But imbalances do not have to damage your relationship. As a leading lady you must simply maintain awareness of your responsibilities, commitments, and unique functions within each sector of your life. It is not a question of fragmenting yourself, separating your professional persona from your self required to operate in a domestic setting. No, we've already discussed the problems that can arise when you try to fill too many different roles and lose sight of your core self. What I'm talking about is recognizing what you are called to do in a particular situation. There are times when cost control and increased productivity must take precedence in your mind, but there are also moments when bandaging a scraped knee or comforting the tired heart of your weary mate is the priority of the day. As a woman, you have so many talents and fulfill so many needs. You must learn to be a wise steward of your gifts and administer them with a sense of timing that serves the greatest good.

I strongly advise you working women not to bring the office home with you. This can often make your man feel like "the little woman," a feeling that women don't enjoy either. The need to vent every frustration or flaunt every success must be timed well with sensitivity and the awareness that the whole world does not revolve around your career. Most jobs that pay those higher-level incomes also come complete with a set of troubles, stresses, and office espionage. While having good communication that enables you to have a sounding board at home is indispensable, it may be a wise habit to take turns discussing each other's day so that there is a sense of equality and shared importance. Share what is relevant to each of you and really listen to each other's concerns. Remember that you are teammates, working in tandem to support each other and bring the victory home.

If there is an imbalance in the level of prestige attached to your professions, I urge you to support your husband and deflect any disparaging remarks or actions made against him. Some people might pass a snide comment in an attempt to belittle your mate, or try to persuade you that he's not good enough for you. "Come on, girl, you know you can do better." "Don't you think you should be with someone who can keep up with you?" "Honey, that man is just keeping you down. How can you expect to go anywhere when you're tied to a guy like that?" Just stay away from them. They are petty and insecure, degrading others so they can raise themselves up. And if you have to interact with them, for professional or personal reasons, then to thine own self and to your man be true. Ladies, you know how to put a person in their place, guide the conversation back on track, and throw away their condescending comments like sour garbage. Protect your spouse and your relationship like a mother bear protects her cubs.

Finally, if your relationship is unequally yoked economically, there are ways to restore equality to your partnership without your man having to take on a second job. While his financial contributions may not rival yours, it may be that there are other areas of life in which he exceeds your ability or expectation. So while it may appear that economics tilt the balance away from equality, he may bring qualities that no amount of money can ever buy. His contribution then restores balance despite whatever salary discrepancies may exist. For example, he may be a great father, an ardent lover, a source of comfort to you, and be able to fill a void that your career does not. Acknowledge his areas of contribution. He may not even know them himself. He may not know how important it is to you to have him in your life. He may not know how watching him love your children adds so much to your life and provides an answer to your prayers. He may not know that his loving you and holding you gives you a special sense of intimacy for which there is no substitute. The lack of that intimacy would leave you cold and lifeless, empty and feeling unappreciated. Tell him. Tell him how you feel about these other areas so that you can balance your yoke and stay your course together for years to come.

Seven Tips for Balance As You Succeed

HERE ARE A few simple tips that will help you gain and maintain a sense of balance, a balance that is essential as you become more and more successful.

1. Keep your work at work and your heart at home.

Many women have learned how to play the corporate game and to manipulate the office politics so that they can further their own careers. These women often devote themselves to every detail of every project and are clearly resistant to delegating to their employees. They work long hours and find themselves working on projects at home, planning social events for the company and developing presentations that would impress Bill Gates. Then one day these women discover that their careers have taken over their lives. This wake-up call often comes in a moment of crisis. Maybe they get laid off and without a job they realize they have no identity. Or perhaps their spouse refuses to play second fiddle anymore and walks out of their marriage and out of their life. Dazed and confused, these bright, capable ladies realize that they have given so much and are now left with nothing.

No matter how passionate you are about your career interests, work on strong boundaries that protect your true priorities. Give 110 percent when you are at work, but don't compromise relationships for promotions and don't confuse your leadership style in the office with who you are as a leading lady inside. The paperwork, e-mails, phone calls, and meetings will always be there, with or without you. Your children, your husband, your sense of a larger purpose require your complete attention when you are home.

2. Acknowledge your husband verbally and frequently for his contributions and strengths rather than providing him with an encyclopedia of his weaknesses.

This doesn't mean you need to ignore his mistakes or live in denial concerning his flaws. No, I'm simply saying that you need to avoid taking him and his many contributions for granted before it's too late. No matter how many times you may have told him how much you appreciate the meal he cooked or the repair he made on your car, he still likes to hear it. When you get caught up in the busyness and hectic pace of corporate life, it's easy to overlook his contributions and take them for granted. Gratitude and appreciation foster mutual respect and create a lasting style of positive communication between valued partners.

3. Reprimand those in your life who feel obligated to make derogatory statements that would demean or degrade your husband.

At her company picnic, Elisa overheard another VP whisper to her secretary, "I wonder where Elisa found *him*—looks like he just stepped out of the projects!" The two snickered and cast eyes at Elisa's husband, George, who didn't quite fit in with the well-tailored linen suits and seersucker shirts of the other husbands. It wasn't the first time Elisa had heard offhand comments made about her spouse, and she knew George was self-conscious about his image and appearance among her work crowd. She decided she'd had enough. Coming up behind her two snide co-workers, Elisa said, "I wouldn't be where I am today without George, and I'd appreciate not hearing another word about what you two think of him." Her firm tone and set eyes took her colleagues by surprise. They got the message and dispersed.

It's not easy to confront the gossips and the rumormongers, the critics and the petty socialites who thrive by picking apart others. And you may not need to confront them every time—sometimes it takes away their power when they are ignored. But sometimes you must stomp out the sparks of cruelty and ignorance before they firebomb the foundation of your most important relationship. "Keep your heart with all diligence, for out of it spring the issues of life. Put away from you a deceitful mouth, and put perverse lips far from you" (Proverbs 4:23–24).

4. Share equal interest in his occupation and interests, even if they do not yield the same economic benefit as yours.

If you've been married or in a relationship for a while, then you know that sometimes you must choose to love and respect your husband by sharing in his interests just as he should share in yours. He may not like to go shopping, but he's willing to go with you because he likes to see you happy and he enjoys spending time together. Similarly, you might not enjoy the same sports he follows, but you're willing to root for his team because it's important to him. For some reason, this mutual sharing of individual interests seems to become harder if there's inequity in each other's paychecks. But the need is even greater then, I believe, because this economic wedge can become a social wedge as well. Now that you're making six figures, he may fear that you're too elite to attend his favorite hockey game or too busy to hear about his volunteer tutoring for at-risk kids in the inner city. Don't let the money separate you from investing in each other's lives, a far greater investment than any stock dividend or 401K plan can ever yield.

5. Make sure that you have an agreement on financial philosophies—who handles what monies, etc.

Although I've counseled hundreds of couples by now, I'm still surprised by how many come to see me because they argue about money. Of course I know money's important and gets to the heart of our individual selfishness as we seek to run our household and balance our needs with our wants. No, what surprises me is that two bright, successful people will sit before me and complain about their finances and then sheepishly admit that they have never followed a budget or delegated responsibilities for their various obligations and accounts. He thinks she's doing it and she thinks he's doing it and then the bills go unpaid and the money's spent before either of them realizes it. With one couple I saw, he prudently administered their account while she spent discretionary funds without discretion. He then resented towing the line while watching her spend without apparent limits. He needed to enjoy some of the fruits of his labor while she needed to be a bit more responsible with her purchases.

Both partners must clearly communicate their expectations and function as a team if you are going to keep money from coming between you. You must develop a shared mission statement regarding your finances and how you will each contribute to your goals. If this is an area you haven't considered yet, I humbly recommend that you and your spouse read my thoughts on these very important matters in my other books *The Great Investment* and *Maximize the Moment.*

6. Honor him as your covering.

So much has been misunderstood regarding the way men and women are to relate to one another's roles in their marriage. While it's clear that culture and society affect how we view gender roles, some things remain inherent in the essence of masculinity and femininity as God created us. While you may not need your husband to hunt for food or protect you from marauding tribes, you still need his covering, the protection that comes from your affiliation with who he is as your husband. This principle is explained with a clear sense of balance in mind as Paul describes it in his letter to the Ephesians.

> *Wives submit to your husbands, as to the Lord.*
>
> *For the husband is head of the wife, as also Christ is head of the church; and He is the Savior of the body.*
>
> *Therefore, just as the church is subject to Christ, so let the wives be to their own husbands in everything.*

Husbands, love your wives, just as Christ also loved the church and gave Himself for her, that He might sanctify and cleanse her with the washing of water by the word,

that He might present her to Himself a glorious church, not having spot or wrinkle or any such thing, but that she should be holy and without blemish.

So husbands ought to love their own wives as their own bodies; he who loves his wife loves himself.

EPHESIANS 5:22–28

So often the first half of this passage is taken out of context and used to suppress women and rob them of their voices and the unique contributions they make to their marriage. But being subject to your husband as you are subject to the Lord does not mean becoming a simpering doormat. It does mean respecting and honoring the unique role your husband plays in the partnership. It doesn't mean that you passively subvert your will and accept his decisions without question or qualification. It does mean that you have a safe place to relax and let your guard down, a calm haven of security in which you are protected and nurtured. If you are always on the defensive, protecting and controlling your own interests, then you miss out on one of the incredible blessings of having a husband.

Headship is not intended to be used by the man to dominate or rule like a monarch. It is a privileged position of trust and confidence, a place of looking out for the rest of the body and making the best decisions for the health and well being of the body. Headship is intended to be a covering for the woman, not a curse. We see this emerge clearly in the second half of this passage in which husbands are instructed to love their wives as Christ loves the Church. A husband should wash and cleanse his bride with gentleness and a desire for her purity. His authority should be exercised for her welfare, not his own aggrandizement. This takes a secure partnership based on mutual trust. She trusts him to know how to proceed in the way that will best further their shared goals and dreams. He trusts her to share the fuel of her life-giving spirit in all they endeavor. There is no jealousy or power struggle or egotistical manipulations of either individual—it is a seamless team of two blended into a unity so solid that God intends for it to reflect Christ's relationship with His bride the Church. Such unity relies on mutual submission, preferring each other in love. This is the secret to a successful marriage, no matter who makes the most money.

Many successful women squirm under the headship of their husband rather than snuggle into the security it should afford them. They are so used to leading in the office or at the board meeting that it requires a relinquishment of their career authority for them to relax in the relationship with their man. However, this allows them time to enjoy being nurtured and protected, to reconnect with their softness and femininity, which should provide balance to their lives.

7. Avoid allowing your professional life to cannibalize your personal time together.

It seems so simple to list your marriage as a priority over your job. But when it comes down to those heat-of-the-moment choices, it becomes very difficult to recognize what's at stake. Your boss wants you to work late to finish an important report on the night your husband has secured a baby-sitter and planned a romantic dinner at your favorite restaurant. I'm not saying there aren't times when you reschedule your date night and finish the report. But for too many successful ladies, it's a notorious habit, one that will eventually cost them greatly when they discover that while they've achieved a record-sales award, there is no one at home waiting to toast their accomplishment. The cannibal of career will always eat as much as you feed it. Promise your husband that you won't feed it the sweet food from the wedding banquet of your marriage relationship.

Even if you must schedule couple time months in advance to protect it from the encroachment of your career, then sit down with him and nail down dates and plans. Then stick to your calendar and don't allow the intrusion of the urgent at work to eclipse the investment in the vital at home.

God's Daughter

NOW THAT WE have studied the attributes of a virtuous wife as they relate to the practical matters of life—caring for her family and contributing to her household—we need to explore her spiritual character.

She stretches out her hands to the distaff,
And her hand holds the spindle.
She extends her hand to the poor,
Yes, she reaches out her hands to the needy.
She is not afraid of snow for her household,
For all her household is clothed with scarlet.
She makes tapestry for herself;
Her clothing is fine linen and purple.
Her husband is known in the gates,

When he sits among the elders of the land.
She makes linen garments and sells them,
And supplies sashes for the merchants.

PROVERBS 31:19–24

At this point, you might be throwing up your hands in frustration, wondering what spinning and sewing have to do with spirituality. And if this is what it takes to be a virtuous wife, you might as well quit now; you can barely sew on a button, much less spin your own fabric and create tapestries and clothes. But do not worry, dear sister, for I believe this passage is not meant to be taken literally. We must look at the symbolic meaning behind the words to find the example we need to emulate.

This virtuous wife spins the flax and sews fine garments, but what exactly is she making? First we are told that she is not afraid of snow for her household because her household is clothed in scarlet. Does this mean she designed red clothes for them to keep them warm during the winter? Likely not. No, I think this means that she is not fearful for her family because they are protected by God. The ultimate protection we have, the greatest gift that God has ever bestowed upon us, came in the form of His Son Jesus Christ, through whose blood we are saved. Scarlet represents the sacrificial blood of Christ, and to be clothed in His blood is to be forgiven and to find salvation in a relationship with God. Therefore, the leading lady of Proverbs 31 is comforted by the fact that her family is covered in the protection of our Lord.

Now, obviously, that protection doesn't come directly from the virtuous wife, but I believe the writer of Proverbs is implying that it is through her that her family is covered. It is not uncommon for the matriarch of the household to be the spiritual backbone in the family. I see it in my own church. Grandmothers and mothers keep the fires of faith burning in the home. Often, they are the ones to gather the family on the Sabbath, to lead the children to the Word of the Lord. When everyone seems to be tangled in the busyness of business, running from meeting to meeting, soccer practice to dance class, the women ground the family in the Source of all Life. And thus it is that the virtuous wife is not fearful for her family, for she has placed them in the Hands of God.

We're also told that the virtuous wife clothes herself. She dresses herself in fine linen and purple. Purple has always symbolized royalty, and in donning purple clothing, the virtuous wife is displaying her regal status as a daughter of the King, His Majesty the Lord. But it is not just her garments that indicate that she is a princess of God, but her actions as well. She blesses others as God has blessed her. First we're told that she cares for the poor and needy and gives them what she can. She also blesses her husband. Verse 23 tells us that "her husband is known in the gates, when he sits among the elders of the land." You may wonder why we are given this one sentence about her husband in the middle of a lengthy description of the woman. I believe this just goes to show that what a woman does impacts her husband's world, his reputation, his life. By living her life in the Lord, the virtuous wife becomes an asset to her husband. He is known in the gates in part because she is known and respected. He is blessed by her virtue.

Finally, the virtuous wife makes garments and sells them and supplies sashes for the merchants. By using the gift God has given to her, by working with her hands, she gives back to others. He blesses her with the skill to make fine garments, and she in turn sells them to others, blessing them with the garments' quality and blessing her household with financial gain. But the virtuous wife is not greedy. While she is making products to sell, she is also making sashes for her fellow merchants. They may be her colleagues or even her competitors, but she still blesses them with the talents God has given her.

Yes, the virtuous wife certainly conducts herself as a princess of God. The verse concludes with further description of her royal behavior and the rewards that such a woman can expect to reap.

Strength and honor are her clothing;
She shall rejoice in time to come.
She opens her mouth with wisdom,
And on her tongue is the law of kindness.
She watches over the ways of her household,
And does not eat the bread of idleness.
Her children rise up and call her blessed;
Her husband also, and he praises her:
"Many daughters have done well,
But you excel them all."
Charm is deceitful and beauty is passing,
But a woman who fears the LORD, she shall be praised.
Give her of the fruit of her hands,
And let her own works praise her in the gates.

PROVERBS 31:25–32

Once again, the virtuous wife's attire is discussed. Now we are told that strength and honor are her clothing. As a daughter of God, she is clothed in His strength and honor. His strength is her strength, and it is through Him that she can accomplish all. And it is for this reason that she rejoices. She has no worries, no fear, for she is wrapped in the power of the Lord.

This woman also speaks with wisdom. Proverbs says a lot about exercising wisdom in our speech. She speaks what God has given her to speak and doesn't use her knowledge to cut others down. No, her speech is ruled by the law of kindness. She is discerning and discreet, saying what needs to be said, but saying it in a way mindful of how it will be received. She doesn't use her words to inflict harm on anyone.

The virtuous wife also is attuned to the needs of her family. She pays attention to her surroundings but also prepares for what her family may need in the future. She watches their steps and does all she can to provide a clear path for them. She knows that she can't just sit back and rest on her laurels because all is well for the moment. She knows she must do what needs to be done so that her family is provided for now and in the future.

For all her hard work, her children rise up and bless her, and her husband sings her praises. She has lovingly and wholeheartedly cared for her family, and the natural result is that they love and honor her in return. But even if this woman goes unappreciated by her family, or if her good works are not noticed beyond the sphere of her immediate family, there is One who will always applaud her performance. The last four lines of this verse make that clear. We are told that charm and beauty are fleeting, but a woman who fears the Lord shall be praised. As we discussed earlier, this fear is reverence, this fear is awe, and a woman who praises God's glory and acts in service to Him will receive great rewards.

She will receive the fruit of her hands. It has already been established that she was a hard worker and an astute businesswoman.

She has likely received the rewards of her labor in a safe and successful home, financial security, and the love and honor of her family, but there is more to come. For in the last line we are told she will also receive her heavenly rewards. She will find that as she enters the gates of heaven, her Father will greet her and echo the praise her husband utters in verse 29: "Many daughters have done well, but you excel them all."

I hope that you are inspired and not overwhelmed by this woman. She is certainly amazing, but so are you. Each one of you is a daughter of God. He offers all of us His strength and honor. He provides all the resources you need to be a true leading lady. The key to the virtuous wife's success is encapsulated in verse 30: she fears the Lord. She dedicates all that she does to His purposes. Take her example to heart. The only way even to begin to try to fulfill the ideal described in this passage is with the Lord's blessing. Look to Him and live as a daughter of the King. Wear the royal robes of a princess and let His magnificence shine through you.

Yes, the virtuous wife is a true all-star player, but I think now it is obvious that her excellence is attributed to her following the plays designed by her Coach. All her efforts are for the good of herself, her team, and her Lord; everything she does serves all three. This should come as no surprise, for when a woman walks the path God has set before her, her blessings extend to touch everyone in her life.

PART THREE

Encore:

Legacy of a Leading Lady

CHAPTER TEN

Monuments and Moments

HAVE YOU EVER walked into an empty room and caught a waft of a sweet scent clinging to the air? No one is in the room, but the lingering perfume leaves undeniable evidence that someone was there. In fact, this person continues to have a definite effect on the room despite their absence.

In much the same fashion, there have been people in my life who are no longer on this earth but have a left a lasting impression on me. My present experiences are somehow shaped, affected, and altered by the lingering impact of those who have gone before me. I can almost see them smile or hear the faint sound of fading laughter. Gone but not forgotten, these shadows of love adorn my soul, giving me a history that has shaped my destiny in manifold ways.

My parents are both now deceased. My father passed many years before my mother, leaving her to finish the training process in my life. Yet, although they are both gone, they forever will remain a part of me and my siblings. A seed cannot be extracted from the tree it produces. Nor can rain be separated from the ocean it fills. Likewise, our parents will always be a part of us. We each have some trace of them, some residual effect that helps define who we are today.

When I started to write this book about leading ladies, my mother immediately came to mind. She was truly a leading lady of her time, a superstar who shined brightly in the lives of her family and those blessed to know her. I am proud to say that who I am today is a reflection of her. There are few times when I stand to do anything in public that I cannot catch a glimpse of my mother's legacy affecting and influencing my every move. At every speaking engagement, her teaching style directs my words. For every decision I am called to make, her wisdom guides me. She is ever present, watching over me and somehow influencing all that I will ever be. She, like the rich fragrance of an exotic perfume, cannot be dismissed by the absence of her body. She is still here in my speech, my style, and my actions. She is the thirst I have for life, the strength of my stance, and the rigid spine that causes my shoulders to remain erect even when my faith slumps and my body grows weary and my mind perplexed.

I am also aware of her presence that lives on in my mind and in my heart, in the building blocks of my character, the kind of man I am, the kind of husband and father I have turned out to be. As a master teacher with a gifted voice herself, she inspired me and taught me how to speak in public before crowds of people. As an entrepreneur and savvy businesswoman, she bequeathed to me an eye for opportunities and an ear for possibilities. As a fountain of wisdom and insight into human nature, she instilled in me a compassion for all people and a desire to listen to their hearts and not just their words.

Although she passed from this world several years ago, she lives on through hundreds of moments that run through my mind on any given day. I'm not alone, for her legacy extends to her other children as well as countless friends, students, and loved ones. She left a legacy so much larger than her life that it's difficult to measure its impact.

Consequently, her monument lies not in some slab of marble or in any of her possessions that have been passed on to me and my siblings. No, her monument is comprised of moments. The look she gave me as a little boy when I'd fallen and bloodied my knee—not just compassion, not just tenderness or comfort, but a special glance of caring and connection that a mother personalizes for each of her children. Moments when, even after I was an adult, she could still put me in my place. Moments when she shared my blessings and told me how proud she was of me. Moments at the end of her life when the flicker of recognition in her eyes as I walked into her hospital room made my heart soar and ache at the same time.

Like a mosaic of colorful quilt pieces lovingly stitched together by her lifetime's presence, these moments form a living monument that continues to comfort, inspire, and protect the lives of all it envelops. Her impact ripples throughout my life, my children's lives, and someday, even their children's lives. You do not have to have known someone directly to experience the blessings of their inheritance. The bonds of relationship become parlayed into innumerable influences on those we meet each day. It is her legacy. And it is one of the greatest gifts a leading lady can bestow on her children and successors.

Regardless of your age—fifteen to ninety-five and in between—all women are aware of wanting their lives to count, of wanting to have an impact, to leave behind an offspring borne of dreams and the labor of her life's energy. But still, many of us don't consciously think about leaving a legacy for a couple of reasons. For one thing, we associate legacy with dying and no one really likes to spend much time thinking about their own demise. Similarly, we don't consider the investment we are making in our legacy right now at this moment. Often, we assume that our legacy is something that will be revealed years and years from now, long after we're gone. We feel as if we don't really have any control over what we'll leave behind us.

But that's the same kind of thinking that abdicates your decisions to other people and blames other events for your place in life. No, you are no victim, my sister, nor is your legacy some vague, distant surprise to be discovered at the bottom of a Cracker Jack box. Just as you pursue the calling of greatness on your life, so, too, do you pursue the investment in what you will leave behind. You are a trailblazer, widening the path as you proceed along the journey of faith toward the greatness that is your calling. Others will follow you and your example in order to achieve their own pinnacles of success.

If you want to move beyond mediocrity, if you want to commit to fulfilling the unique and special purpose burning in the furnace of your soul, if you want to sustain your dream throughout a lifetime of triumphs and trials, then you must invest. Like a studious stockbroker scanning each day's business report for an emerging company, you must invest in each day so that you can accumulate a lifetime portfolio of memorable moments.

All women want to leave a legacy, just like men want to leave one. Certainly there are people who think that the more houses and estates, sports cars and antiques they leave behind, the greater their legacy and therefore the greater their significance. But most of us know that so little of what a person leaves behind is in the actual form of silver tea sets and stocks in blue-chip companies. No, the really valuable items left behind are more intangible, more unique, and more powerful than the material goods that get parceled out in someone's will.

I believe many more women than men recognize this truth. They inherently know the greatest gifts they leave behind cannot be contained in a vault. Perhaps it's because women inherently seem to value the relational and the emotional more than men. But as more and more women pursue the opportunities opening around them, they become more and more distracted. The demands of being a career woman, mother, wife, community leader, and so on weigh on the woman's soul. Surely out of all that's she's doing there is significance. Sadly, however, many women reach the end of their lives before they realize that they may have sacrificed too much and invested too little for what matters most.

Business or Blessing

YOU SEE IT time and time again. Women and men who excel in their chosen professions at the expense of what life is all about. Until one day they become a living cliché, like the washed-up movie star trying to maintain her appearance of decades long past, living in denial about the emptiness of her life now that her time on screen has ended. Or the entrepreneur who devoted herself to so many new ventures that there was no time for old friends, and when she finally regained her perspective on what matters, all her friends had moved on.

We've asked the question before, but now as we begin to think about the legacy a leading lady wants to leave beyond her performance, it's essential to rethink priorities. Do you know what you want out of life? You may say success or excellence or greatness, and that's good. But what, exactly, does success look like on any given day in your life? Do you know what kind of significance you want to have? Do you know what kind of legacy you want to leave behind? And better yet, do you know what it will cost you on a daily basis to establish that kind of endowment?

If all you want out of life is to make money, then your life is simple. It's not hard to work diligently, invest wisely, and emerge with fat bank accounts. Similarly, if you want to be famous for your job, and that's what you want most out of life, then you can promote yourself until your name is a household word. Or if you want to be a great athlete, then you simply devote yourself from childhood on to the necessary discipline of training and competition. You see, virtually any of these apparently elusive goals is attainable—if you are singularly focused on it and it alone. But it is within the context of real life, of relationships, of making decisions for the kind of life you want, the quality of your marriage, or the bond between you and your children, that complexity and challenge set in. Balance once again becomes essential if you are to succeed not just in one area of your life but in the entire theater of your life's performance.

In my ministry, I meet a lot of women who want to have it all and seem to have it. They want the successful career, the loving marriage, 2.5 children and a dog. They want a nice house in a nice community, where they can be active in their church, their children's schools, and the social scene. They run from business meetings to PTA meetings. When they're not carpooling the kids to dance class, they're making cupcakes for the church bake sale. Like a circus clown, they juggle many things in the air at once. They are the problem-solvers at the office, the tutors who help with homework; they contribute to their community, and at night offer a loving heart, a listening ear, and the soft arms of comfort for their husbands. They offer so much to so many, and quite frankly they are happy to give what they can. It is nice to be needed, and satisfying to know that you can make a difference in others' lives. But these women get tired. Competing needs pull at them, a tug-of-war with their time and energy. Sometimes it just gets overwhelming.

The Scripture says that to whom much is given, from her much is required (Luke 12:48). The question then arises, how can a woman manage all that she has intellectually, spiritually, and maternally without depleting, short-circuiting, and collapsing into a puddle of muddled mayhem on the floor? I am glad you asked.

Many women I counsel ask me how to stay focused on so many different important areas of their lives at once. As I shared with you a few pages back, I find the model in Proverbs 31 a wonderful model to incorporate. Depending on where they are in their search for balance, some women find this model a little overwhelming. The woman described in this passage feels too much like a Superwoman. This woman is too perfect, too righteous, too resourceful, too savvy. They want women closer to where they are, warts and all.

Then I direct them to another classic scene of two sisters and a very special guest.

Now it happened as they went that He entered a certain village; and a certain woman named Martha welcomed Him into her house.

And she had a sister called Mary, who also sat at Jesus' feet and heard His word.

But Martha was distracted with much serving, and she approached Him and said, "Lord, do You not care that my sister has left me to serve alone? Therefore tell her to help me."

And Jesus answered and said to her, "Martha, Martha, you are worried and troubled about many things.

"But one thing is needed, and Mary has chosen that good part, which will not be taken away from her."

LUKE 10:38–42

It's a simple scene that encompasses much of the fretting and inner turmoil that so many people experience as they attempt to make choices in their lives. And I believe we will only continue to experience more and more of the complexity of such decision making in our twenty-first-century, consumer-ruled society. As more opportunities open up, more choices are available.

Our lives have become like a trip to the supermarket. Recently, I stopped off at the grocery store to pick up a bottle of salad dressing for our family's dinner that night. There were not only four dozen varieties made by five different brands, there were so many other variations! Fat-free, low-cal, creamy, vinegar-based, oil-based, sweet, sour, sweet-and-sour, fresh herbs, dried herbs, no herbs, restaurant style, home style, café style, steakhouse style—I'm not kidding. These were all real varieties of salad dressing on the supermarket shelf. My head spun from reading so many different descriptions of something that I thought would be relatively simple to pick out.

The more choices we have, the more difficult it is to make a decision. Each option sounds better than the last. Just when I thought I had settled on the dressing I would buy, my eye caught sight of another bottle, and that tempted me as well. I'm embarrassed to say that I walked out of there with two shopping bags full of salad dressing, determined that I would try each one.

But there is quite a bit of difference between buying condiments and allocating your time. While my indecision simply resulted in a larger grocery bill, uncertainty about how to prioritize your responsibilities is not so easily solved. I'm reminded of a friend of mine who recently hosted a dinner party. She sent out handmade invitations. The menu was a feast fit for a king. My wife and I arrived at our friend's home and we were extremely impressed with the presentation. The table was set with the utmost care. A beautifully arranged floral centerpiece filled with flowers picked from the perfectly manicured garden added elegance to the room. Our hostess greeted us and seated us and then raced off to the kitchen to put the finishing touches on some hors d'oeuvres. When she reappeared, she was bearing a try of delectable delights. She is a fabulous cook and these treats were absolutely delicious. Everyone at the party was raving about the food, but the compliments went unheard, for the cook was back in the kitchen working on dinner. She barely sat through the meal—dessert was in the oven—and when the last bite of soufflé was finished, she was already busy starting on the cleanup. None of the guests could find one complaint about the dinner, but as we left that evening, we all felt disappointed. Oh, we had had a terrific meal, all right, but we could have gotten that at a restaurant. No, what we really missed was the company of our gracious host.

I know she meant well. She wanted to please us, to make the evening an enjoyable one. Yes, there were a lot of things to do, but that's what it takes to throw a successful party, isn't it? Quite frankly, I think everyone who was there that night would agree that, although we were treated to an evening right out of *Better Homes and Gardens,* we would have much rather made do with some cheese and crackers and good conversation and camaraderie with fine friends.

This same situation occurred with Martha and her houseguest, not just any houseguest, but the man who had brought her brother back from the dead. Wouldn't you want to do everything in your power to ensure he had a warm, gracious environment with a delicious meal on the fire? This woman becomes the Martha Stewart of her day, racing to sweep, dust, wash, clean, chop, knead, bake, stir, pour, and pout. It's not that she particularly enjoys all this work, evidently—if that were the case, then she wouldn't care what her sister did in the meantime. No, it's that she feels obligated to do it—obligated to do it so that she can feel good about herself as a hostess.

How many acts of "service" do you feel obligated to perform? How many "ministries" are you working in so that you can feel good about yourself as a giving, Christian woman? How much are you resenting those women who seem to be rested, refreshed, and more in tune with God than you are? Are you more Martha or more Mary? More business or more blessing? It's so easy to create a merit system of chores and busyness by which to grade ourselves and our faith. We all know that hard work is necessary, right? If I don't do it, nobody else will. If you want something done right, do it yourself.

Someone once sent me an amusing Christmas card that said that if God had only sent three wise women instead of the three wise men, then Jesus' birth would have gone a lot smoother. Three wise women would have brought practical gifts—a crib for the baby, some diapers, and a warm casserole for the holy family. It made me chuckle, but it also hits on that truth that so many women cling to—women know best what needs to be done and they get it done when no one else does.

Not to denigrate the incredible efforts of women, but so often some women assume these burdens because they haven't focused their priorities. They haven't thought about weighing what they perceive as needing to be done with a larger, more long-term point of view.

Martha knows what needs to get done to make sure her guest is comfortable. There's a lot that needs to get done, and her sister should help her. So Martha tells Jesus to tell Mary to get busy! Evidently she didn't think her sister would respond to her own rebuke, so she asks Jesus to use His authority and status as a guest to get Mary moving. The only problem is, Jesus stops poor Martha cold in her tracks. It's almost as if He said, "Martha, who asked you to do all this stuff anyway? I came to see you and listen to you, not to inspect your clay pots and dust bunnies." The Master tells this type-A woman, "But one thing is needed, and Mary has chosen that good part, which will not be taken away from her."

If you are going to lead a life's performance that produces a meaningful legacy and not merely an entertaining show, then you must take His words to heart. Each day you will be forced to make decisions that will have a significant impact on both your daily performance and your lifetime legacy. And from my experience, it's not always an easy choice. The difficulty is usually not in having to choose between what appears good and what appears evil—those choices are rather easy. The real difficulty is choosing from among several good options, several necessary possibilities, many urgent demands. Do you take the promotion that means working more hours but also more money, or do you start looking for another job with fewer hours so you can spend more time with the kids? Do you spend the income tax refund on a new roof or on braces for your twelve-year-old? Do you agree to make the costumes for the church's Easter pageant, or use that time to have some alone time with your man?

So how are we to choose? With so many difficult choices caught in our daily crossfire, how are we even to consider which ones will contribute to the legacy we want to leave? It seems so simple, too simple. Jesus says that only one thing is needed and that its goodness cannot be taken away from us when we choose it. This is our legacy part. This is the part that blesses us, perhaps not in the moment, but long after we are gone.

In Mary's case, the one thing she chose was to value the relational, the finite, limited opportunity over the occupational, ceaseless necessity of cooking and cleaning. Certainly homes have to be swept and meals have to be cooked. But they always will—part of the frustration my wife has always had with housekeeping is that with five kids, nothing stays clean and orderly for long! Chores will always need doing. But can we recognize those rare moments when those duties can wait because something much more precious has presented itself to us? It might be as simple as allowing yourself an hour or two in your favorite chair with a cup of coffee and your Bible rather than going on-line and checking your accounts like you usually do during that time. It might be enjoying the presence of your children home from school rather than worrying about whether they're going to mess up your clean carpets. It might be volunteering to give your time to others instead of thinking that your time is too valuable for you ever to consider working for free. For the work you accomplish can be undone, the dishes will be dirtied again, the floors muddied. But you cannot take away the indelible memories of time with your Lord, your children, or with those in need. Those gifts establish a legacy that continues long after the last supper is eaten and the last carpet is vacuumed.

Estate Tax

ALL GREAT LEGACIES carry a price tag. When a multimillionaire dies, his estate is given a value based on the difference between his assets and liabilities. That figure, if above a certain level, is then taxed, and this is known as the estate tax. Even though this tax is just a small portion of a much larger inheritance, there's an intangible price that has already been paid. How much time was given to secure such wealth? How much time was wasted worrying and fretting over the estate tax garnered by the government after he dies? How much energy was expended trying to spend, shop, and consume the enormous amounts of money earned? How much time was used to secure insurance and protection, security and bodyguards for the vast storehouses?

This is where you have to get serious with your definition of greatness. It's one thing to measure success by the numbers in your bank account or the square footage in your ten-bedroom villa, by the price of a stock share or the stock of your portfolio. It's another thing to measure success by the intangibles of mothering a son or a daughter, perhaps single-handedly. Or to evaluate greatness by the number of young women you mentored or ministered to in your community. How do you measure the enrichment of your husband's life by all that you gave to him? How do you tabulate the value of the work ethic you established in your co-workers?

I'm reminded of a conversation I had with a dear older woman in my church many years ago. She came to me in confidence, seeking prayer for a young woman she was mentoring in a women's Bible study. The young woman had confided to the older woman that she was tempted to have an affair with a wonderful man she'd met at work. This man seemed to be everything that the young woman's husband was not—attentive, romantic, thoughtful, sensitive. The young woman said that she knew it would be wrong to get involved with her handsome co-worker, but she was afraid she couldn't help herself. She asked her Bible study leader what she should do. The older woman told me that she had told her that she knew exactly how she felt, that she, too, had once been tempted to stray in her lifelong marriage. "What stopped you?" I asked her, just as the younger woman had asked. "The knowledge that I would have to live with myself, for one thing," the dear old saint replied. "And the expectation that someday some young gal would ask me why she shouldn't."

There is no substitute for integrity, dear lady. It is in short supply. Here was a woman who knew what it meant to be fully human, to suffer the anguish of extramarital temptation among the many other temptations of a lifetime, and to maintain her faith for the long haul. That has weight, my sister. That is character that leaves its impact on the lives of others in ways that continue to ripple throughout time. From my one example, think of the impact this older woman's honesty and integrity had on the lives of so many others—not just her family, but this younger woman's husband, her children, even the man she was tempted by. Every life touches another in ways seen and unseen. What sacrifices are you willing to make today so that you will have greater resources out of which to give in the future?

As you can see, I'm not even talking about financial resources, although savings and retirement plans are good to have. I have encouraged women for years to build up their financial portfolios and diversify their holdings. But this is a different type of diversification. It is the kind of accumulated wealth that cannot be accounted for in columns with your accountant. No, I'm talking about the strength of character developed over a lifetime of storm-tossed losses and silent disappointments. How will you weather your temptations today in order to give shelter to others in their times of need? I challenge you to invest in the invisible accounts of others every chance you're given.

Competing Children

AMONG THE MANY challenges that face women on the road to success is the complex assortment of competing dreams operating within them. What do you do when what you want in one area conflicts with what you desire in another? Good decisions and mature choices are the vital nutrients of a well-nourished soul. Even when we remember Jesus' words to Martha and are on the lookout for the one necessary choice to fulfill His goodness, which cannot be taken away, we may still feel divided. We want to bask at His feet and we want the house clean and the dinner cooked. We want to unleash our creativity in our new business venture and in our relationships with our husband and children. As more and more variables compete for our time and energies, it can become difficult for us to discern what our legacy will be. As a result, we find ourselves forcing what we want our legacy to be into a neat spot on the shelf of the future. But what we forget is that God has already established the place for our legacy. Like a master artist painting the intricate beauty of an autumn landscape, He has left vacancies on the canvas that can only be filled by the bright color we produce.

One leading lady who discovered this the hard way was a loving mother and wife who wanted only the best for her children and her future. Let's see what happened when she attempted to take the paintbrush out of God's hand and color in her own bold strokes.

> *Isaac was forty years old when he took Rebekah as wife, the daughter of Bethuel the Syrian of Padan Aram, the sister of Laban the Syrian.*
>
> *Now Isaac pleaded with the LORD for his wife, because she was barren; and the LORD granted his plea, and Rebekah his wife conceived.*
>
> *But the children struggled together within her; and she said, "If all is well, why am I like this?" So she went to inquire of the LORD.*
>
> *And the LORD said to her:*
> *"Two nations are in your womb,*
> *Two peoples shall be separated from your body;*
> *One people shall be stronger than the other,*
> *And the older shall serve the younger."*
>
> *So when her days were fulfilled for her to give birth, indeed there were twins in her womb.*
>
> *And the first came out red. He was like a hairy garment all over; so they called his name Esau.*
>
> *Afterward his brother came out, and his hand took hold of Esau's heel; so his name was called Jacob. Isaac was sixty years old when she bore them.*

So the boys grew. And Esau was a skillful hunter, a man of the field; but Jacob was a mild man, dwelling in tents.

And Isaac loved Esau because he ate of his game, but Rebekah loved Jacob.

GENESIS 25:20–28

Once again, we find a barren woman suffering through her lack of children until she becomes able to conceive as a gift from the Lord. Like Sarah and Hannah, Rebekah wants to birth children who will carry her legacy into the future. And even during her pregnancy, she senses the inner turmoil between her two children. The twin sons within her seem to be vying and competing for attention or favor even *in utero.*

I believe many of us experience a similar kind of tension within us as we are in the process of birthing our dreams. One possibility seems to contradict or challenge another possibility, one dream seems mutually exclusive of the other. It's important to note that Rebekah turns to God for insight into her problem. She asks, "If all is well, why am I like this?" Can you relate to her question? How many times have you sensed an undercurrent of fear or foreboding even in the midst of productive times? Many successful women cannot enjoy their present successes because they fear the unseen effects their choices will have on their futures. Some of these women will come to me for counseling or stop me after a service and confide, "I don't know what's wrong with me. Everything seems to be going well. But if everything's so good, then why can't I be happy?" While many factors may influence the circumstances of each individual, often I find that these women are wrestling with their own definitions of success. They reach a certain pinnacle of financial prosperity or domestic productivity, perhaps after a long drought of barrenness and longing, they achieve their goal, and then they feel let down that there's not more fulfillment in the accomplishment.

While we may not always have as clear an answer as Rebekah receives, I believe it is important to take these feelings and fears to the Lord. Ask Him for insight into the turmoil washing over you. Ask Him for security and protection for your future and for the life of the dream you are birthing. Learn to take your strength and fulfillment from Him instead of relying on accomplishments to nourish your soul. No matter how great the achievement, its ability to define you or satisfy your soul remains limited. Don't expect success of any kind to replace your reliance on your Lord.

After Rebekah births her twin sons, she realizes the source of the inner skirmish she felt inside during her pregnancy. They couldn't be more different than night and day! Perhaps if you have children you can appreciate some of what this mother experienced. As a father I have enjoyed observing and learning the personalities and hearts of my own five children, including my twin sons. While some similarities exist in resemblances and physical features from child to child, each one is incredibly different and unique from his or her siblings. One is quiet and easygoing while another is high energy and extroverted. Another loves finding out what makes things tick while his brother wants to get lost in the power of music. One child seems to have been born picky about what she eats and wears while her sister enjoys whatever she discovers on her plate or in her closet.

Yes, our children are incredibly unique and distinct in the special differences coloring each one. Rebekah immediately recognized the differences in her two sons. Although they were twins, they were more like two sides of a coin than peas in a pod. Esau was red and hairy, even as a baby. He grows into a little outdoorsman, off hunting and running through the fields, bringing his daddy whatever wild creature he happened to snare. Jacob, on the other hand, is mild-mannered and smooth-skinned. He's a mama's boy and enjoys the indoors and, if his deceptive ways are any indication, the life of the mind. And I'm sure the brothers recognized the differences in each other as well. It doesn't take long before one negotiates an incredible trade from the other.

> *Now Jacob cooked a stew; and Esau came in from the field, and he was weary.*
>
> *And Esau said to Jacob, "Please feed me with that same red stew, for I am weary." Therefore his name was called Edom.*
>
> *But Jacob said, "Sell me your birthright as of this day."*
>
> *And Esau said, "Look, I am about to die; so what is this birthright to me?"*
>
> *Then Jacob said, "Swear to me as of this day." So he swore to him, and sold his birthright to Jacob.*
>
> *And Jacob gave Esau bread and stew of lentils; then he ate and drank, arose, and went his way. Thus Esau despised his birthright.*
>
> GENESIS 25:29–34

Have you ever watched your kids hammer out a deal that you knew was far from equitable? One little boy offers a stick of gum to another little boy in exchange for his latest video game. Hardly a fair trade, but one that both parties have agreed to accept nonetheless. It's only later, as the flavor of the gum wears off and the little boy realizes how temporary his choice was compared with how enduring his video game is, that the truth sets in. With Esau we see a similar dynamic. He's tired and hungry and nothing else matters, especially something as intangible and irrelevant as a birthright. Jacob shows himself to be just as shrewd a hunter as his brother here, for he has prepared a clever trap in order to obtain his desired prey.

Have you found yourself in Esau's position before? You're stressed, you're bone-weary, and you're famished. It's been a long day after a string of long days, and nothing matters more than a good meal and an uninterrupted night's sleep. Then suddenly your teenaged daughter wants to talk to you about something important. Then suddenly your boss needs your new ideas—you know, the ones that might land you a promotion—by first thing tomorrow morning. Then suddenly your husband wants to discuss your family's finances and plan how to save to send the kids to college. If it's not one thing, it's another. How can you possibly concentrate and listen to the words you know are important when you are so physically distracted? Couldn't these other things wait?

It's so tempting to postpone, duck out, or ignore the legacy moments when they creep up on you at a bad time. It's not hard to remember why they're important, it's simply next to impossible to remember why they're essential to right now, in the midst of your fatigue, your depression, your own need. But the enemy wants to trick you out of these legacy moments by selling you a cheap bowl of soup. If the devil can distract you from the issues of eternal consequence through the use of the urgent, then he can leave the rest to you. Who hasn't made a bad decision when exhausted, hungry, bored, or lonely? Before you judge Esau and think him merely stupid or naive, remember that human weakness resides in all of us.

And what about his brother Jacob? Perhaps you find yourself

relating to him more easily. You have no problem taking advantage of situations or the needs of others if it will secure the legacy you think you deserve. It could be anything from exploiting customers to increasing your business output to manipulating family members to be indebted to you. Maybe you've even accomplished such a feat under the guise of ministry. You take a meal to a sick friend in exchange for your friend's allegiance on an issue at the church business meeting. You offer to listen to someone who is clearly troubled just to gain information about mutual friends. Like Jacob the supplanter, the trickster, you revel in seizing any opening for advantage and purchasing it with the lowest possible price.

As you can guess, neither of these sons of Rebekah provides us with a good model for leaving a legacy. We want to avoid having our dreams sold cheaply, like Esau handing over his birthright. You may think that selling the patent for your whimsical little invention is a good idea. After all, there are a lot of bills left to pay and Christmas is coming, and that extra $500 from that Internet company sure would come in handy. And when would you really have time to actualize your ideas, let alone see about having them produced in volume to sell? There are certainly hard times when we have to liquidate our assets and use any and all resources at hand. But too often women sell their ideas, their dreams, their birthrights far below their true value. Dare to hold onto your dream until the time is right to see it come to life on its own. Trust God to bring it about in a way that will honor its value and yours, not diminish them. For that is what Esau experiences after the stew has filled his belly and indigestion has replaced his hunger. "Thus Esau despised his birthright." If you sell your dreams too cheaply, if you trade your legacy in for immediate gratification, then you will despise all that you had once longed for. The sweet flavor of hope and fruition will sour on your tongue and sicken your spirit.

Learning to manipulate and exploit opportunities based on the weakness of others does not equate to a fulfilling legacy either. If, like Jacob, you become so intent on stealing others' ideas, possessions, husbands, or legacies, then you will only perpetuate a lie that will tarnish whatever genuine legacy of your own you might have had. Leading ladies trust God for the inheritance of their birthrights. They don't have to feel insecure in what they don't have or in what they see others possessing. They have a patience and a class that sets them apart from the connivers and tricksters of the world.

All in the Family

ARGUABLY, THOUGH, WE might say that both sons have inherited their weaknesses, for their parents display similar kinds of flaws. We have already seen the way each parent plays favorites with the sons, Isaac with Esau and Rebekah with Jacob. But the exploitation perpetrated by the younger brother on his hairy twin is only the beginning. For as Isaac's eyesight dwindles in his old age, his wife's cunning only becomes sharper and more acute. When the old father asks his favorite son to hunt some game and bring it to him for a meal, the crafty Rebekah is listening.

> *Now Rebekah was listening when Isaac spoke to Esau his son. And Esau went to the field to hunt game to bring it.*
>
> *So Rebekah spoke to Jacob her son, saying, "Indeed I heard your father speak to Esau your brother, saying,*

'Bring me game and make savory food for me, that I may eat it and bless you in the presence of the LORD before my death.'

"Now therefore, my son, obey my voice according to what I command you.

"Go now to the flock and bring me from there two choice kids of the goats, and I will make savory food from them for your father, such as he loves.

"Then you shall take it to your father, that he may eat it, and that he may bless you before his death."

And Jacob said to Rebekah his mother, "Look, Esau my brother is a hairy man, and I am a smooth-skinned man.

"Perhaps my father will feel me, and I shall seem to be a deceiver to him; and I shall bring a curse on myself and not a blessing."

But his mother said to him, "Let your curse be on me, my son; only obey my voice, and go, get them for me."

GENESIS 27:5–13

No matter how many times we see it in others, in ourselves it can always be justified. We deceive. We lie. We cheat. We betray. Like Rebekah, you want only the best for your children. You want only to see your little one get what he deserves. You want only to see your dream have all the opportunities to come into a glorious life. But at what cost, my sister? How far are you willing to go to obtain what you think you must have?

Mothers make many sacrifices for their children. My own mother often worked several jobs at once in order to support our family. She often went without new clothes or nice things for herself so that she could keep us all clothed and fed. Sacrifices are noble and godly, fueled by love and enabled by hope. But you must not confuse holy sacrifices for your family or for your dreams with the crooked paths of deception. Because she could not wait for God to fulfill His promise concerning her offspring, Rebekah felt compelled to make things happen for herself.

While Jacob certainly displays these deceptive tendencies as we've seen, his mother must bear a large share of the weight of responsibility in this scheme to steal his father's blessing. She overhears her husband and other son and perceives it as a must-act situation. She comes up with the idea for Jacob to bring in some savory food as if he were Esau. She counters Jacob's fear of being discovered with two other ingenious ideas. First, she will cover her smooth son with animal skins and his brother's clothing. Second, she will assume any curse or liability he incurs if the near-blind Isaac does indeed discover their ploy.

Once again, I must ask you, how far are you willing to go to get what you want? Certainly the deception and betrayal executed by Rebekah harms her marriage and her relationship with both sons. She clearly does not trust her husband's judgment regarding which son will receive his favored blessing. She clearly does not respect her son Esau if she is so quickly determined to put her favorite up to impersonating him. And she doesn't respect Jacob either, for she will not allow him to stand as a man and confront his father and his brother for who he is. Instead she dresses him up as an impostor and uses subterfuge to acquire what she believes will secure her legacy. Finally, and worst of all, she violates her Lord by not trusting Him to fulfill His seeds of greatness in her life or the lives of her children.

Rebekah's scheme goes according to plan, but just as Isaac finished blessing Jacob, Esau walks in and finds that his brother has cheated him out of his birthright yet again. Although he manages to secure a secondary blessing from his father, he vows to kill Jacob. Now Rebekah, who wanted so much for her favorite son, fears for his life, and so she sends him away. She knows that through her betrayal she's lost the love of Esau, and she doesn't want to lose Jacob, too. So Jacob leaves and the family is torn apart.

Now some people might argue that Jacob wouldn't have gotten his birthright and his father's blessing without trickery, without Rebekah's deceitful intrusion. He would not have fulfilled God's prophecy for His greatness, would not have run away and wrestled the angel at Peniel and been given a new name that would establish him as God's nation, Israel. While we can argue theological smoke circles in all kinds of interesting ways, I believe that what's truly remarkable about this story is the way God fulfills His promise despite the thick webs of deceit and trickery the mother-son team had spun. What I think we can learn from this is that, once again, God transforms our botched attempts at greatness with His miraculous interventions on our behalf. His vision for our legacy is so much greater than what we ourselves could ever dream up.

Your desire to have a lasting legacy, long after the stage lights of your performance have faded to darkness, is a natural and vital longing. No one stays onstage forever. So what do you do when the music stops? What will you have left when the contracts end? Your desire to leave a legacy of substance should be used to nurture and strengthen your efforts along the burgeoning path of God's action plan for your life. However, it is a joint effort between you and God. You must never assume that you know what is best, when is best, or how is best without His stamp of approval. Even when He has promised you that your dream will come alive, don't presume that you have license to violate His laws or His love. Wait and see what He has in store for you.

Monuments of Mite

IMAGINE AN ELDERLY African-American woman, gnarled by arthritis and wearied from a lifetime of hard labor, hanging clothes out to dry on a line in her tiny yard in Hattiesburg, Mississippi. For more than seven decades this woman has earned her living by taking in the soiled bundles of laundry left on her front porch and transformed them into neat stacks of clean shirts and starched pants. Even after the various ailments of old age set in, including the debilitating arthritis, this woman continued to wash, dry, and iron the dirty clothes of the numerous families, both white and black, who used her excellent service. She doesn't own a car but walks everywhere she goes in her tiny community, including the grocery store and church.

Now imagine this same little old lady seated at a large round table covered with white linen, polished silver, and exquisite crystal. On her right sits President Bill Clinton, who seems delighted to engage this gentle woman in conversation. Surrounding them in this posh Washington dining hall are some of the most prominent political and civic leaders in the country. It is the dinner of the Congressional Black Caucus.

What catapulted this ordinary washerwoman into the extraordinary echelons of the elite? It is her amazing legacy, embodied in a single gift she made just after she had retired from her laundering at age eighty-seven. You see, Miss Oseola McCarty donated $150,000 of her life savings to the University of Southern Mississippi to establish a minority scholarship fund for deserving students with financial need. With her simple, frugal, and hardworking lifestyle, Miss McCarty's gift caught everyone by surprise and inspired many people to contribute their own donation to her scholarship fund. According to a press release by the university, at the time of her gift Miss Oseola said, "I want to help somebody's child go to college. I just want [the scholarship] to go to someone who will appreciate it and learn. I'm old and I'm not going to live always." Although she completed only the sixth grade before having to drop out and support her family, this incredible woman always valued education and the opportunities it affords. Despite the fact that she had never married nor had children, Miss McCarty did not want to allow this to keep her from giving to those in need.

Such an inspiring example reminds me of the gift of the widow's mite.

> *And He looked up and saw the rich putting their gifts into the treasury,*
>
> *and He saw also a certain poor widow putting in two mites.*
>
> *So He said, "Truly I say to you that this poor widow has put in more than all;*
>
> *"for all these out of their abundance have put in offerings for God, but she out of her poverty put in all the livelihood that she had."*
>
> LUKE 21:1–4

Here is this poor widow who puts the equivalent of two pennies into the collection box and Jesus regards her contribution as greater than any other. For He knows that her gift is a true sacrifice. The rich may have given a lot more money, but it is only a tiny portion of their wealth. But here is this woman who has given all that she has. It's easy to give out of our abundance. But leaving a legacy requires a much steeper price. We must be willing to give of ourselves in ways that will require suffering, in ways that will extend the labor pains of our dream far beyond what we thought we could endure.

Seek to emulate the might of the widow's mite, or the surprising generosity and foresight of women like Oseola McCarty, and you will leave a legacy just as great. What is it that you most want to leave behind when your body departs this earth? What changes will you have accomplished, what sacrifices will have been made so that your monument will endure in the thousands of precious moments you have planted in those you knew? If you want to achieve your status as a leading lady, then consider what great performances will set the standard for what you give on life's stage.

As I have had several plays on tour across our country, I have often watched with fascination as the leading lady would exit out the back door, after the show, and embrace the cool breeze of the evening. Many nights I watched the cast, tired and exhausted, board buses and load into cars headed back to hotel rooms or airports. As the players and crew called loved ones or checked on their children, I learned a lesson that I will share with you. While what you do onstage is notable and noble, what really counts is what remains when the show is over. What do you have left when the lights go down? My sister, I am glad you are proud of what you do. But what matters most is who you are. Leave something behind that points to who you were. And if you can leave nothing behind, leave someone behind who can glean from your wise impartation. I am certain you can have a tremendous impact. As I watch my fingers pound the keyboard, I can smell the perfume of my mother and I can feel her hand on my shoulder. She and I both want to encourage you that there is more to life than success. There is also a successor.

CHAPTER ELEVEN

Birthing Your Dreams

IN THE PENTHOUSE apartment of a luxury building in the old, established part of the city there's a woman. She stands at the window looking out at the flickering lights of the world around her. So much is going on out there. From her perch high above the town, she imagines couples walking along the street hand in hand, young people joking and laughing and doing what young people do. Somewhere out there, a young mother tucks her child into bed and reads a story to send her baby off to sleep. Perhaps somewhere there is a woman just like her, looking out a window, watching the world, until the hum and buzz of her household pulls her back inside to a teenage son asking to borrow the car, a young daughter who needs some advice, a loving husband who envelops her in his arms and whispers "I love you" in her ear.

But the woman in the penthouse is alone. She turns from the

window and surveys her surroundings. The apartment is absolute perfection, filled with the finest furnishings, opulent and plush rugs, and artwork that could rival the collections of some museums. She walks around the room looking over the precious mementos of her career: plaques and degrees, certificates and statues, letters from presidents and governors, paperweights and portfolios. When she had checked *The Wall Street Journal* that morning, her company continued to head the list of Standard & Poor's fastest-growing investments. What a career she has had as the firm's first female CEO. She had worked hard and advanced quickly, earning accolades and an astronomical salary—not to mention the many perks and company stock options. She was the envy of all her colleagues.

The woman smiles as she recalls her high-school reunion all those years ago. When she had walked into the room, all eyes were on her. She had made sure she wore her best outfit—it had cost a fortune, but it fit her well in all the right places. Oh, and she looked good, too. She had made sure of that. A little nip here, a tuck there, and hair and makeup from the finest salon in town ensured that she looked at least twenty years younger than everyone else in the room.

She had been married at the time. Her husband was handsome and rich, a great catch by anyone's standards. But their competing careers and diverse interests had torn them apart. Since then, there had been a trail of casual love affairs, several corporate alliances, but there was never anyone serious. Although many tried, no man was able to compete with the lifestyle her successful career afforded or the time and energy it required. There was passing consideration given to children, to charity work, to friendships and community.

But there was never enough time, enough hours in the day, to accomplish any of those things and maintain the career and standard of personal care that was necessary to keep her looking young, beautiful, and successful in everyone's eyes.

But time had won in the end. Crow's-feet and laugh lines could no longer be hidden by makeup, and there was only so far cosmetic surgery could go. Her once taut body bore the signs of aging and gravity. And what of her career? Well, her mind just wasn't as sharp as it used to be. Details began slipping and fading into the recesses of her memory. Board members subtly began indicating it was time for her to retire, time to bring "new blood" into the company. The harsh reality was that she was no longer needed there.

So what was it all for? She worked so hard and now what was she left with? She's alone and lonely, and a mere ghost of her former self. Now photographs are the only testaments to the beauty she once was. Sure, she has all the money she could ever need, but really, what's left to buy? All the hours, all the energy she put into her career, and it doesn't even matter anymore. She's no longer an asset to the company; she has nothing left to give. New talent has been brought in and now they will be the new stars. Will anyone remember what she gave to the company? Will she be remembered as a pioneer who shattered the glass ceiling in a male-dominated industry? Is that even how she wants to be remembered? What legacy will she leave behind?

A Lingering Melody

WHY DO SO many women question their contributions when the stage lights go down? What keeps a woman from knowing that her performance as a leading lady was incomparable and inimitable? While there are numerous obstacles to leaving a worthwhile legacy, perhaps the most insidious is realizing that you have bought into someone else's standard of success. By the time this realization sinks in, it may feel like it's too late to change.

Many women spend their entire lives searching for the purpose and the cause that will give their lives meaning. What they often don't realize is that God has already provided them with the resources and raw materials for establishing a significant legacy in the lives of those around them. But these women often fail to see what is literally before them because they are so intent on measuring their worth by false standards, either someone else's definition or their own skewed perception based on comparisons and competition with someone else.

This statement is not one I make lightly, for I realize that many women struggle throughout their lives trying to grasp their purpose and their legacy. Yet some women, even in the midst of the most fortunate and successful circumstances, remain dissatisfied and disenchanted. These ladies remind me of Rachel and of her battle to birth greatness throughout the deceptive turns of her relationship with Jacob and her sister, Leah. Rachel was a beautiful woman, and much loved by her husband, Jacob, but she believed that her life was void of meaning because she was not as fertile as her sister. Instead of relishing the relationship she had with Jacob, she felt she had to compete with her sister.

Beware When You Compare

Now Laban had two daughters: the name of the elder was Leah, and the name of the younger was Rachel.

Leah's eyes were delicate, but Rachel was beautiful of form and appearance.

Now Jacob loved Rachel; so he said, "I will serve you seven years for Rachel your younger daughter."

And Laban said, "It is better that I give her to you than that I should give her to another man. Stay with me."

So Jacob served seven years for Rachel, and they seemed only a few days to him because of the love he had for her.

GENESIS 29:16–20

As you may know if you are familiar with this love triangle, Laban deceives Jacob and gives him Leah, the older daughter, on his wedding night, a discovery that Jacob does not realize until the next morning. Laban claims that he couldn't marry off his youngest without her older sister being married. Then he squeezes seven more years of labor out of his nephew before he will give him Rachel. If you remember that Laban is Rebekah's brother, then once again we see how deception tends to run in this family.

However, Jacob's love for Rachel is so intense and loyal that he works off his time and marries his first choice, even as his less attractive, unloved wife Leah bears him four sons. Rachel, by contrast, suffers her barrenness. The fact that Leah can give Jacob children and she can't infuriates Rachel.

You see, Rachel is the beautiful daughter, the one fair of face and form, and Leah's eyes were "delicate" or weak, which likely means she was cross-eyed. It seems likely that Rachel was used to attracting more attention than her older sister. Rachel may have even been spoiled as the youngest daughter—Laban certainly seems reluctant to part with his baby girl. Now all of a sudden, life is not turning up roses for her as it has for most of her early life. Although she has the adoration of a loving husband, a man willing to work fourteen years to secure her marriage, she does not have the next logical piece of her life's puzzle. She doesn't have children. So Rachel proceeds so that she can once again enter the race and pass her sister on the track.

> *Now when Rachel saw that she bore Jacob no children, Rachel envied her sister, and said to Jacob, "Give me children, or else I die!"*
>
> *And Jacob's anger was aroused against Rachel, and he said, "Am I in the place of God, who has withheld from you the fruit of the womb?"*
>
> *So she said, "Here is my maid Bilhah; go in to her, and she will bear a child on my knees, that I also may have children by her."*
>
> GENESIS 30:1–3

Like a spoiled child throwing a tantrum, Rachel demands that Jacob give her a child. If her sister can bear Jacob children, she should be able to as well. After all, she's always won out when compared to her sister; she's prettier and she's better-loved. But Jacob knows that only God can bless his wife with a baby and gets angry at Rachel's outburst. But Rachel will not be put off. She knows what she wants and she's used to getting it. So she comes up with a plan to force her dream into fruition. Like Sarah with Hagar, Rachel uses a surrogate to produce a child for her husband. She sends Jacob to her maid, Bilhah, so that she can bear children for Rachel.

Consolation Prizes

WE'VE TOUCHED BEFORE on this toxic tendency women have to compare themselves, but as we reflect on the components of a truly great legacy, we must realize the incredible damage a lifetime of comparing can do to that woman's soul. With Rachel, it's not just that she wants to figure out a way to produce a child; she seems intent on keeping up with her sister regardless of the method or the cost. She has bought into someone else's vision of success and tries to inflate her own dream with borrowed air. She believes that she can compensate for her inability to birth a child by "borrowing" someone else's womb, her maid's.

So often when women feel cheated of the life's dream that they hold dearest to their hearts, they compensate by finding "consolation prizes." We have all done it at one time or another. You may not have lined up a surrogate mother to carry your husband's child, but you may have set your sights on making more money than anyone in your family after you realized that your father would always prefer your older sister to you. Maybe you struggled with being jealous of someone else's looks, sense of humor, or creativity. When you realize that you can never top their abilities, you find something that you can beat them at. You find something that makes you feel good—for all the wrong reasons.

Don't get me wrong; we all need to discover those areas that are uniquely designed for our talents and desires. But you will never fill your full potential by motivating your quest with jealousy or spitefulness. Succeed in your chosen fields because those are the ones that send your heart racing and your spirit soaring, not because you need to one-up someone and put them in their place.

It is very easy to get caught up in the comparison game, partly because we learn by observing those around us. If I ask you to stop right now and describe the impact you want to have on those around you and your world after you're gone, it's only natural that you will think of women you want to emulate. Having successful women to model after is a true blessing. As we've seen throughout our journey in this book, you need strong role models and healthy mentors who nurture and inspire your success like Olympic runners passing the baton in a relay of faith. So maybe in thinking about what you want to leave behind, you focus on the compassion of Mother Teresa, the courage of Rosa Parks, the generosity of Oseola McCarty, the perseverance of Cathy Hughes, and so on. That sounds like a great recipe for success, doesn't it? Yes, indeed. It's so positive to wander through the art gallery of great leading ladies and choose colors and brushstrokes that you admire and want to incorporate onto your own canvas.

The danger arises when you set yourself up to be measured on their scale without their life circumstances, talents, or personalities. When you tell yourself, "I am successful only if I become as compassionate as Mother Teresa," or "I'm a failure unless I create a company as successful as Radio One," that's when the recipe turns into a volatile mixture of disappointments and bitterness waiting to be ignited by your anger. No one can be another Mother Teresa or Maya Angelou. We had those originals and don't need another. More important, no one else can be you but you! You must observe and emulate without attempting to conform to someone else's standards and achievements. You have your own race to run, and while you can learn about pacing and breathing by studying those who have run ahead of you, only you can finish your race and break the Finish Line God has established for your unique course.

One-Up-Womanship

Then she gave him Bilhah her maid as wife, and Jacob went in to her.

And Bilhah conceived and bore Jacob a son.

Then Rachel said, "God has judged my case; and He has also heard my voice and given me a son." Therefore she called his name Dan.

And Rachel's maid Bilhah conceived again and bore Jacob a second son.

Then Rachel said, "With great wrestlings I have wrestled with my sister, and indeed I have prevailed." So she called his name Naphtali.

GENESIS 30:4–8

The competition between the sisters has now become a wrestling match. And notice how quickly Rachel uses God to support her manipulations. But, dear sister, keep in mind that just because your plan may succeed, it doesn't necessarily mean that its fulfillment is God's best plan for your life. When you don't wait on Him, it can become very tempting to give Him the credit in the short term so that you can dodge blaming yourself in the long term. But it's easy to see that Rachel is in complete control here. She's the one who gives her maid to her husband as yet another wife. She's the one who gets to name the children of this other woman. And, most glaring of all, her clenched fists of control is her statement concerning the naming of the second son by Bilhah. "I have had a great struggle with my sister, and I have won," (Genesis 30:8, NIV) declares this competitive woman. Notice this declaration does not say that she has struggled with God over her barrenness, or that she has anguished over feeling jealous of her husband's relations with her sister. No, she declares that it's between her and her sister! She and Leah have the ultimate sibling rivalry here. Consequently, it becomes a one-up-womanship between the two sisters. Leah learns from Rachel's example: she offers her maid Zilpah to Jacob and increases the breeding contest (see Genesis 30:9–13). Back and forth it goes, with no sign of ending in sight.

Do you have grudge matches with certain women in your life? Or on a broader scale, ask yourself how often you compare yourself to other women. Think back over your day today. Was there a woman on the bus whose fine clothes caught your attention and envy? How about the teenager on her way to school with the toned body that you couldn't get no matter how much you worked out? Did you vow to work harder only after you heard your boss compliment your co-worker? Don't be too surprised if you think of half a dozen comparisons that you made without even realizing it.

Unless I'm greatly mistaken, it's a system our society perpetuates by bombarding women with messages about their age, looks, and sexuality, as well as what it means to be a "success." Advertisements display youthful beauty with petal-pink cheeks and unblemished skin, silky hair and tiny waists. Most television and movie heroines who get the man at the end share these physical features. The message becomes loud and clear: Ladies, if you want to be a winner, then you need to look young, beautiful, and sexy.

And I'm sure you've watched those television shows that take us into the homes of the rich and famous. We tour through their mansions, admiring their custom-built homes with their decorator-designed interiors. We see their state-of-the-art kitchens, their Olympic-size pools around which they throw the most fabulous parties, and of course we end up in the master bedroom suite. These romantic chambers paint a picture of perfection, for here a perfect couple spends perfect nights in perfect matrimonial bliss.

In many ways, though, our media images and cultural pressures provide only background noise for the comparisons a woman makes with those more personal acquaintances around her. Her sisters, her mother, her girlfriends, her co-workers, her friends at church, on and on. She looks at these other women and finds some way that she doesn't measure up. If she's single, she looks at her married friends and envies their domestic lifestyle. Or perhaps she sees her friend purchasing the luxuries her high-paying job affords, and thinks she could never be that rich or that successful. And even if she feels superior in some area or another, she always feels lacking in some respect. There is always someone who is richer, thinner, prettier, smarter, more talented, etc.

The best antidote I know for this terrible poison is to consider the source of your creation. God never asks us to compare ourselves with any other person. Indeed, I think it's an insult to Him when you look at another woman and think, "I wish I looked like her. I wish my lips were fuller. I wish I were smarter. I wish I had her talent. I wish I *were* her."

God designed you with tenderness and forethought. He uniquely fashioned you to bear His image and no one else's—your individual beauty can never be duplicated. Like the most complex, exquisite snowflake sparkling across the winter sky, you are unlike any other creature who has ever lived or ever will live.

When you buy into the comparison game, you are really saying,

"God, I think you made a mistake with me. I know you meant well, but you failed here. You could have made me taller, darker, lighter, smarter, thinner, but you didn't. So I guess you messed up with me." But who are you to criticize the Lord of everything? He has looked at you His creation and pronounced, "She is good. I will bless her." Do you second-guess Him? You display an incredible amount of pride and folly when you attempt to place your human standard on the Divine's creation.

It's ironic in a way. I attend many church and social events related to my ministry, and it never ceases to amaze me how much trouble ladies go to in order to look a certain way. Yes, they want to dress appropriately for the occasion and the season, but they also want to stand out as an original, someone with her own sense of style. Heaven forbid two ladies show up at the party in the same dress! These women wouldn't want to be accused of copying someone's "look." But they don't apply this same principle to the way they view their beauty, their personalities, and their abilities. They compare themselves to other women and want to look like them, act like them, succeed like them, be like them.

Let me tell you, if you play the comparison game, you will never be satisfied with your life. You will never enjoy the peace and joy that come from knowing who you are and what you are called to. You will always feel like you are playing catch-up, always outside the circle, always one success away from regaining the lead against the other "opponents."

You must overturn this competitive board game and regain your unique sense of beauty and purpose. Move toward the place where you are fully aware of the fact that your God made you exactly, intricately, and wondrously who you are. You are a designer original for which there is no comparison! If you quit comparing yourself to others, then you will discover a new and different standard of success rather than appropriating theirs. You will regain your own power and grow in healthy confidence, because you will no longer be shuffling from trend to trend and person to person. When you refuse to play the comparison game any longer, then you will find yourself less intimidated by what others think of you. If they want to continue comparing themselves to you and competing, then that's their problem. But you, my sister, will be a free woman. You will become free to discover the unique aspects of God's glory that He has waiting just for you.

Blinded by the Present

UNFORTUNATELY, RACHEL WASN'T to this point just yet. Her scheme to "win" by having her maid bear Jacob's children fails; Leah sends her maid, Zilpah, to Jacob and Zilpah has two children as well. Rachel still desperately wants to bear a child and will do whatever she can to achieve her goal. So when Leah's son, Reuben, comes back from the field with mandrakes, a plant thought to increase fertility, Rachel begs for some. She even offers up her husband to get her hands on this plant that may help her fulfill her dream. "And Rachel said, 'Therefore he will lie with you [Leah] tonight for your son's mandrakes' " (Genesis 30:15). But again Rachel's plan fails. In fact, it backfires completely, for Leah conceives another child. Actually, in time, Leah gives Jacob three more children.

But then, finally, after all of Rachel's machinations and manipulations, a most unexpected event occurs.

Then God remembered Rachel, and God listened to her and opened her womb.

And she conceived and bore a son, and said, "God has taken away my reproach."

So she called his name Joseph, and said, "The Lord shall add to me another son."

GENESIS 30:22–24

Just when it seems that Rachel has reached the bottom of her bag of tricks, God reminds her of His goodness and His grace and gives her what she has connived after for so long. Curiously enough, it's not enough. Still caught up in the throes of comparison to Leah, Rachel names her son Joseph, meaning "may Yahweh add," as if to ask God for yet another son. She's not satisfied with the goodness God provides for her because she's already moved on to the next thing.

Do you know people like this, who never seem to truly appreciate what they have at present because as soon as they attain something they're on to the "next big thing"? Many women I see caught up in this often share similar circumstances to Rachel's. They seem to have life by the tail. They appear to have everything a woman could want. And yet there is always a longing, a sense that something is missing, that they need something more. No matter how much they have, no matter how much they achieve, they think they need more. I believe they feel this way because they are not secure and self-confident in their identity as a daughter of God. They don't trust that He has created them in absolute perfection or that He provides all they need to fulfill their Divine purpose.

Despite having her son, Joseph—her own baby and not her maid's—Rachel only seems to grow in her discontent. Even when the Lord grants her the request of another son, still her bitterness oozes out of her disgruntled dreams. She does birth another child, a child whose passage requires the price of her own life, but it is not enough for her.

> *Then they journeyed from Bethel. And when there was but a little distance to go to Ephrath, Rachel labored in childbirth, and she had hard labor.*
>
> *Now it came to pass, when she was in hard labor, that the midwife said to her, "Do not fear; you will have this son also."*
>
> *And so it was, as her soul was departing (for she died), that she called his name Ben-Oni; but his father called him Benjamin.*
>
> *So Rachel died and was buried on the way to Ephrath (that is, Bethlehem).*
>
> *And Jacob set a pillar on her grave, which is the pillar of Rachel's grave to this day.*
>
> GENESIS 35:16–20

Throughout all her struggling and striving and planning, her comparing and competing, Rachel never found rest. Here at the end of her life she is still trying to give birth. She has not reached a point of contentment with her life's accomplishments, has not made peace with herself for who she is, has not stored up the fruit of her labors so that she might relax and relish God's goodness. Finally, she is moving to a place of rest and abundance (Ephrath means "house of bread" and is another name for Bethlehem), a place where descendants would carry out the lineage of the Messiah. But Rachel cannot see that far ahead. She feels like a failure as she grinds her body and tries to expel the baby coming into life even as she is leaving her own. She cannot see that the two sons she has birthed are destined for greatness. Joseph, her first son, is of course his father's favorite, which gets him in trouble with his numerous jealous brothers. However, as you may know, the story has a happy ending ordained by God, for Joseph delivers Israel from the devastating famine that would surely have obliterated their nation had he not risen to power in Egypt. Benjamin, this son of her passing, becomes the forebear of all kings of Israel. But Rachel does not see this, and so she names her second son, Ben-Oni, which means "son of sorrow." It's as if all of Rachel's grief, sorrow, and bitterness culminate in the birth of this child. She's leaving this world and she doesn't think she's leaving a significant legacy behind.

But Jacob changes the child's name and symbolically foreshadows the vast legacy of his leading lady, by rechristening him Benjamin, which means "son of my right hand" or "son of my strength." A vast difference from son of sorrow! If Rachel had not spent her life comparing herself to Leah, perhaps she could have appreciated all that she had and all that she was. Perhaps if she had had faith in God, she would have known that He would carry her legacy far beyond the limits that she herself could see. She becomes blinded by her present and does not have the faith to have hope in her future. God's present to her was not one that she would get to fully unwrap in her lifetime, and so she felt as if she had received nothing but an empty box. She becomes blinded by her present.

Shadowboxing

"AM I BIRTHING anything significant?" No matter when your mortality stares you in the face, this is the question that stares back at you like the barrel of a gun. Whether you have raised a dozen kids and another dozen grandkids, whether you have built companies or starred in motion pictures, whether you're just starting your life or reaching its conclusion, this question reverberates like an echo in a canyon. You may know that you have accomplishments and even worthwhile relationships. You may know that you can't take money with you and that beauty is fleeting. But still you wonder, what will remain of your presence on this earth once your time onstage has been completed?

Certainly, you are not the only one to ask this question. In Ecclesiastes, the Poet muses on the meaning of life and faces the same dilemma for measuring significance.

> *For what has man for all his labor, and for the striving of his heart with which he has toiled under the sun?*
>
> *For all his days are sorrowful, and his work burdensome; even in the night his heart takes no rest. This also is vanity.*
>
> *For who knows what is good for man in life, all the days of his vain life which he passes like a shadow? Who can tell a man what will happen after him under the sun?*
>
> ECCLESIASTES 2:22–23; 6:12

It seems apparent that even people who have lived their entire life birthing the dream that God appointed for them may have doubts at the end of their lives. It seems to be human nature to shadowbox, as I call it, to dart and parry with the what-ifs and might-have-beens of life. So many leading players may not be able to see the fruits of their labors; there may be only silent fields plowed and seeded. That's why we must not use our own perceptions as the standard for whether we leave a successful legacy. In Ecclesiastes, the Poet, after evaluating the different standards of meaning and success, concludes that all our human striving is "vanity of vanities." However, he also points out that God has set an alarm clock of mystery and greatness in our hearts—we are eternal beings created for eternal purposes. "He has made everything beautiful in its time. Also He has put eternity in their hearts, except that no one can find out the work that God does from beginning to end" (Ecclesiastes 3:11). No one is entitled or imaginative enough to fathom the vast purposes and awesome narrative God is weaving throughout the lives of all humans in time and space. The only way we can feel confident of our life's performance is when we know that we have obeyed our King and lived for His purposes. Only He knows the grand scheme of His design and our role in that royal tapestry.

Have you birthed anything significant? It's a sobering question, dear sister. But it's one that you must face if you are to stay focused on your true identity and your true calling. Otherwise, your mind will drift and your spirit will sag as you observe all those around you. You will lose sight of your finish line and settle for someone else's dead end if you aren't in the process of answering this question on a daily basis.

Only you and God can set the standard of greatness by which to measure your accomplishments and evaluate your legacy. And rarely do you know the full extent of your impact—only God can see the big-screen, high-definition picture of your life's intersection with so many others. Don't assume that you will be able to see your full impact in this lifetime. Trust Him with your dreams, even the ones that do not seem to grow beyond a tiny sprout in your lifetime.

Realize that even after you have passed from this life's stage, so many of the seeds you planted will continue to grow and thrive into vast forests of greatness. Live for the day when your dreams are birthed and you can hear Him exclaim, "Well done, my daughter, you good and faithful servant!"

CHAPTER TWELVE

Divine Divas

MY WIFE AND I arrived at the auditorium in New York in a limousine provided by the music company. We were amazed by the many celebrities hovering around the entrance, eliciting screams of recognition and flashes of cameras from the fans and reporters. When our driver opened the door for us and we made our way out of the limo, I panicked because I figured that none of the fans surrounding the barricaded premises would recognize us. Most looked at us, trying to figure out what sitcom they had seen us on or what news show we anchored, until finally they realized that they didn't know us at all, therefore we must not be that important. But a few ladies over in the corner took our picture and one of them shouted out my name. I was so happy I almost gave them all a twenty-dollar bill—I didn't mind not being famous; I just didn't want them to boo us or throw tomatoes at us for wasting their film. I will always believe that God planted those ladies, obviously from someone's church, to spare us the embarrassment of coming into the Grammy Awards without the traditional greeting of fans and flashbulbs.

The city was abuzz as usual, but this night was even more electrifying than normal. It was the night of the much-revered Grammy Awards, one of the most prestigious events in the music and recording industry. People were dressed in tuxedos and fabulous gowns, smiling and milling through the auditorium to find their seats. Tickets were difficult to attain but had been given to us by our own record label, and so we were making an evening of it. I could not believe that our work with "Woman Thou Art Loosed" had been nominated. So my wife and I put on our Sunday best to attend that evening's ceremony, although by then we knew that the actual Grammy in our category had gone to another nominee. No matter, it was still such an honor to attend the event. I will never forget watching Bill Gates as he walked right past me, dressed in his distinguished suit and looking quite successful. Then I saw Danny DeVito, an actor I have enjoyed watching on television and in many motion pictures. Boy, I had come a long way from where I grew up in the hills of West Virginia!

As Serita and I sat in the auditorium and watched the numerous celebrities around us make their way down the aisle to present or receive an award, I was so awed by each act and presentation made. But the life lesson I was to learn that night far exceeded the excitement I experienced over these celebrity sightings. You see, that was the night that I learned what versatility and creativity can do in the life of a real lady who has mastered her craft.

Well into the ceremony, a hush went through the crowded, star-studded auditorium. Evidently, there was a problem backstage. One of the world-renowned performers scheduled to sing had suddenly taken ill halfway through the live, televised awards program. The producer could simply cut the scheduled highlight of the show, but then the timing of the entire broadcast would be thrown off course. No, someone was needed to fill in for the ailing superstar. But it would be an impossible job—the world's greatest tenor, Luciano Pavarotti, had planned to sing the famous aria "Nessun dorma" from Puccini's opera *Turandot*, complete with a seventy-two-piece symphony orchestra. And if the selection didn't intimidate anyone willing to stand in, then the glamor and grandeur of the event would: the 1998 Grammy Awards. Anyone willing to substitute for the great Pavarotti would be performing unrehearsed before hundreds of music-industry insiders, producers, and executives, not to mention the countless professional musicians and singers. Of course, then there was the matter of the twenty-five million television viewers, and that was just U.S. viewers and didn't include the millions watching overseas!

When a bright star suddenly dims, where do you turn to find another source of illumination? Another superstar, of course. One firmly planted in the skies of success in her own right. Informed of the situation with Pavarotti's illness, Aretha Franklin agreed to the producer's desperate request to sing the aria. With only eight minutes to prepare backstage, the Queen of Soul took the stage as the lights went down and the beautiful operatic melody was ushered in by the strings of violins. All of us held our collective breath.

Certainly, this extraordinary lady was a living legend in her own right, with more than fifteen Grammys of her own—more than any other woman. She was the first female ever admitted to the Rock and Roll Hall of Fame. In 1968, the R&B sensation graced the cover of *Time* magazine, the first African-American woman to appear on its venerable cover. But an operatic aria was a far cry from the glorious soul tunes this legend was accustomed to singing. Was she setting herself up for embarrassment?

From the moment the powerful yet delicate instrument of her voice hit the first note—still in Pavarotti's key, three steps lower than her own—no one could believe their ears. The heart-wrenching emotion, the Italian lyrics, the exquisite synthesis of voice and virtuoso melted the audience and laid to rest any doubts about the simply amazing talent, courage, and giftedness of the amazing Aretha Franklin. As difficult as it might have been to believe, the Soul Lady performed with the trained operatic professionalism of a Jessye Norman or Beverly Sills. Stunned and delighted, the cheering crowd gave her a standing ovation and begged for an encore from this genre-crossing superstar. She bowed demurely and thanked the applauding throng for their gracious reception of her offering.

What a class act! Long before she stepped in to fill the shoes of a male Italian opera singer, Miss Aretha had established herself as the premiere artist of countless R&B, soul, gospel, and pop classics. Throughout the course of a career now spanning into its fourth decade and showing no signs of letting up, this woman has become the epitome of what every leading lady aspires to be. In one word, a diva.

Defining Diva

WHAT DOES IT mean to be a diva? The word itself derives from Latin and is the feminine form of the word *divus,* meaning "god." So diva means "goddess." During the Italian Renaissance, the word became appropriated as a musical equivalent of the stage term "prima donna," a leading lady of first-rate talent, and usually with a first-rate ego. Today a diva is not just a superstar with an attitude but a woman who has earned her place of prominence on life's stage through her faithfulness to her unique calling and to her Lord. She has embraced the special talents and abilities entrusted to her, weathered the life-storms of disappointment and loss, and emerged stronger and more resilient than ever. Like a vintage wine crafted with care from the finest grapes of the heartiest vineyards, this kind of leading lady becomes only more exquisite as she ages. She has learned to give herself away to those around her and beyond, pouring the sweet essence of her wine into each glass at her table.

You know her when you see her. She may be young or middle-aged or older; the truth is that she appears timeless in her beauty regardless of her chronological age. She catches the eye of every person in a place when she enters, whether it's with fanfare or a demure nod of greeting. There's simply something about her that you can't quite put your finger on. It's not a sense of entitlement or an elitist attitude of superiority. It transcends culture and economic status, goes beyond the education one receives from a university or charm school. In her eyes you see a full range of emotions burning in a complex conflagration of passion for life. There's a twinkling hint of humor, a compassionate spark of understanding, a flicker of gratitude, a blaze of humility, and a touch of confidence fueled by a lifetime of being onstage as a leading lady. She is a diva. With a natural grace and a transcendent poise, she commands the room without lifting a finger. Men find themselves attracted to the vitality and unself-conscious ease with which she returns their gaze. Women find themselves wanting to draw closer to this magnetic creature's radiant femininity and undeniable strength.

Although it's unclear and indefinable when a leading lady crosses the threshold of her own greatness and becomes a diva, it's always apparent when she has emerged on the other side. There's no longer any sense of regret or resentment clouding her eyes about what might have been in her life. For she knows that her God has allowed all the odd assortment of events and emotions, losses and gains, to shape who she is as His beautiful creation. Her confidence is at ease and does not need to inflate itself every five minutes by checking her appearance in the mirror or fishing for a compliment. She is at peace, and all cross-purposes in her life have been rechanneled to form a unified foundation of excellence in all that she endeavors.

Can you see yourself as this woman, this extraordinary diva? What obscures the view? It might be helpful to reflect on the legacies of the divas who came before you so that they may bolster your faith and strengthen the resolve to believe that your legacy extends far beyond what you can see.

With this in mind, let us walk down the corridor of the Leading Lady Hall of Fame and revisit some of our prior examples and mentors. Let us pause briefly before the women who grew into their roles under God's direction and left us with a legacy that continues to enrich our own purposes and inform our choices today. Let us consider what it means for us to grow into our role as a diva, as an authentic leading lady totally at home with herself, her purposes, and her Lord.

Lost and Found

PERHAPS THE FIRST leading lady turned diva whom we linger before takes us back to where we started, with Jesus' mother, Mary. From the tender vulnerability of her innocent trust in the awesome God of the universe to father her Child, to her thoughtful nurturing of the boy Messiah, Mary displays so many facets of a woman's beauty yielded unto the purposes of her God. And it was never easy. Back at the beginning of our journey, we examined the way Mary chose to submit and relinquish her future plans and hopes so that God could fill her with His greatness as she took her place onstage. But overcoming her fear of the angel and accepting God's invitation was only the beginning of a lifetime battling the tension between hope and loss.

Yes, it's a delicate and lovely scene to consider Mary birthing the Christ Child in a manger on a mild winter's night in Bethlehem, straight out of our Christmas cards and nativity sets. But at the other end of this scene is a disturbing, heart-wrenching tableau of anguish and grief, a mother watching her firstborn Son be murdered by the state like a common criminal. At the other end of the stable in Bethlehem is the cross of Calvary, and our Lord's mother was there from start to finish. She had watched her baby boy grow and become strong in spirit, filled with wisdom and marked by the grace of the God who was His Father (Luke 2:40). Later, as He grew into boyhood, she searched high and low for Him throughout the narrow cobblestone streets and alleys of Jerusalem during Passover. When she and Joseph found their Son conversing with the teachers in the Temple, she could not understand why He had let them worry so, but she was relieved to have Him back nonetheless.

Then she lost Him at the height of His ministry. She likely knew the prophecies of Scripture and what they foreshadowed for her Son. Even stronger was probably her mother's intuition warning her that her baby's life was in danger and soon to be taken from her. But nothing could prepare her for that awful image of seeing the Child she had pushed and birthed into this world hang from two crossed beams of wood above her.

Now there stood by the cross of Jesus His mother, and His mother's sister, Mary the wife of Clopas, and Mary Magdalene.

When Jesus therefore saw His mother, and the disciple whom He loved standing by, He said to His mother, "Woman, behold your son!"

Then He said to the disciple, "Behold your mother!" And from that hour that disciple took her to his own home.

JOHN 19:25–27

Can you imagine such an agonizing scene as this surreal experience Mary found herself in? Looking up at the cross where her firstborn Son was nailed, she had to have felt the pain from his oozing wounds. Every mother knows what it is like to feel her baby's hurts. While some onlookers viewed Jesus as a prophet, a good teacher, a heretical charlatan, or some even as the Messiah, Mary saw Him as her baby boy. She saw the small infant wrapped in swaddling clothes in a dusty, smelly stable. She recalled a toddler's first teetering steps and His first attempts toward the sound of language. This woman had raised Him and loved Him and supported Him throughout His lifetime in the ways that only a mother can. And now she had to stand next to the instrument of His death and let Him go. She had to relinquish her baby into the hands of His Father, the Father whose Spirit had descended upon her to conceive the Child in the first place, the Father she knew but had not seen.

And what are Jesus' dying words to her? Words of comfort as He seeks to make sure she is cared for. There is no time for long good-byes or articulations of what she means to Him. He must simply transfer her care to His disciple John.

What can prepare a leading lady for this kind of tragedy? Does any mother ever truly expect to outlive her child? Does any mother ever expect to endure the jeers and taunts, the vicious rumors and violent abuse of her children? What could possibly comfort her at a time like this? There are no words of solace, no gifts of consolation that can ease her shattered heart. There is no place left to run. Mary had followed Jesus as far as she could go physically. As grueling as the dusty steps along the route to Golgotha, she had followed His tortuous path to the spot where the Roman guards spiked nails into His open palms and crossed feet. She trembled as the soldier's spear unleashed a fountain of blood and water from His side. She dared to gaze into the anguished eyes of this Man who was God, this Messiah who was still her baby. It was more than she could bear, and yet she went as far as she could go. And now, the only thing she can do is trust in the Father's care of Him and the Father's care for her. Mary knew that her only alternative was to give herself to the same God to whom she had entrusted her Son. The same God who had chosen her among all other women of all time to bear His Son into this cruel world, a world that would crucify Him.

Perhaps you can identify with this part of Mary's story. You know that you have committed to accept the call God has placed on your life and to sow the seeds of greatness for your appointed destiny. You have birthed some of that greatness already, perhaps. You have watched some of your dreams come alive and flourish like giddy children rolling on a lush green hillside. Only now they've rolled off the bottom of the hill and been swallowed up by a dark canyon of calamity or unexpected disaster. Perhaps your business has dwindled in the wake of a struggling national economy to the point where now you must watch items be auctioned off and windows boarded up for good. Maybe your ministry no longer attracts the supporters it needs to continue its successful outreach. You may have lost your job, or your husband, or even one of your precious children. Dark clouds may have rolled into the theater of your life's performance like billowing smoke, choking and obscuring the pure, clean air right out of your lungs. You are no longer sure of your place onstage, the spotlight has dimmed, and the audience seems distant and coldly critical of your attempts.

The doubts set in and the tears mount like a flood line rising behind the walls of a crumbling dam. Were you wrong about your dream? Did you misunderstand God and what He seemed to promise you? Is this a bitter turn that the enemy has engineered in order to crash the course of your life's path? Will your legacy mock the potential you once displayed in the opening act of life's great play?

Dear sister, this is when you must summon the strength, courage, and confidence of a truly divine diva. This is when you must resist the urge to quit, to squander, to weep without hope, and to resign yourself to the death of a crucified dream. As the old Gospel preachers used to bellow from the pulpit, "Today is Friday, but Sunday's coming!" Yes, today may see the death of your baby, your dream, your vision of future greatness, but do not think that God does not bring life back to the dead. Do not think that Good Friday is the closing day of your dream's production. Easter Sunday is right around the corner, and so is your Day of Pentecost!

Revived by the Spirit

MARY EXPERIENCED THIS. Three days after her Son's death, His tomb was found to be empty. Some whispered about grave robbing by His disciples and scoffed about fraudulent claims He'd made, but she knew. Like all great leading ladies of faith, Mary knew that her Son was alive again.

And might she have known that her Son would live again in her in the Spirit? Notice that even after Christ's ascension into heaven, Mary is still following in His footsteps.

> *Then they returned to Jerusalem from the mount called Olivet, which is near Jerusalem, a Sabbath day's journey.*
>
> *And when they had entered, they went up into the upper room where they were staying: Peter, James, John, and Andrew; Philip and Thomas; Bartholomew and Matthew; James the son of Alphaeus and Simon the Zealot; and Judas the son of James.*
>
> *These all continued with one accord in prayer and supplication, with the women and Mary the mother of Jesus, and with His brothers.*
>
> *When the Day of Pentecost had fully come, they were all with one accord in one place.*
>
> *And suddenly there came a sound from heaven, as of a rushing mighty wind, and it filled the whole house where they were sitting.*
>
> *Then there appeared to them divided tongues, as of fire, and one sat upon each of them.*
>
> *And they were all filled with the Holy Spirit and began to speak with other tongues, as the Spirit gave them utterance.*
>
> ACTS 1:12–14; 2:1–4

What must have been going through Mary's mind as she sat in the upper room with her other children and the followers of the One Child she had watched ascend into the heavens just days before? When the fire tongues fell, what did she imagine to be happening? Perhaps she was the only one not truly astounded by His presence descending upon them and into them. She would recognize this feeling of His Spirit, for she had known it so well during the months He grew and kicked inside her. And now once more she carries Him inside her, a new kind of pregnancy, a conception of promise. This time He was more than an embryo or a promise. He was, in fact, a prayer answered. Out of all the sorrowful tears she had cried, out of the vacant place in her heart carved out on Calvary that fateful afternoon, now there was a new but familiar presence.

Mary is truly a leading lady of incredible faith, endurance, and hope. Her lifetime was spent birthing the Savior and then birthing Him again. So often this is the lesson that we must learn if we are to survive the valleys of the shadows in our lives and live again to see the splendor of success kindled like a tongue of fire. He will revive us and rekindle our quenched dreams. Like the languages of the Spirit emerging in the power of His descent into the disciples' lives, you may have to wait to discover a new language in which to speak your greatness, sing your hymn, or write your masterpiece. Ask for His presence and remember, divas never give up!

Portraits with Power

AS WE STROLL down the hall of this museum of faithful lives, let's review some more of our leading ladies and reconsider them as the divas they became through the impact of their ongoing legacies. Let's not forget the other great mother we studied earlier in the book, Eve, the first mother of our human race. Although she succumbs to the pressure of the enemy and sacrifices her initial greatness for a few succulent bites of bittersweet fruit, Eve also carries the seed for another great hope within her. Although she endures the terrible double loss of her firstborn sons, one to death and one to exile, she learns that God has not finished with her yet. She lives to see the birth of her son Seth, the progenitor of Christ's lineage. "And Adam knew his wife again, and she bore a son and named him Seth, 'For God has appointed another seed for me instead of Abel, whom Cain killed'" (Genesis 4:25). Throughout the terrible travails of her sorrowful and weary life, her Seth-experience loomed ahead of her to establish her legacy as one of tenacity, perseverance, and redemption.

Or consider another saint in the sisterhood who knew what it meant to wait and wait and wait, like a parched earth for drops of cool, sweet rain. Sarah saw her hope languish throughout her century on this planet. She was a faithful wife to a wealthy man, a man whom God chose to receive His convenant for greatness. Only the covenant involved Sarah, too, for God promised that He would use them to populate His people into a mighty race. He promised them so many descendants that they would be like sands on the beach or stars in the night sky. But then time dragged on and on and still no conception, no baby, no future. So Sarah attempts to outsmart God by using her maid Hagar as a surrogate for birthing this great promise of procreativity. Finally, as an old woman, long beyond her monthly cycles of being a fertile woman, long after she had begun to give up hope, long after she had laughed at the prospect, then the impossible became the tangible baby named Isaac. "And the Lord visited Sarah as He had said, and the Lord did for Sarah as He had spoken. For Sarah conceived and bore Abraham a son in his old age, at the set time of which God had spoken to him" (Genesis 21:1–2). Can you bear to see your cynical laughter of doubt transformed into the joyous, irrepressible outburst of celebration like this diva experienced?

A few steps down and we pause at a pure white canvas adorned with a single red thread. At first we may be tempted to think there's some mistake, as if the crimson cord has fallen off the frayed cuff of another passerby. Then we remember, ah yes, the woman with the scarlet letter and shame-faced past, dear sister Rahab. Known by reputation and history as a woman willing to sell her body and its sensual services to men with enough money, Rahab found herself forced into a handful of tense, life-threatening moments that would forever alter the way she saw herself and her future. Betray the king and risk the wrath of all of Jericho, or trust the fresh voice of this new God whispering in her soul? Turn over the spies to the king's soldiers or harbor them in hopes of a dangerous gamble? She is shrewd and used to taking care of herself, but nothing could have prepared this woman for these kinds of split-second choices. It was basically a conflict, not of invading Jews and outraged Canaanites, but of Rahab's character. Her dilemma gnawed at the very conflict of her callused heart: whether to trust God or man. What was the mettle of her being?

You know the answer if you've read this far along. But keep in mind that it's always easier to applaud a leading lady as a diva after her performance has been completed and the reviews written. Hindsight affords us a deeper appreciation of the bravado, courage, and foresight of this transformed diva. But let us not lose sight of the incredible risk, danger, and fear that Rahab must have endured in her journey of faith. Surely she wondered if the spies would remember their promise, let alone where she lived and the symbolic flare of scarlet cord hanging out her bedroom window. Surely she wondered if she had made the right decision by betraying her countrymen.

Surely she wondered if this new God revealing Himself to her could really be trusted with her life and the lives of all those she held most dear. No matter the scourge of her past or her fear of the future, Rahab acted with finesse and courage to secure her legacy as a diva of faith. "By faith the harlot Rahab did not perish with those who did not believe, when she had received the spies with peace" (Hebrews 11:31).

What decisions looming in your life right now require your courage and faith? What actions must you take to follow up on the directions provided by the Lord's prompting? Are you willing to extend your own scarlet cord in order to lasso the legacy of a lifetime?

Energy Crisis

ALTHOUGH THERE ARE so many leading ladies and divas we can admire and give thanks for, let us stop and consider one more before we move on. Her role may seem small in comparison to some of the stellar parts we have seen performed by other leading ladies. However, I believe she affords us a glimpse into the fundamental power source of a divine diva with such directness and clarity that it takes our breath away.

We have talked much about how you are created to be a giver of life, a giver of hope, a giver of sustenance to those around you. We have talked a great deal about never giving up, never quitting, never letting the flame of your passionate calling be snuffed out as you carry it into the winds of the future. We have seen leading ladies, like Eve or Sarah or Jesus' mother, wait for the birth of their dreams beyond what seems possible or plausible to their human understanding. But this next portrait I want to unveil is one that must speak to every woman's heart if she truly wants to fulfill her destiny as a leading lady.

Whether you're just starting out or just burning out, you know what it means to give until you give out. That's the kind of woman we find in the early days of the Christian Church, a kind and good woman, generous to a fault, birthing the greatness of her faith through all she did for those around her. But it came with a price, perhaps an unexpected price if the reaction of those around her is any indication.

> *At Joppa there was a certain disciple named Tabitha, which is translated Dorcas. This woman was full of good works and charitable deeds which she did.*
>
> *But it happened in those days that she became sick and died. When they had washed her, they laid her in an upper room.*
>
> *And since Lydda was near Joppa, and the disciples had heard that Peter was there, they sent two men to him, imploring him not to delay in coming to them.*
>
> *Then Peter arose and went with them. When he had come, they brought him to the upper room. And all the widows stood by him weeping, showing the tunics and garments which Dorcas had made while she was with them.*
>
> *But Peter put them all out, and knelt down and prayed. And turning to the body he said, "Tabitha, arise." And she opened her eyes, and when she saw Peter she sat up.*
>
> *Then he gave her his hand and lifted her up; and when he had called the saints and widows, he presented her alive.*
>
> *And it became known throughout all Joppa, and many believed on the Lord.*
>
> ACTS 9:36–42

Dorcas gave life to those around her. From her kindnesses and charitable deeds to the beautiful handiwork of her self-designed clothing, she was an extraordinary woman. She seems like the kind of solid, dependable, and compassionate woman who becomes the lifeblood of the community, the cornerstone of the church, and the conduit of grace for those in need. She knows what it means to give birth to her dreams and share her ample bounty of goodness with all those around her.

But it seems likely that she gave to everyone but herself, as all of a sudden she takes sick and just up and dies. Dorcas had depleted her own internal resources until there were no defenses, no hidden provision, no internal wellspring from which she could draw new strength, new power, new life.

Have you found yourself in the crosshairs of the sniper of self-depletion? You give and give and give, listening to the trials and tribulations of the friends and family who clamber over your sympathetic heart. You give and give and give, taking the warmth of soothing provisions to those who are sick and hungry and discouraged. My sister, you give and give and give, providing encouragement for the downcast and hope for those who stand on the precipice of despair, attempting to jump. It may feel good for you to give so much of yourself because you know that it's part of your nature, part of the very essence of your identity. But then suddenly you find yourself with an empty gas tank on a deserted highway with nothing but a darkened horizon looming in the distance.

And you may or may not see it coming. Whether it's the physical toll of skipping meals and losing sleep as you're always on the go, or the emotionally draining pull of the swirling tides produced by so many other people's hurricanes; whether it's the run-down and lethargic demeanor of fatigue or the numbed sting of burnout, you find yourself sick. And then you lose yourself as surely as if you'd vanished off the face of the earth into a mineshaft to the core of our planet.

You're not physically dead, but you know that the life has all drained out of you. I recall the statement of a once vibrant matriarch in our church, a woman who had raised three children of her own as well as two grandchildren. She had salvaged her husband's small business and single-handedly begun a ministry to the children of women in prison in our community. One fine spring day this woman collapsed on the sidewalk as she was getting into her car. Her daughter found her and rushed her to the hospital. Doctors ran tests and checked measurements but could not find anything wrong with this strong and otherwise healthy lady. But she remained fatigued and weak and unable to regain her intense focus and high-energy style of meeting life head-on. I visited her in the hospital and prayed for her recovery, and as I was leaving, I said, "Get well, sister." She looked at me with a strange expression in her eyes for a moment and then said simply, "I don't have the energy for that right now. I don't have any energy for myself anymore." Although I wasn't able to articulate it then, I somehow understood what this vibrant lady was communicating. She was like Dorcas and had simply run out of her energy source.

Dorcas's friends were devastated and couldn't imagine the extent of losing such a life force in their community. They laid her out in an upper room, sent for Peter, and then gathered the souvenirs of Dorcas's generosity to them to show the disciple. But then, curiously enough, Peter sends them all out. He knows that even after her body is dead, if other people are around she will somehow try to give to them instead of to herself. So the widows and spectators are forced outside while Peter goes in and prays.

He prays and speaks to the woman by name and gives her the imperative, "Arise." She opens her eyes, sits up, and takes Peter's hand as he helps her reacquaint herself with the flow of blood circulating through her body and the rhythm of her heartbeat drumming in her ears. She is alive. God has restored her through the miracle of this disciple's healing prayer over her.

Two important lessons emerge for you from this extraordinary leading lady's resurrection. First and foremost, realize that God will not abandon you when you are down. If there's any common denominator recurring throughout all the performances of the leading ladies we've studied, it is the faithful presence of their Director, nurturing and guiding, instructing and loving, molding and shaping their destinies. While you may give until it hurts to those around you, while you may dedicate your life in loving service to your kids, your spouse, your ministry, your church, your business, your art, your dream, know that He will restore your resources. Those people benefiting from your gifts may not realize the cost to you, may not appreciate the quality of what you offer, and may not remember to thank you properly.

But God never forgets any of the sacrifices and labors of love that you extend in pursuit of your legacy. He sends Peters into your life to voice the prayer of healing and offer you a hand to get back on your feet. He has the power and can restore the heartbeat of your dream and the breath of wind needed to fill your sail and return you to your passage across life's sea.

The second vital lesson we must take away from the resurrection of Dorcas is the need to be alone with your power source. You must not neglect yourself if you want to fulfill your destiny as a leading lady. Don't get caught up in the life-draining role of martyr as an excuse for not taking better care of your body, your mind, and your spirit. You must replenish what God gives you by resting and waiting upon Him. Without the rest of fall and sleep of winter, fruit trees and rosebushes would not be able to bring forth fruit and flowers when the spring rains and summer suns stimulate them again. Even the most productive farmland must be allowed to lie fallow if it is to remain productive.

Similarly, when the time comes for you to rest, you must get yourself alone with your Father and keep the spectators and beneficiaries of your goodness outside. It will be hard to keep them waiting sometimes, but you will not restore life to your heart or clarity to your vision if you do not have the solitude and sustenance of time alone. In the intimacy of your prayers and the privacy of your supplications, you will discover enormous power to sustain you for the long haul of a lifetime performance. If you are to weather the numerous challenges and assaults, the frequent changes of course and monotony of the mundane, then you must nurture this relationship with your divine Director above all else. This is the fuel that kindles and rekindles the spark of confidence in the eyes of a diva. This is the power source unleashed to sustain her perspective when she is temporarily blinded by storm clouds, fog-strewn nights, and oncoming traffic. He is the rain pouring down into the parched patches of your dusty soul.

Relay Race

LINGER AT THIS portrait of Dorcas and know that her revival can inspire your own restoration. Like the other lives of the leading ladies we've examined, Dorcas has passed her torch to you. With the precise timing and synchronized rhythm of the fastest relay team, these leading ladies have passed on their faith, their talent, and their illumination to one another and now to you. They each have known how difficult it can be to keep the fires of greatness burning when the wind was against them and the path seemed dark. They all know how excruciating it can be to run with the swollen ankles and bruised dreams that inevitably occur on this marathon of faith.

You know that you have seeds of greatness growing and blossoming within you. If you didn't believe that you would not have read this book up to this point—you would have likely never read it in the first place. But you have heard God's calling on your life and you have answered it by taking your place onstage, by being willing to grace the spotlight with the energy and talent that only you can pour forth. The time has come now, dear sister, for you to embark on the next leg of your journey. You have many sisters in the gallery of faith urging you on, cheering for you, encouraging you and admonishing you to complete your journey and birth your dream.

> *Do you not know that those who run in a race all run, but one receives the prize? Run in such a way that you may obtain it.*
>
> *And everyone who competes for the prize is temperate in all things. Now they do it to obtain a perishable crown, but we for an imperishable crown.*
>
> *Therefore I run thus: not with uncertainty. Thus I fight: not as one who beat the air.*
>
> *But I discipline my body and bring it into subjection, lest, when I have preached to others, I myself should become disqualified.*
>
> 1 CORINTHIANS 9:24–27

You are in the race, dear lady, and you know that your legacy of greatness awaits you. You know the stakes are high. This is not merely for a blue ribbon or a garland of ivy leaves around your head. This race is for the golden imperishable crown that your loving Creator wishes to place on you as you cross the finish line. It is the ultimate Academy Award, the only acknowledgment of your life's performance that matters. Discipline yourself with this higher goal in mind. Run not with uncertainty but with certainty. Fix your eyes on the prize and do not be discouraged or discounted no matter what obstacles may temporarily obscure your path. Know that God Himself has chosen and ordained you as His Leading Lady.

Perhaps life will challenge you to do something you have never done before. Maybe you have been asked to sing the song, say the speech, face a challenge that you would never have expected for yourself. You are the woman for the job, on a mission filled with wonderment and excitement. But enough of this rambling, the show is about to begin. The curtain is going up on the next act of your life. You have everything you need to dazzle the earthly audience surrounding you and to garner the heavenly applause of He who loves you most. You are a divine diva destined for greatness beyond what your imagination can conjure. Go out into the awaiting spotlight, dear woman, and, as they say in the theater, break a leg!